MEXICAN AMERICANS

MEXICAN AMERICANS

Resources to Build
Cultural Understanding

by

LOIS B. JORDAN

1973

Libraries Unlimited, Inc.

Littleton, Colo.

Library of Congress Card Number 72-94302
International Standard Book Number 0-87287-059-6

LIBRARIES UNLIMITED, Inc.
P.O. Box 263
Littleton, Colorado 80120

TABLE OF CONTENTS

PREFACE

Mexican Americans: Resources for Young People to Build Cultural Understanding is a selective annotated bibliography of materials suitable for young adults in junior high school, senior high school, and college. The aim is to bring together a selection of books, 16mm films, 35mm filmstrips, 8mm film loops, recordings, slides, transparencies, and other audiovisual media which provide information on the historical backgrounds, cultural heritage and contemporary social, economic and political problems of Mexican Americans. While non-print media are included in the bibliography, the emphasis is on books. In addition to the two main sections of the work, there are four appendixes providing information on a selected number of periodicals, associations and organizations, and notable Mexican-American personalities.

Recently a number of bibliographies and filmographies have been published in this subject area. However, these are frequently issued by libraries and are not always readily available. Examples of such works are *La Raza in Films* (68p.), compiled by Cynthia Baird and issued by the Latin American Library, Oakland, California, and *Mexican-Americans, A Selected Bibliography* (73p.), issued by the University of Houston Libraries. The first list includes Spanish language and English language films while the latter bibliography is an unannotated list and is restricted to books and articles. While these two lists are aimed at the public at large or university students in Mexican American studies, and there are other guides to materials for children, there is a notable lack of bibliographies covering a wide range of material and topics for young people in junior and senior high schools. This bibliography hopefully fulfills that purpose.

It is hoped that this list of materials will lead the young Mexican American to a better understanding of his heritage, and that the resulting sense of dignity, security, and pride will help him to compete as an adult citizen with people from other cultures while still retaining his own. At the same time his Anglo peers, through reading of the cultural roots of their Mexican-American fellow student, may acquire respect for these roots and a deeper appreciation of cultural differences as reflected in art, music, and literature.

Entries in Part I: Print Materials are subdivided into Mexico's History, Mexican Americans in the United States, The Arts, Literature, Biography, and Fiction, then are further subdivided by specific periods and subjects. Entries in Part II: Audiovisual Materials are subdivided by medium. Full bibliographic information is followed by a descriptive annotation. This list represents an effort to evaluate English language materials relating to the Mexican American and does not include books in the Spanish language; however, some audiovisual material is in the Spanish language or is available in both Spanish and English. The selection has not been limited by date, but emphasis has been placed on materials published within the past ten years.

Several out-of-print titles are included because of their excellent presentation of the subject matter or background material; they are still available on many library shelves. If a book is out of print, the abbreviation "o.p." appears at the end of the bibliographical information. Books on the junior high school level are designated by a lower-case "j" to the left of the entry. The Reference section

(Appendix D) offers sources for additional reading. The author, title, and subject indexes facilitate access to the numbered entries in Part I: Printed Materials and Part II: Audiovisual Materials. Page numbers are used in the indexes to locate authors, titles, and names of individuals and organizations listed and described in the four appendixes.

Appendix A is a selective listing of Mexican-American personalities who have achieved notable positions in government or education or fame in the sports or the entertainment fields. These biographical notes are intended to provide students with an awareness of the contributions of some Mexican Americans in a wide range of careers and activities and does not purport to be a comprehensive directory. The second appendix is a listing of the Chicano Press Association as received from the Association as of April 1, 1972, and a sampling of the many hundreds of periodicals and newspapers of interest to the Mexican American. Entries for the periodicals and newspapers include title, address, frequency of publication, subscription price, date of establishment, language, and a brief description of the purpose or objective of the periodical or newspaper. The third appendix lists a variety of the many Mexican and Spanish American organizations, whether social or political. The name of the association, address, scope, date established, membership and type of organization is given for each listing whenever this information was available.

In addition to the usual standard book selection criteria of theme, illustrations, and language, these books were considered in terms of knowledge of subject matter, imagination, truthfulness, understanding, the degree of involvement of the Mexican or Mexican-American characters, the values and attitudes developed in the book, and the book's contribution to the total picture of this minority group. Materials in this work have also been selected to represent treatment of such basic areas as religion, language, the family, education, economics, health, government, and recreation.

Thematically, the books were examined for values and attitudes, enrichment of experience, and the promotion of understanding and sympathy toward the development of a self-concept on the part of the minority person.

The literature of fiction and biography does much to give the young reader an appreciation of the customs, the patterns of life, and the emotions of people who have a different cultural heritage. Fiction can be especially valuable as an aid to forming self concepts and constructive attitudes. The reader often develops sympathy and appreciation through identifying with a fictional character and vicariously experiencing his problems. James L. Summers' powerful present-day story of a Chicano youth, *You Can't Make It by Bus*, gives insight into the slights, the subtle insults, and the feeling of degradation of spirit experienced by a member of a minority group. Everyone who is young, eager, and in search of his future will identify with Paul Guevaro and Lura Golden in the perplexities of their love and in Paul's search for his heritage.

In *Across the Tracks*, by Bob and Jan Young, the social problems of a young middle-class Mexican-American girl are vividly pictured. Betty Ochos is the first of her group to run for a high school office. During the contest some Anglo students scrawl "spic" across her election posters. The majority of the school, ashamed of the incident, supports her campaign and subsequent election. The prejudice, racial barriers, and mixed feelings of the youthful Mexican

Americans are fully developed within the framework of the plot, while the realistic treatment of the attitudes contributes to developing an understanding of cultural differences. Because the derisive name "spic" is treated by the authors as if it were a disaster, the reader very easily understands the pernicious effect of such language in books for young people.

Dialect in earlier literature was often derisive, condescending, and insulting to the Mexican character. In the literature today authors either choose to use no dialect at all or use just enough to suggest a Spanish accent. In some few titles dialect treatment is awkwardly handled, but this is primarily due to poor writing rather than to malicious intent.

Throughout their history Mexican Americans have been subjected to prejudice and discrimination in areas of education, civil rights, jobs, and social activities. As an example, many of the incidents in Whitney's *A Long Time Coming* show the prejudice and discrimination against migrant Mexican-American workers in the local canning factory. This novel presents the blinding traumatic force of prejudice and the cruel results of acts of intolerance. Christi Allard's growing insight and sympathetic understanding of the situation cause her to help solve the problems. The author, basing her story on actual incidents which she witnessed, presents a very realistic story.

Prejudice against Mexican Americans and one young teacher's efforts to combat it figure prominently in the plot of Erdman's *My Sky Is Blue*. Jinny, seeking a change in her life, leaves a promising teaching career in a large city school to teach in a rural school in New Mexico. Here in a one-room school she encounters prejudice against a Mexican-American family. Rosie, an Anglo girl, torments the Garcia children, creating a disturbing situation in the school and in the village. Jinny, while helping Rosie change her attitude, at the same time instills a cultural pride in the Garcia family. This good junior novel of romance develops interest in teaching and also shows a way of combating prejudice.

Stereotyping or caricaturing is another factor to be considered in material on the Mexican American. From the earliest encounters between Americans and Mexicans the Americans have not hesitated to record indignity and scorn for the "greasers" through caricaturing and stereotyping. "El Mexicano Through the Eyes of the Gaucho" is the title of a revealing article in an issue of *La Raza* (Vol. 1, No. 4) about stereotyping of Chicanos and racism in Anglo advertising and literature. The article questions, "Do all Mexicans wear sombreros, serapes and mustaches? Clearly, these things are not true, but are too often generally accepted and perpetrated by keeping alive such racist symbols as 'el frito bandito.'

"The frito bandito is an example of the stereotyping of Mexicans and Chicanos in the form of a comic cartoon character. The character is depicted as a thief, and is recognizable as a Mexican because he wears a sombrero, has a big mustache and speaks with a pseudo-Mexican accent in English.

"Another example is the Elgin watch advertisement: 'Your new Elgin is better than the Elgins Zapata was willing to kill for in 1914. It's a good thing Emiliano Zapata is gone. He'd be stealing Elgins as fast as we could make them.' This Elgin advertisement insults a great historic leader of the Mexican people by implying that he is a thief and a killer. The *La Raza* article indicates how racism is manifested by other forms of stereotyping in newspapers, books, magazines and TV commercials."[1]

Edward Simmen's new book, *The Chicano: From Caricature to Self-Portrait*, is an interesting and enlightening work. This anthology consists of a series of short stories by or about Mexican Americans, arranged in chronological order: I, From the Beginnings to 1930: Early Caricatures; II, Through the Depression to 1940: Realistic Profiles; and III, From World War II to the Present: Portraits and Self-Portraits of the Awakening Minority.

Excellent material has been found and included in the bibliography to represent the criteria of basic cultures. As is usually the case with minority groups, education is the field which contains the most material. Three basic books are: Charles B. Brussell's *Disadvantaged Mexican American Children*, Herchel T. Manuel's *Spanish Speaking Children of the Southwest: Their Education and Public Welfare*, and George L. Sanchez's *Concerning Segregation of Spanish Speaking Children in the Public Schools*. These books and others (such as Leo Grebler's statistical survey of educational retardation, *The Schooling Gap: Signs of Progress*, and Vera P. John and Vivian M. Horner's new work, *Bilingualism*) present a telling picture of education for the Mexican American.

The lack of thorough studies of religious influences on the Mexican American is surprising. Authors too often present a superficial view of religious institutions and are not greatly concerned with religious development. Julia Nott Waugh's *The Silver Cradle* is an excellent work describing the Mexican American festivities, and Jose E. Espinosa describes the religious art in New Mexico in his *Saints in the Valleys: Christian Sacred Images in the History, Life and Folk Art of Spanish New Mexico*. A study exploring the history of the church generally in the Southwest, utilizing survey data on Catholic practice from San Antonio and Los Angeles, is to be found in a work by Grebler and others, *The Mexican American People*.

Studies of "The Family" have been brilliantly recorded in the remarkable books of Oscar Lewis: *Five Families* (1959), *The Children of Sanchez* (1961), and *A Death in the Sanchez Family* (1969). The books grew out of intimate studies of Mexican families. *Five Families* chronicles the activities of a typical day in the lives of five Mexican families representative of rural village life, slums, working class, and upper class. *The Children of Sanchez*, focusing on one family studied in the previous book, is a realistic picture of the culture of poverty. *A Death in the Sanchez Family* gives the reaction of each member of the Sanchez family to the death of old Aunt Guadalupe. The novel *Chicano*, by Richard Vasquez (1970), is an absorbing family saga which traces the Sandoval family through several generations—from its roots in a village in northern Mexico during the revolution of 1910 to the present-day barrio in East Los Angeles. The novel clearly depicts the family role of the Mexican American from the dominant role of the male to the fact that the collective needs of the family supersede the needs of each individual member.

Depressing and shocking as they may be, three books painfully survey the economic deprivation among Mexican Americans: Frank G. Mittelback and Grace Marshall's *The Burden of Poverty* (UCLA Project, 1966), Arthur J. Ruble's *Across the Tracks: Mexican Americans in a Texas City*, and William Madsen's *Mexican Americans of South Texas*.

[1] "La Raza Attacks Racism for Profit," *Interracial Books for Children*, III (1971), 6.

Closely related to the economic studies are those of health. An interesting study of divergent medical practices is *Cultural Differences and Medical Care: The Case of the Spanish-Speaking People of the Southwest*, by Lyle Saunders. A later study giving the reader insight into attitudes toward modern medical practices is the work by Margaret Clark, *Health in the Mexican-American Culture*, with a focus on health practices in a California community. A recent study, *Health Status and Practices of Mexican Americans*, by A. Taher Moustafa and Gertrude Weiss, reports on Mexican-American mortality rates, morbidity characteristics, mental illness, and health attitudes and practices.

Materials relating to government and government agencies are found throughout the literature; many of these reports have been issued by the Commission on Civil Rights. *The Mexican American*, prepared by Helen Rowan, covers the kind and scope of problems facing the Mexican-American community today in five areas where major problems exist: 1) civil rights and the administration of justice, 2) education, 3) employment, 4) public policies and agencies for assisting the Mexican American, and 5) the Mexican American's growing sense of identity. Another report by the United States Commission on Civil Rights, *Mexican Americans and the Administration of Justice in the Southwest*, is the official report of the Commission presented to the Congress and the President of the United States. Based on extensive field investigations through the Southwest, the report documents harsh treatment by law enforcement officers as well as the lack of adequate representation by counsel and proper bail procedures.

Almost no material is found on the recreation of the Mexican American other than those of holidays and festivals. In *A Treasury of Mexican Folkways*, Frances Toor gives authentic historical descriptions of Mexican fiestas, dances, and songs, many of which have been carried over into the way of life of Mexican Americans.

The materials in this bibliography represent and reflect the culture and heritage of a society in a variety of experiences and periods of history, both political and social. Some books and articles which do not meet the standard criteria of good literature have been included because of distinctive characterization, outstanding historical background, exceptional subject matter, or timeliness of the subject. It is hoped that this bibliography will be of assistance to students, teachers, and librarians in selecting suitable materials about Mexican Americans. In future editions new materials will be included, and readers' suggestions for additions of relevant works to the bibliography will be appreciated.

INTRODUCTION

The Mexican American of the United States is referred to by a number of names: he is designated as Spanish American, Mexican, Latin American, Spanish-speaking, and Chicano. It should be noted that each term denotes a particular philosophy regarding self-identification. To consider the Spanish-speaking a homogeneous group with a given set of characteristics and qualities is therefore to stereotype. In this bibliography, "Mexican American" has been chosen as the closest thing to a suitable term for this group. These people have a bond with Mexico which they should be able to acknowledge with pride, for that nation is the homeland of their forefathers as well as the origin of their culture and historic roots. The Mexican-American society of today has evolved in the course of many years. The social relationships that have developed between the Anglo American and the Mexican American may be best understood if seen in historical perspective.

The first white people to migrate into what is now the American Southwest were Spanish-speaking. During the period of Spain's colonial expansion they settled portions of the Southwest even before the founding of Plymouth in 1620. Between 1528 and 1602, a handful of Spaniards had explored the borderlands: from Galveston to San Diego, from Sonora to Santa Fe, from the west coast of Mexico to Monterey. If myth set them in motion, it was the Indians who lured them still farther from their bases with tales of gold and silver, always seeking to draw them out of the Southwest. Where they had expected to find cities of gold, they found mud villages and uninhabited desert wastes. Something of this initial disappointment must have influenced their subsequent policy: they neglected California from 1542 until the arrival of Fray Junipero Serra at San Diego in 1769; Texas was ignored for a century; and 40 years elapsed before the settlement of New Mexico was undertaken.

The colonization of New Mexico—"the first white colony in the trans-Mississippi West"— was a by-product of the discovery of rich silver deposits at Zacatecas in 1548. Juan de Onate, one of the four richest men in Mexico, set forth in 1598 to colonize New Mexico. Cabeza de Vaca had entered the borderlands from the southeast, and Fray Marcos and Coronado from the southwest by way of Sonora; but de Onate moved directly northward to El Paso and then up the Rio Grande to a point near Santa Fe. The colonists managed to establish a series of settlements and by 1630 had founded some 25 missions. These initial settlements were extinguished in 1680, when the Indians revolted and drove the Spaniards from New Mexico.[1] Twelve years later, Diego de Vargas reconquered the province, made peace with the Pueblo Indians, and laid the foundations for settlements which survive to this day. By 1890 there were an estimated 23,000 Spanish-speaking people in the five-state area of the Southwest.

Soon after the 13 colonies gained their independence from England, the migration of English-speaking people into the Southwest began. Mexico, its own independence newly-won from Spain, encouraged such migration. This vast Southwestern area, stretching from the Western border of Louisiana to the Pacific, belonged to Mexico. She was anxious to see it settled and developed, and

[1]Carey McWilliams, *North from Mexico: The Spanish-Speaking People of the United States (Philadelphia: J. B. Lippincott Company, 1949)*, p. 24.

few Mexican colonists were moving there. So the government of Mexico granted large blocks of land to contractors who would bring in colonists. The response was large and prompt. By 1835 there were 25,000 to 35,000 American farmers, planters, and traders in Texas, with more on the way.

The deluge dismayed Mexico, and she tried to check it by cancelling land grants. The Texans became irked and in 1836 they revolted against Mexican overlordship and won their independence. Shortly afterward, Texas was admitted to the Union. A dispute broke out between the United States and Mexico over the southwestern boundary of Texas, the result of which was the Mexican War and the loss by Mexico of nearly all that remained of her northernmost empire. To the United States were ceded much of New Mexico, most of Arizona, the future states of California, Nevada and Utah, and part of Colorado and Wyoming. Five years later the Gadsden Purchase added a strip of land between the Gila River and the present southern boundary of Arizona and New Mexico, completing the American acquisition of what is now the Southwest.

Thus, by one of history's ironies, the majority became a minority. Spanish-speaking people who had been the first whites to settle the Southwest became, if not an alien group, an alienated group. They were Americans, yes, but with a language and culture different from the language and culture of the region in which they found themselves. Today in the Southwest a cultural and linguistic gulf still exists between Mexican Americans—the "invisible minority," as they have been called—and Anglo Americans.[2]

The 1970 federal government census identifies more than six million Mexican Americans living in the United States. Until 1965, the geographical placement found most Mexican Americans in the five Southwest states of Arizona, Colorado, California, New Mexico, and Texas. During the period from 1965 to 1970, massive migrations of Mexican Americans into the Midwest states of Illinois, Michigan, Indiana, Ohio, and Wisconsin took place. The resulting concentration in urban environments caused a tremendous impact on young people, both Mexican American and Anglo American, in schools and social life, due to the diversity among groups in customs, aspirations, and attitudes. This bibliography can serve to make people in these states aware of material that would be useful in working with Mexican-American youth and in broadening the knowledge of the English-speaking youth.

Differences in culture have always existed, but the need for better understanding of the various cultures is now more critical. Do books have the power to build bridges of cultural understanding? Books play a unique role in human relations and can do much to provide the perspective needed in order to appreciate the problems of other people. Thus, wide reading concerning the rich cultural and historical background of Mexico should help the English-speaking youth to form an understanding and appreciation of the Mexican-American youth. By the same token, wide reading on the part of the Mexican-American youth will enhance his sense of ethnic identity by enabling him to become aware of outstanding and respected members of his group and to learn of their contributions to America—in short, he will become familiar with himself as a member of an important segment of our society.

[2]National Education Association, *"The Invisible Minority" in the United States: A Reader*, ed. by John H. Burma (Cambridge, Mass.: Schenkman Publishing Co., 1970), p. 104.

PART I

PRINTED MATERIALS

1. MEXICO'S HISTORY

GENERAL

1. Alba, Victor. **The Mexicans: The Making of a Nation.** New York: Frederick A. Praeger, Inc., 1967. 268p.
Mexico demands constant interpretation as it cannot be understood solely in terms of its physical face or historical exploits. This updated explanation, which considers all facets, gives the reader an excellent insight into Mexico and the culture of its people.

2. Brandenberg, Frank R. **Making of Modern Mexico.** Englewood Cliffs, N.J.: Prentice-Hall, Inc., 1964. 379p.
An interpretation of the causes and effects of the Mexican Revolution, and of the present health and probable direction of the Mexican nation.

3. Burns, E. Bradford. **Latin America: A Concise Interpretive History.** Englewood Cliffs, N.J.: Prentice-Hall, Inc., 1972. 256p.
Provides a complete overview of Latin American history from pre-Columbian civilizations to the present. Rather than detailing the individual histories of each country, the author unifies his treatment by emphasizing the major trends, cultural themes and institutions in Latin American development during broad chronological periods. In this century attention is given to the struggle of the Latin American nations, focusing on the major revolutions, to exchange their colonial heritage for a more equitable society.

4. Caldwell, John C. **Mexico.** New York: Frederick A. Praeger, Inc.,
j   1962. 244p. o.p.
An easy-to-read comprehensive history.

5. Carter, Hodding, and Betty W. Carter. **Doomed Road of Empire: The Spanish Trail of Conquest.** New York: McGraw-Hill Book Company, 1963. 408p.
This book tells of the royal road that ran from Saltillo, Mexico, to Natchitoches, Louisiana, and initially lay entirely within the borders of Mexico. The people and the events bound up with the history of this thoroughfare from the 1500s through the 1800s are described in a leisurely way by authors whose feeling for the dramatic is exemplified in a chapter on the Alamo.

6. Cline, Howard F. **Mexico: From Revolution to Evolution, 1940-1960.** New York: Oxford University Press, Inc., 1962. 374p.
Mexico presented from post-revolutionary chaos to an industrial empire. The 34 chapters of the book are grouped in broad segments including perspectives and legacies, the land, the people, political evolution, the institutional revolution and the economy. Almost 100 statistical tables, maps, and diagrams supplement the text. An excellent analysis of the profound changes of the last two decades. The work concludes with a section on Mexican policy and place in the world.

7. Cline, Howard F. **The United States and Mexico**. Rev. and enl. ed.
    Cambridge, The American Foreign Policy Library. Cambridge, Mass.:
    Harvard University Press, 1963. 484p.

In this revision of the 1953 edition, the author reviews the salient features—
geographical, historical, political, economic, and social—of Mexico in the past
and the present. He stresses the remarkable transformation of the Mexican
domestic scene and of Mexican international relations.

8. Coy, Harold. **The Mexicans**. Illustrated by Francisco Mora. Boston:
j   Little, Brown and Company, 1970. 326p.

The story of Mexico from the pre-Columbian times to the present, emphasizing
the efforts of the Mexican people to throw off the yoke imposed by Spain and
to forge themselves into an independent nation. Pronunciation guide is included.

9. Credle, Ellis. **Mexico: Land of Hidden Treasure**. Camden, N.J.: Thomas
j   Nelson & Sons, 1967. 224p.

An introductory book for the junior high age covering history, arts and crafts,
family life and culture of both the Spanish and Indian population, education
and present-day economic conditions.

10. Cumberland, Charles C. **Mexico: The Struggle for Modernity**. New
    York: Oxford University Press, 1968. 394p.

Excellent history of Mexico from pre-Columbian period to the present. Social,
economical, and cultural trends receive closest attention in relation to it. The
structure of Mexican society in critical times of upheaval and change is portrayed. The author also discusses the practices of the Aztecs, the Conquest, and
the independence movement.

11. Dozer, Donald M. **Latin America: An Interpretive History**. New York:
    McGraw-Hill Book Publishing Company, 1962. 618p.

Readable and brilliant survey slanted from the right.

12. Ewing, Russell C., ed. **Six Faces of Mexico: History, People, Geography,
    Government, Economy, Literature and Art**. Tucson, Arizona: Univer-
    sity of Arizona Press, 1966. 320p.

Each of the seven authors writes in his area of specialization to present a picture
of Mexico through history, social customs, ethnic backgrounds, geographical
features, cultural factors, economy and political institutions. The book is a
useful comprehensive reference on Mexico, with summaries and bibliographies
at the end of each section.

13. Fagg, John E. **Latin America: A General History**. 2nd ed. New York:
    Macmillan Company, 1969. 814p.

A factual and illustrative general history of Latin America, with chapters on
Mexico and relations of the United States to other Latin American states.

14. Hancock, Ralph. **Mexico**. New York: Macmillan Company, 1964.
j   117p.

A good survey of Mexico past and present. The author writes with authority and the book has broad coverage and a balanced treatment. The writing style, however, is rather wooden and the book lacks the impact of Hobart's *Mexican Mural* (Harcourt, 1963), although that is written for a somewhat older reader. The first half of the book describes the early civilizations of Mexico, the second half the recent history. Mr. Hancock gives a good deal of the sort of information that will be useful to visitors to Mexico; he also describes festivals, the growth of literacy, the arts, the political science, and some aspects of the relationship between Mexico and the United States. An index, a list of suggestions for further reading, and a list of recording are appended.

15. Hanf, Walter. **Mexico**. Chicago: Rand McNally and Company, 1967.
j   126p. o.p.
Pictorial history of Mexico from ancient times to the present.

16. McNeer, May. **The Mexican Story**. Lithographs by Lynd Ward. New
j   York: Farrar, Straus & Giroux, Inc., 1953. 96p.
The story of Mexico from the early Mayan civilization through Montezuma's magnificence, the glory of Cortes, down through the great figures of Father Hidalgo, Maximilian, Juarez, Diaz, to Villa and modern man.

17. Morner, Magnus. **Race Mixture in the History of Latin America**.
Boston: Little, Brown & Company, 1967. 178p.
An excellent readable piece on the concept and history of Latin American mestizaje from the conquest period to modern times. A penetrating summary of the history of interracial relations.

18. Parkes, Henry Bamford. **A History of Mexico**. Rev. ed. Boston:
Houghton Mifflin Company, 1960. 460p.
One of the highly rated English language histories of Mexico covering the pre-conquest period to current times. Originally published in 1938. The revision adds a new concluding chapter and bibliographical references.

19. Paz, Octavio. **The Labyrinth of Solitude: Life and Thought in Mexico**.
Translated by Lysander Kemp. New York: Grove Press, Inc., 1961.
212p. Reprint of 1959 Mexico edition.
This work is the essay of the distinguished Mexican poet discussing the character and culture of his country through the motives, symbols, and aspirations of the Mexican. He equates Mexican history with the psychological, intellectual growth of the Mexican man and explains that Mexican history has always been a search for selfhood though stifled by cultural forms from foreign models, and the Catholic Church.

20. Quirk, Robert E. **Mexico**. Englewood Cliffs, N.J.: Prentice-Hall, Inc.,
1971. 152p.
A history of Mexico from the earliest times to the present. Explaining contemporary Mexico in terms of its cultural, political, economic, and social development. An excellent bibliographical essay is on pages 216 to 247.

21. Ramos, Samuel. **Profile of Man and Culture in Mexico.** Translated by
Peter G. Earle. Texas Pan American Series. Austin, Texas: University
of Texas Press, 1963. 198p. Original Spanish edition, Mexico 1934.

The purpose of the study is to present an analysis of the historical forces that
have molded the Mexican national character. The author states that the Mexican
suffers from an inferiority complex resulting in anti-social character traits. This
complex was created in colonial times and became more acute after Mexico's
independence, when Mexican leaders looked to European countries for culture.
An eminently readable evaluation of Mexican character. In this edition the
author's 1951 essay entitled "Concerning Mexican Character" is appended.

22. Sierra, Justo. **Political Evolution of the Mexican People.** Translated by
Charles Ramsdell. Austin, Texas: University of Texas Press, 1970.
420p. Reprint of 1969 edition.

This excellent translation based on the 1948 Spanish edition contains notes and
new introduction by Edmundo O'Gorman with a prologue by Alfonso Reyes.
This excellent history of Mexico from the beginning to the Diaz regime reveals
the writer's acute perception of Mexican development.

23. Simpson, Lesley Byrd. **Many Mexicos.** 3rd rev. ed. Berkeley, Calif.:
University of California Press, 1966. 389p. Reprint of 1952 edition.

This work, first published in 1941, is an entertaining, well-written general introduction to Mexican history from pre-historic times to the present, stressing the
many widely divergent geographical areas, cultures, and traditions. The author
is knowledgeable and perceptive in his interpretation of the "Many Mexicos."

PRE-HISPANIC TIMES

24. Benson, Elizabeth P. **The Maya World.** New York: Thomas Y. Crowell
Company, 1967. 172p.

The curator for the pre-Columbian collection at Dumbarton Oaks in Washington
has written an account of the world of the ancient Maya of southern Mexico and
Guatemala. The author concentrates upon the achievements of the Maya of the
classical period and discusses the work of archaeologists in solving the mysteries
of Maya civilization.

25. Bernal, Ignacio. **Mexico Before Cortez: Art, History and Legend.**
Translated by Willis Barnstone. Garden City, N.Y.: Doubleday &
Company, Inc., 1963. 135p.

Art, history and legend in antiquities. A good coverage of Mexico history to
1519.

26. Coe, Michael D. **Mexico.** New York: Praeger Publishers, Inc., 1962.
244p.

Describes the main pre-conquest culture in Mexico.

27. Duran, Diego. **The Aztecs: The History of the Indies of New Spain.** Edited and translated from the Spanish by Doris Heyden and Fernando Horcasitas. Introduction by Ignacio Bernal. New York: Orion Publishers, Inc., 1962. 384p.

Utilizing in part pre-Hispanic manuscripts which have since been lost, this sixteenth century chronicle is of great importance to the study of Aztec civilization. Duran, a Dominican missionary writing some 50 years after the Conquest, had a sympathetic understanding of Indians which was rare for his time. The present translation includes the history of the Aztecs from their mythical origins to the Conquest; it omits the sections about rites and the calendar.

28. Duran, Fray Diego. **Book of the Gods and Rites and The Ancient Calendar.** Translated and edited by Doris Heyden and Fernando Horcasitas. Foreword by Miguel Leon Portilla. Civilization of the American Indian, Vol. 102. Norman, Okla.: University of Oklahoma Press, 1971. 450p.

The chronicles of the sixteenth century on the ancient Mexicans were the forerunner of modern Mesoamerican ethnography. Among the most thorough were the writings of Diego Duran, an obscure Dominican friar who spent most of his life absorbing the language and culture of the Aztecs. His *Book of the Gods and Rites* is a detailed description of the religious life of the Aztecs, while The Ancient Calendar is a guide to their intricate system of measuring.

What is remarkable about Duran's work is the painstaking research based on the use of native informants, pre-Hispanic manuscripts and paintings, plus his own observations. Like *The Aztecs*, this work has been translated into English for the first time and edited brilliantly by Horcasitas and Heyden, whose knowledge of Nahuatl and Mesoamerican culture has contributed so much to our understanding of the world in which Duran worked. After 400 years of obscurity, Diego Duran now stands as one of the very best ethnohistorians of Mesoamerica.

29. Hardy, Jorge E. **Pre-Columbian Cities.** Translated by Judith Thorne. New York: Walker & Company, 1972. 384p.

A study of the ancient cities before the Spanish invasion in the sixteenth century.

30. Joyce, Thomas Athol. **Mexican Archaeology: An Introduction to the Archaeology of the Mexican and Mayan Civilizations of Pre-Spanish America.** Handbook to Ancient Civilization Series. New York: Hacker Art Books, 1969. 384p.

First published in 1914, this work arranged by topic covers tribal history, religion, calendar, writing, social organization and material culture of Mexican and Mayan antiquities. This book is one of the best in the early writing of prehistoric culture.

31. Larralde, Elsa. **The Land and People of Mexico.** Rev. ed. Portraits of
j the Nations Series. Philadelphia: J. B. Lippincott Company, 1964. 160p.

A wide-ranging survey of pre-conquest and later history, of economic changes, art and religion in the lives of people, and some goals for the future.

32.   Norman, James. **The Forgotten Empire**. New York: G. P. Putnam's
      Sons, 1965. 159p. o.p.
History of the Mayan people reconstructed by means of biographical sketches
of the explorers and archeologists who uncovered the mysteries of this ancient
empire, among whom the names of Stephens, Catherwood, Maudslay, Thompson,
and Ruz stand out. As a summary of the archeological achievements and of still
puzzling aspects of the Mayan empire, this is a useful and interesting book.

33.   Padden, R. C. **The Hummingbird and the Hawk: Conquest and
      Sovereignty in the Valley of Mexico, 1503-1541**. Columbus, Ohio:
      Ohio State University Press, 1967. 319p.
Brilliant, imaginative, and carefully documented reconstruction of the mythic
world of the Aztecs. It centers upon the role of the God Huitzilpochtli and
argues that his cult was the sustaining force of Mexican imperialism. Cortez
quickly realized the connection between Aztec sovereignty (Montezuma) and
Huitzilpochtli. He would liberate the subject tribes from Aztec rule by conquering in the name of the Virgin Mary. Padden shows that the conquest was a
psychological and religious victory as much as a military one.

34.   Peterson, Frederick A. **Ancient Mexico**. New York: G. P. Putnam's
      Sons, 1959. 313p.
An authoritative introduction to Mexican pre-Hispanic cultures.

35.   Soustelle, Jacques. **Daily Life of the Aztecs on the Eve of the Spanish
      Conquest**. New York: Macmillan Company Publishers, 1961. 319p.
First published in French, this documentary tells of the vast achievements of the
Aztecs at the beginning of the sixteenth century before the invasion of the
Spaniards. The daily life of the Aztec people, their social customs and structure
are related in this important work.

36.   Spores, Ronald. **The Mixtec Kings and Their People**. Civilization of
      the American Indian Series, No. 85. Norman, Okla.: University of
      Oklahoma Press, 1967. 269p.
An important cultural history, based on manuscripts and native pictorial documents, of the sixteenth century Mixtec people of Northwestern Caxaca before
the Conquest and Spanish rule.

37.   Thompson, J. Eric S. **The Rise and Fall of Maya Civilization**. 2nd ed.
      Norman, Okla.: University of Oklahoma Press, 1966. 415p. o.p.
This books deals with the new material relating to the Maya civilization, the
depopulation of the Maya central area, the archaeological post-contact of periods,
Mayan religion and myth, and major preoccupations of that people.

38.   Vaillant, George. **The Aztecs of Mexico: Origin, Rise, and Fall of the
      Aztec Nation**. Revised by Susannah B. Vaillant. Garden City, N.Y.:
      Doubleday & Company, Inc., 1962. 340p.
A detailed history of the preclassic and classic cultures of Mexico, describing the
Toltecs and the Aztec culture. The work contains notes and a bibliography.

39. Blacker, Irwin, and G. F. Ekholm. **Cortes and the Aztec Conquest.**
j   New York: Harper & Row Publishers, Inc., 1965. 153p.
A well-researched history of Cortes' conquest of Mexico. Illustrated with many paintings, drawings, and artifacts of the period.

40. De Fuentes, Patricia, editor and translator. **Conquistadors: First-Person Accounts of the Conquest of Mexico.** Preface by Howard F. Cline. New York: Grossman Publishers, Inc., 1963. 250p.
An extremely interesting collection of letters and chronicles in which Cortes and some of his followers reported the first stages of their sixteenth-century explorations in the new world. With the exception of the "third letter" of Cortes these narratives have hitherto been unavailable to the public.

41. Diaz Del Castillo, Bernal. **Discovery and Conquest of Mexico.** New York: Farrar, Straus & Giroux, Inc., 1956. 478p.
The first English version ever to be made generally available in this country of what all scholars agree is the most detailed and, apart from Cortes' own official reports, the most accurate first-hand account of the Spanish overthrow of Montezuma and the Conquest of Mexico.

42. Diaz Del Castillo, Bernal. **True History of the Conquest of Mexico: Written in the Year 1568.** March of America Series. Ann Arbor, Mich.: University Microfilm, 1966. Reprint of 1800 edition. 480p.
An exact reproduction of the 1800 edition. The work gives the unique presentation of two points of view of the sixteenth century Spanish conquest of the Aztec Empire.

43. Gardiner, Clinton Harvey. **The Constant Captain—Gonzalo de Sandoval.** Carbondale, Ill.: Southern Illinois University Press, 1961. 221p.
The story of Gonzalo de Sandoval, who became a captain under Cortes and who greatly aided Cortes in the conquest of Mexico.

44. Gibson, Charles. **The Aztecs Under Spanish Rule: A History of the Indians of the Valley of Mexico, 1519-1810.** Stanford, Calif.: Stanford University Press, 1964. 657p.
This classic on the history of the Indians of the Valley of Mexico traces the changes in the life of the Aztec people as a result of the conquest by the Spaniards. Chapters relate to the religious, political, economic, and social subjects of the Indians.

45. Glubok, Shirley, and L. Tillett, eds. **The Fall of the Aztecs.** New York:
j   St. Martin's Press, Inc., 1965. 114p.
An abridged edition, for young people, of the English classic *Discovery and Conquest of Mexico.*

46. Greenleaf, Richard E. **The Mexican Inquisition of the Sixteenth Century**. Albuquerque, N.M.: University of New Mexico Press, 1969. 242p.
A definitive study of the Mexican Inquisition based upon a thorough examination of materials in the Archivo de la Nacion, Ramo de la Inquisition in Mexico, D.F. A clear well-written analysis of the development of the Mexican Inquisition from the time of the Spanish Conquest to the establishment of the Tribunal of the Holy Office in 1571 and for 30 years thereafter.

47. Horgan, Paul. **Conquistadors in North American History**. New York: Farrar, Straus, & Giroux, Inc., 1963. 303p.
An account of all the early explorers, conqueros, and adventurers who brought Spanish civilization and faith to the New World. The book covers about 250 years of the early history of the discovery, exploration, and pillaging of Central America and the southern portions of our present-day United States. All the names, famous and infamous are there: Columbus, Cortes, Coronado, De Soto, Narvaez, Cabeza de Vaca, Onate, down to Diego de Vargas, the last of the Conquistadors. An excellently researched book.

48. Innes, Hammond. **The Conquistadors**. New York: Alfred A. Knopf, Inc., 1969. 336p.
The brutal destruction of the Aztec and Inca civilizations in Mexico and Peru under the swords of two of Spain's most ruthless explorer-conquerors, Cortez and Pizarro.

49. Johnson, William Weber. **Captain Cortes Conquers Mexico**. Illustrated
j   by Jose Cisneros. World Landmark Books. New York: Random House, 1961. 186p.
The Spanish expedition from its departure from Cuba to the destruction of Tenochtitlan.

50. Jones, Oakah L., Jr. **Pueblo Warriors and Spanish Conquest**. Norman, Okla.: University of Oklahoma Press, 1966. 225p.
Jones, a scholar in the field, has delved deeply into original sources to tell the story of the Spanish reconquest of the Pueblo Indians and the latter's subsequent employment as auxiliaries in Spanish campaigns against hostile tribes.

51. Keating, Bern. **Life and Death of the Aztec Nation**. New York: G. P.
j   Putnam's Sons, 1964. 159p.
Based on the legend of the return of the great white god which influenced the Aztec when Cortes came to the Valley of Mexico.

52. Leon-Portilla, Miguel, ed. **The Broken Spears: The Aztec Account of the Conquest of Mexico**. Adapted from original codices paintings by Alberto Beltran. English translation by Lysander Kemp. Boston: Beacon Press, 1962. 168p.
English translation of *Vision de los Vencidos* (1959), translated from Nahuatl by Angel Maria Gabribay K. An interesting work that presents the accounts, chronicles, and poems of Nahuatl writers. Conquest of Mexico is described from the Indian point of view.

53. Prescott, William Hickling. **The History of the Conquest of Mexico.**
Abridged edition. Harvey C. Gardiner. Chicago: University of Chicago
Press, 1966. 413p. Originally published in two volumes by Dutton
in 1909.
The definitive history of the period. A brilliantly told story of the conquest of
Mexico by Cortez and a handful of Spanish soldiers who invaded the Empire
of Montezuma contrary to the orders of Cortez' superior officer.

54. Prescott, William Hickling. **Prescott's Histories: The Rise and Decline
of the Spanish Empire.** Irwin R. Blacker, ed. New York: Viking Press,
Inc., 1963. 568p.
Includes Ferdinand and Isabella, conquest of Mexico, conquest of Peru, and
Philip II. Excellent in content and a very readable text.

55. Sunset Editors. **The Sea of Cortez.** Menlo Park, Calif.: Lane Magazine
and Book Company, 1966. 96p.
Brief history with beautiful photographs.

COLONIAL TIMES

56. Bannon, John Francis. **The Spanish Borderlands Frontier, 1513-1821.**
New York: Holt, Rinehart and Winston, 1970. 308p.
This book traces the stages in Spanish exploration, colonization, and expansion
on three "corridors": the Western, the Middle, and the Eastern. Bannon presents
a thorough and an animated picture of development along the "corridors" leading
to California, Arizona, New Mexico, and Texas.

57. Benitez, Fernando. **Century After Cortes.** Translated by Joan McLean.
Chicago: University of Chicago Press, 1965. 296p.
Mexico during the sixteenth century. A description of the life of the Spanish
ruling class.

58. Cameron, Roderick William. **Viceroyalties of the West: The Spanish
Empire in Latin America.** Boston: Little, Brown & Co., 1968. 276p.
The Spanish empire and its viceroyalties in Latin American history in 1830.
Excellent description of the Spanish colonies.

59. Cumberland, Charles C. **Mexican Revolution: The Constitutionalist
Years.** Texas Pan American Series. Austin, Texas: University of Texas
Press, 1972. 488p.
Traces Mexico's course through the anguish of civil war to the establishment of a
tenuous new government, the codification of revolutionary aspirations in a
remarkable constitution, and the emergence of an activist leadership determined
to propel Mexico into the select company of developed nations.

60. Ricard, Robert. **The Spiritual Conquest of Mexico.** Translated by
Lesley Byrd Simpson. Berkeley, Calif.: University of California Press,
1966. 423p.

An essay on the apostolate and the evangelizing methods of the mendicant orders in New Spain, 1523-1572, the period that the author identifies as the Golden Age of the missionary movement.

61. Simpson, Lesley Byrd. **Ecomienda in New Spain: The Beginning of Spanish Mexico.** Rev. and enl. ed. Berkeley, Calif.: University of California Press, 1966. 265p.
A well-documented account of the fief system in Mexico history during the Spanish regime, giving the relations between ecomenderos and the crown, restrictive legislation, and the weaker ecomienda of the late sixteenth century.

62. Tannenbaum, Frank. **Mexico: The Struggle for Peace and Bread.** New York: Alfred A. Knopf, Inc., 1950. 293p.
A survey of the events which have shaped present-day Mexico. Mexican history is traced from the colonial era, but the main emphasis is on the economic, social, and political developments of the country. A penetrating analysis of Mexican thinking.

63. Thomas, Alfred Barnaby. **After Coronado, Spanish Exploration Northeast of New Mexico, 1696-1727.** Civilization of the American Indian Series, No. 9. Norman, Okla.: University of Oklahoma Press, 1969. 307p. Reprint of 1935 edition.
An interesting collection of documents gathered from the archives of Spain, Mexico, and New Mexico. The range of these materials covers the 280 years between Coronado (1541) and the end of Spanish rule in North America (1821).

MODERN HISTORY

64. Atkin, Ronald. **Revolution: Mexico Nineteen Ten to Twenty.** New York: John Day Company, Inc., 1970. 354p.
A review of the political, social, economic, and military factors that contributed to the popular uprising whose consequences shaped modern Mexico's history. Each of the major figures who played a part in the events both Mexican and foreign is portrayed, including Porfirio Diaz, Pancho Villa, Emiliano Zapato, Alvaro Obregon, and General John Pershing.

65. Benson, Nettie Lee, ed. **Mexico and the Spanish Cortes, 1810-1822.** Latin American Monograph Series, No. 5. Austin, Texas: University of Texas Press, 1966. 243p.
Eight essays on the history of the Spanish legislative body in nineteenth century Mexico cover the election of Mexican deputies and their role in the Cortes, freedom of the press, the effect of the Cortes on Church reforms. The essays, which contain new material, make a valuable contribution.

66. Brenner, Anita. **The Wind That Swept Mexico: The History of the Mexican Revolution of 1910-1942.** New ed. Texas Pan American Series. Austin, Texas: University of Texas Press, 1971. 316p.
A new edition of the original 1943 work in which 184 historical photographs,

assembled by George R. Leighton, present the history of the Mexican Revolution. A sympathetic survey of the Mexican Revolution.

67. Brooks, Nathan Covington. **Complete History of the Mexican War, 1846-1848**. Chicago: Rio Grande Press, Inc., 1965. 558p.
This is a reprint of a book first published in 1849. It is valuable as a period piece and because it contains pertinent military information and the complete Treaty of Guadalupe Hidalgo.

68. Chidsey, Donald B. **The War with Mexico**. New York: Crown Publishers, Inc., 1968. 192p.
This narrative of the 1830s and 1840s covers the United States' controversy with Mexico from Goliad and the Alamo to Chapultepec. Those interested in further reading on this period will find the well-chosen bibliography useful.

69. Clendenen, Clarence C. **Blood on the Border: The United States Army and the Mexican Irregulars**. New York: Macmillan Co., 1969. 384p.
Border relations between the United States and Mexico from the 1850s to the American intervention in Juarez in 1919. The author has written a military history of events based on the literature and on interviews.

70. Connor, Seymour V., and Odie B. Faulk. **North America Divided: The Mexican War, 1846-1848**. New York: Oxford University Press, 1971. 300p.
A new approach to the Mexican War, which sets aside the preconceived bias of most historians and places the blame for the war on both Mexico and the United States. Asserting that the war between the United States and Mexico is largely misrepresented in conventional studies, the authors, who are professors of history in two Southwestern universities, attest to the responsibility for initiating the war on the part of factions in both Mexico and the United States. The conflict is set within the context of the nineteenth century political and military thought and to illustrate, through documented accounts of the course of the war, the issues and events that influenced the final outcome. An extensive, annotated Spanish-English analytical bibliography is appended, arranged by subject with a concluding main entry list by author.

71. Cosio, Villegas Daniel. **The United States Versus Porfiorio Diaz**. Translated by Nettie Lee Benson. Lincoln, Neb.: University of Nebraska Press, 1963. 259p.
A history of the United States-Mexican diplomatic relations in the first years of Diaz' rule beginning in 1876. Writing from the Mexican viewpoint but with scholarly objectivity, the author details the negotiations over border disputes. Notes and a bibliography are appended.

72. Dawson, Daniel. **The Mexican Adventure**. Freeport, N.Y.: Books for Libraries, 1971. 433p. Reprint of 1935 edition.
The author covers the years of Maximilian's reign as Emperor of Mexico and also European intervention during the years from 1861 to 1867.

73.　　Dufour, Charles L. **The Mexican War, A Compact History, 1846-1848.**
　　　　Translated by Ernest E. Dupuy. Military History of the United States
　　　　Series. New York: Hawthorne Books, 1968. 304p.
Almost totally a military history; when personalities and government policies
are discussed, however, very objective views are presented.

74.　　Hamilton, Charles Walter. **Early Day Oil Tales of Mexico.** Houston,
　　　　Texas: Gulf Publishing Company, 1966. 246p.
The author, who worked in Mexico during the great oil boom from 1912 to
1922, recalls the tales he heard.

75.　　Hanna, Alfred Jackson, and Kathryn Abbey Hanna. **Napoleon III and
　　　　Mexico: American Triumph Over Monarchy.** Chapel Hill, N.C.: University of North Carolina Press, 1971. 350p.
History of Mexico during the European intervention period from 1861 to 1867.
Includes illustrations and an extensive bibliography.

76.　　Henry, Robert S. **Story of the Mexican War.** New York: Frederick
　　　　Ungar Publishing Company, Inc., 1960. 424p.
A well-documented and very readable account of the Mexican war in which
leadership and the people are well viewed.

77.　　Johnson, William Weber. **Heroic Mexico: The Violent Emergence of a
　　　　Modern Nation.** Mainstream of the Modern World. Garden City, N.Y.:
　　　　Doubleday & Company, Inc., 1968. 463p.
An extremely readable history of the Mexican Revolution showing the heroism
of the Mexican people. Heavy emphasis is placed on revolutionary leadership
figures.

78.　　Lieuwen, Edwin. **Mexican Militarism: The Political Rise and Fall of the
　　　　Revolutionary Army, 1910-1940.** Albuquerque, N.M.: University of
　　　　New Mexico Press, 1968. 194p.
The Mexican Revolution, as the author writes, was a matter of one question—
whether the army or the civilians would govern Mexico. The story of how
civilian politicans brought civilian rule to Mexico is a classic in the annals of
political astuteness.

79.　　McClellan, George Brinton. **The Mexican War Diary of General George
　　　　B. McClellan.** Edited by William Starr Myers. New York: Da Capo,
　　　　1972. 97p.
A personal narrative of the war with Mexico in 1845 to 1848, giving the American
scene as written in the diary of this notable general.

80.　　Nicholson, Irene. **The Liberators: A Study of Independence Movements
　　　　in Spanish America.** New York: Praeger Publishers, 1969. 336p.
An intensive study that makes a searching appraisal of the South.

81.   Price, Glenn W. **Origins of the War with Mexico: The Polk-Stockton Intrigue.** Austin, Texas: University of Texas Press, 1967. 189p.

The intrigue of President Polk and Commodore Stockton in the war with Mexico.

82.   Quirk, Robert E. **The Mexican Revolution, 1914-1915; The Convention of Aguascalientes.** New York: W. W. Norton & Company, Inc., 1970. 325p. Reprint of 1960 edition.

The reissue of this study, awarded the Bancroft prize in 1961, again makes available a work of much value for students of Mexican history. Quirk's monograph studies a short but crucial stage of the revolution during which time Zapata, Huerta, Villa, Carranza, Obregon, and other military chieftans struggled for control.

83.   Ramirez, Jose Fernando. **Mexico During the War with the United States.** Walter V. Scholes, editor. Translated by Elliott B. Scherr. University of Missouri Studies, Vol. 23, No. 1. Columbia, Mo.: University of Missouri Press, 1950. 165p.

A scholarly treatment of the war between Mexico and the United States.

84.   Reed, John. **Insurgent Mexico.** 2nd ed. New York: Simon & Schuster, 1969. 325p. Reprint of 1914 edition.

A different approach to modern Mexico is John Reed's kaleidoscopic and journalistic work on the Pancho Villa era. With minor corrections the text of the 1914 edition has been retained. In a new introduction the editors sketch in the events leading to the Mexican Revolution and give a short biography of Reed.

85.   Reeder, Red. **The Story of the Mexican War.** American Military History Series. New York: Hawthorn Books, Inc., 1967. 184p.

This controversial war was filled with picturesque personalities, agonizing campaigns, and maneuvering by President Polk.

86.   Ross, Betty. **Mexico: Land of Eagle and Serpent.** New York: Roy
j   Publishers, 1965. 104p. o.p.

Mexican independence and the leaders from Santa Anna to Pancho Villa.

87.   Ross, Stanley Robert. **Is the Mexican Revolution Dead?** Borzoi Books on Latin America Series. New York: Alfred A. Knopf, 1966. 255p.

The theme attempts to communicate a distinct and elusive image of the Mexican. Significant essays in this book are by Luis Cabrera, Jesus Silva Herzog, Gilberto Loyo, and Moises Navarro.

88.   Ruiz, Ramon, ed. **The Mexican War.** New York: Holt, Rinehart & Winston, Inc., 1963. 118p.

A good introdution to the United States-Mexican War.

89.   Singletary, Otis A. **The Mexican War.** Chicago: University of Chicago Press, 1960. 181p.

This work continues to be a standard among works giving an unobjective account of the Mexican War. Divided equally between an account of the military operations and the intrigues among the U.S. military and civil authorities.

90. Tannebaum, Frank. **Peace by Revolution: Mexico After 1910.** New York: Columbia University Press, 1966. 316p. Reprint of 1933 edition. This excellent book treats the subject of Mexico intellectually and with great sympathy and understanding, since the author traveled extensively in Mexico and was able to make personal contact with Mexican leaders. The work gives first-hand views.

91. Turner, John Kenneth. **Barbarous Mexico.** Texas Pan American Series. Austin, Texas: University of Texas Press, 1969. 322p. A crusading California newspaperman's expose of the Diaz regime. This book has been called the *Uncle Tom's Cabin* of the Mexican Revolution. *Barbarous Mexico* was published serially beginning in 1909 but has been out of print for nearly 60 years. This new edition includes a biographical essay on Turner as well as photographs of the characters involved. A vivid account of life in Mexico under the tyrant Diaz.

92. Werstein, Irving. **Land and Liberty: The Mexican Revolution 1910-1919.** New York: Cowles Book Co., 1971. 214p. A factual picture of the bloodshed which accompanied the overthrow of Diaz, president of Mexico, and of the subsequent struggle for power. Vivid portrayals of such men as Francisco Madero, Pancho Villa, Victoriano Huerta and Emiliano Zapata are given in the text.

93. Werstein, Irving. **The War with Mexico.** New York: Grossett & Dunlap, Inc., 1965. 175p. This account of the United States' war with Mexico discusses actual battles and brings to light the social and political concepts which led to the war.

MEXICO TODAY

94. Avila, Manuel. **Tradition and Growth: A Study of Four Mexican Villages.** Chicago: University of Chicago Press, 1969. 219p. This study sets forth the unique characteristics of four communities today, each of which traces its origin to ancient periods.

95. Brasher, Christopher. **Mexico 1968: A Diary of the XIXth Olympiad.** New York: Sportshelf and Soccer Associate, 1969. 142p. A British sports journalist and former Gold Medallist presents a concise, informal account of the nineteenth Olympiad held in Mexico City in October 1968.

96. Brooks, Nathan Covington. **United States and Mexico.** Rev. ed. Cambridge, Mass.: Harvard University Press, 1963. 484p. o.p. Explores the relationship between Mexico and the United States, considering geographic, historic, political, economic, and social growth.

97.   Dunn, Frederick Sherwood. **The Diplomatic Protection of Americans in Mexico in International Finance and Diplomacy**. New York: Columbia University Press, 1972. 439p.
Prepared under the auspices of Columbia University Council for Research in the Social Sciences. Covers foreign relations between the United States and Mexico, and also Americans in Mexico.

98.   International Congress of Historians of the United States and Mexico. **The New World Looks at Its History**. Proceedings. Archibald R. Lewis and Thomas F. McGann, editors. Austin, Texas: University of Texas Press, 1962. 220p.
Published for the Institute of Latin American Studies, these papers make a readable and interesting story. The essays go far in exploring and debating the frontier concept, maintaining a high professional standard but varying widely in their comments and approach. The editors have compiled a useful index. An interesting examination of the special nature of the history of the new world and the ideas which interested its historians.

99.   James, Daniel. **Mexico and the Americans**. New York: Praeger Publishers, Inc., 1963. 472p. o.p.
History of Mexican-U.S. relations—diplomatic, political, and economic—from the Civil War to the second summer of the Kennedy administration. The author's observation point is located, figuratively, south of the border, so that he helps the U.S. reader see such areas of mutual interest as oil and expropriations, immigrant labor, and lead-zinc quota from the Mexican side. An informative and easy-to-read book.

100.   King, Timothy. **Mexico: Industrialization and Trade Policies Since 1940**. New York: Oxford University Press, 1970. 160p.
King concentrates upon the industrial sector and particularly on how the growth of that sector has been influenced by the Mexican government's policy of stimulating import substitution. He examines this policy critically and suggests that more stress on developing export industries would seem to be the better course of action. Many tables present new data and the extensive index complements the text.

101.   Liss, Sheldon B. **A Century of Disagreement: The Chamizal Conflict, 1864-1964**. St. Louis, Mo.: Washington University Press, 1967. 165p.
The Chamizal conflict symbolized much that had been wrong between Mexico and the United States. An historical analysis of the problems. Maps are included, and also a student edition.

102.   Liss, Sheldon B., and Peggy K. Liss, compilers. **Man, State, and Society in Latin American History**. New York: Praeger Publishers, Inc., 1972. 456p.
History, social and economic conditions of each country are well covered in this new book on Latin America.

103. **Major Trends in Mexican Philosophy**, by Mexico National University. Translated by A. Robert Caponigri. Notre Dame, Ind.: University of Notre Dame Press, 1966. 382p.
Selected papers of the Thirteenth International Congress of Philosophy. Seven essays detail the development and principal movements of Mexican philosophy.

104. Romanell, Patrick. **The Making of the Mexican Mind: A Study in Recent Mexican Thought.** Lincoln, Neb.: University of Nebraska Press, 1952. 213p.
A sympathetic and interesting account of the evolution of Mexican philosophical thought traced through five stages: scholasticism of the Colonial era, the Enlightenment, Antirationalism, Positivism and Antipositivism. Detailed chapters cover the work of Antonio Casco and Jose Vasconcelos.

105. Schurz, William Lytle. **This New World.** The Civilization of Latin America. New York: E. P. Dutton, 1954. 429p.
The impact of Spain on the new world and that of the new world on Spain are comprehensively viewed in *This New World.* A study of the history of various racial and social elements of the colonial period and their importance in present-day Latin America.

106. Worcester, Donald E. **The Three Worlds of Latin America.** New York:
j   E. P. Dutton and Company, Inc., 1963. 189p.
A historical survey of the political and economic development of Latin America from the earliest days of Spanish exploration and colonization. A country-by-country analysis for the nineteenth and twentieth centuries brings each up to 1962.

CIVILIZATION

107. Aaron, Jan, and Georgine S. Salom. **The Art of Mexican Cooking.** Garden City, N.Y.: Doubleday & Company, Inc., 1965. 309p.
Mexican dishes adapted for U.S. kitchens and fascinating comments on the history of Mexican food.

108. Beals, Carleton. **Land of the Mayas: Yesterday and Today.** Photo-
j   graphs by Marianne Greenwood. New York: Abelard-Schuman, 1967. 158p. o.p.
Authoritative, moving portrait of the ancient Mayas and their descendants.

109. Beals, Carleton. **Stories Told by the Aztecs: Before the Spaniards**
j   **Came.** Illustrated by Charles Pickard. New York: Abelard-Schuman, 1970. 208p.
Illustrated stories giving valuable insight into the Aztec civilization before the Spanish Conquest.

110. Bleeker, Sonia. **The Aztec, Indians of Mexico.** New York: William
j   Morrow & Company, Inc., 1963. 610p.

Aztec civilization, history, religion, customs, and conquest are simply and well portrayed. A final chapter covers the life of the Aztec Indians today.

111. Bray, Warwick. **Everyday Life of the Aztec.** New York: G. P. Putman's Sons, 1969. 208p.
After briefly sketching in the setting and history of the Aztecs, the author focuses on the Aztec civilization, detailing everyday life with regard to family, work and pastimes, city and country life, religion, politics, commerce, and warfare. Photographs, maps, and authentic drawings complement the text.

112. Brock, Virginia. **Pinatas.** Illustrated by Anne Marie Jauss. Nashville,
j   Tenn.: Abingdon Press, 1966. 106p.
The traditional uses of the pinata and instructions for making pinatas of various shapes suitable for different holiday celebrations.

113. Bunker, Robert Manson, and John Adair. **The First Look at Strangers.** New Brunswick, N.J.: Rutgers University Press, 1959. 154p.
A well-documented description of Mexican heritage.

114. Cassel, Jonathon F. **Tahahumara Indians.** San Antonio, Texas: The Naylor Company, 1969. 160p.
A writer who stayed, with his wife and son, among Mexico's Tarahumara Indians gives a sympathetic account of these isolated, primitive cave dwellers.

115. Coe, Michael D. **America's First Civilization.** New York: American
j   Heritage Publishers, 1968. 159p.
Discoveries made during the last 50 years and as recently as the 1960s concerning the Olmec Indians of southern Mexico are reviewed by an archaeologist who played a major role in digging up the remains of their culture.

116. Coe, Michael D. **The Maya.** New York: Frederick A. Praeger, 1968. 252p.
The book deals with the geography, cultural development, and life and thought of the Maya. Good for casual reading, it is an excellent account of Maya archaeology.

117. Conrad, Barnaby. **La Fiesta Brava: The Art of the Bull Ring.** Boston: Houghton Mifflin Company, 1953. 184p.
The drama and excitement of "the brave spectacle" are captured in memorable photographs, diagrammatic drawings, and vivid descriptions. An informative volume on the history, techniques, and behind-the-scenes details of the art of the bullfight.

118. Crow, John A. **The Epic of Latin America.** Rev. ed. Garden City, N.Y.: Doubleday & Company, Inc., 1971. 879p.
A revised and updated interpretation of Latin America from the days of the Mayas, Incas, and Aztecs up to the present day.

119. Demaris, Ovid. **Poso del Mundo: Inside the Mexican American Border, from Tijuana to Matamoros**. Boston: Little, Brown Company, 1970. 244p.

A discussion of vice and gambling along the border as linked to Mexican political history and shady southern California financial interests.

120. Ediger, Donald. **The Well of Sacrifice**. Garden City, N.Y.: Doubleday & Company, 1971. 228p.

Engrossing account of the archaeological expedition that probed the depths of the mysterious sacred well at Chichen Itza, on Mexico's Yucatan Peninsula, in search of clues to the baffling ancient Mayan civilization. Photographs.

121. Fagen, Richard R., and William S. Quoky. **Politics and Privilege in a Mexican City**. Studies in Comparative Politics 5. Stanford, Calif.: Stanford University Press, 1972. 224p.

An analysis and study of politics in Jalapa, Veracruz.

122. Fergusson, Erna. **Mexican Cookbook**. Albuquerque, N.M.: University of New Mexico Press, 1967. 128p.

Old Mexican recipes have been adapted for modern U.S. kitchens. This book, in print and often revised since 1934, is a classic source book.

123. Fromm, Erich, and Michael Maccoby. **Social Character in a Mexican Village: A Sociopsychoanalytic Study**. Englewood Cliffs, N.J.: Prentice-Hall, Inc., 1970. 303p.

Over a period of 13 years the authors studied a small Mexican village that had no cultural ties with the past, combining techniques of interview, questionnaires, and direct observation with a grasp of the social and economic condition of the village. This study convinced them that traditional values are often destroyed by modern technology. A technical but stimulating book.

124. Gibson, Charles, ed. **The Spanish Tradition in America**. Columbia, S.C.: University of South Carolina Press, 1968. 257p.

The documentary selections of this volume extend in time from the late fifteenth century, when the larger part of Spanish America declared its independence.

125. Gibson, Charles. **Spain in America**. New York: Harper and Row Publishers, Inc., 1966. 239p. Revised version of the 1904 book by Bourne.

A presentation of Spanish America from the earliest explorers to the modern times, discussing such subjects as the power and influence of the church and the relationship between the Spaniards and the Indians. A careful survey of the present state of knowledge and scholarship, with a critical bibliography.

126. Granberg, Wilbur J. **People of the Maguey: The Otomi Indians of Mexico**. New York: Frederick A. Praeger, Inc., 1970. 168p.

A compassionate and informative account of the Otomis: their fiestas, their superstitions, and their reluctance to enter the twentieth century.

127.   Hayner, Norman Sylvester. **New Patterns in Old Mexico: A Study of Town and Metropolis.** New Haven, Conn.: College and University Press, 1966. 316p.
A comparison of the old and the new in Mexican village and city.

128.   Irwin, Constance. **Fair Gods and Stone Faces: Ancient Seafarers and the New World's Most Intriguing Riddle.** New York: St. Martin's Press, Inc., 1963. 346p.
An illustrated study of the origin of Mexican, Central and South American peoples and their civilization.

129.   Joy, Charles R. **Young People of Mexico and Central America.** Des Moines, Iowa: Duell, Sloan & Pierce, 1962. 152p. o.p.
Students from Mexico and Central America write about their own countries, their home and school life, and what they enjoy doing, plus other activities of interest to young people.

130.   Kessell, John. **Mission of Sorrows: Jesuit Guevavi and the Pimas, 1691-1767.** Tucson, Ariz.: University of Arizona Press, 1970. 224p.
Original title: *Black Robes at Guevavi: Jesuits on the Pima Frontier, 1691-1767.* A fascinating narrative of long-buried historical facts of the efforts of Father Kino and his successors to transform a native rancheria into an ordered mission community. A meticulously researched contribution to the history of the Spanish borderlands.

131.   Lambert, Elizabeth Ortiz. **Complete Book of Mexican Cooking.** New York: Evans Publishing Co., 1967. 320p.
One of the best books on Mexican cooking for North Americans.

132.   Leonard, Jonathan Norton. **Ancient America.** Great Ages of Man Series. New York: Time-Life Books, 1967. 192p.
An account of the rise and fall of the ancient Indian cultures of Latin America, including the Aztecs, Mayas, and Incas based on the testimony of early Spanish chronicles, travelers, sociologists, modern archaeologists and anthropologists.

133.   Lewis, Oscar. **Anthropological Essays.** New York: Random House, 1970. 523p.
A collection of Lewis' anthropological essays written during the 1941-1966 period reflects the transition in his work from the study of tribal society to the study of peasant communities in Mexico and India and on the urban scene.

134.   Lewis, Oscar. **The Children of Sanchez: Autobiography of a Mexican Family.** New York: Random House, 1961. 499p.
Biographical picture of a family of slum dwellers in Mexico City, based on taped interviews with four adult children of Jesus Sanchez. Realistic, earthy picture of the "culture of poverty."

135.   Lewis, Oscar. **A Death in the Sanchez Family**. New York: Random
        House, 1969. 119p.
The reaction of the members of the Sanchez family to the death of old Aunt
Guadalupe. Lewis' main subject is how her life and death reflected the culture
of poverty in which she lived.

136.   Lewis, Oscar. **Five Families: Mexican Case Studies in the Culture of
        Poverty**. New York: Basic Books, Inc., 1959. 351p.
Events and activities of a typical day in the lives of five Mexican families
representative of rural village life, slums, working class and upper class *nouveau
riche* in Mexico City.

137.   Lewis, Oscar. **Life in a Mexican Village: Tepoztlan Restudied**. Urbana,
        Ill.: University of Illinois Press, 1963. 512p.
A magnificent ethnography of a Mexican village. Gathering means were combined
to produce a total picture of a village studied first by Robert Redfield and
described in his *Tepoztlan* (1930).

138.   Lewis, Oscar. **Pedro Martinez**. New York: Random House, 1964. 507p.
A study of a Mexican village family, given in their own words: of the father
born into an Aztec village, joining Zapata's revolutionary army when a young
man, then entering the political life of the village; of the mother; and of the
first son.

139.   Miller, Ann D. **Matadors of Mexico**. Globe, Ariz.: D. S. King, 1961.
  j   307p.
A colorful account of modern bullfighting in Mexico and comments on the
matadors who are most familiar to American aficionados.

140.   Norman, James. **Charro: Mexican Horseman**. New York: G. P. Put-
  j   nam's Sons, 1969. 129p.
Illustrated with photographs, this book encompasses the history and development of the horse in the Western hemisphere and thereby presents an encapsula-
tion of Mexican history.

141.   Parsons, Elsie Clews. **Mitla: Town of the Souls**. Chicago: University
        of Chicago Press, 1936. 590p.
Life in the Zapotecan village of 2,500 in Oaxaca. Explanation of what is
Indian and what is Spanish.

142.   Reed, Alma M. **The Ancient Past of Mexico**. New York: Crown Pub-
  j   lishers, Inc., 1966. 388p.
An up-to-date survey of Mexico's latest archaeological discoveries.

143.   Schendel, Gordon. **Medicine in Mexico: From Aztec Herbs to Betatrons**.
        Austin, Texas: University of Texas Press, 1968. 329p.
The material covered by this book has been grouped under three major headings:
Aztec medicine, the Spanish Colonial Period, and modern Mexican medicines,

from Independence to the present time. The contents of the earlier historical periods are the usual anecdotes about miraculous cures with Indian ingredients or the glamorous accounts of pre-Columbian medicine.

144.   Stone, Idella Purnell. **30 Mexican Menus in Spanish and English.** Los Angeles, Calif.: Ward Ritchie, 1971. 196p.
A new and interesting book of Mexican cookery using materials available in modern supermarkets.

145.   Stoppelman, Joseph W. F. **People of Mexico.** New York: Hastings House Publishers, Inc., 1966. 256p.
A portrait of the Mexican people drawn by a sympathetic and discerning eye.

146.   Thompson, John Eric S. **Maya Archaeologist.** Norman, Okla.: University of Oklahoma Press, 1963. 284p.
Thompson has a thorough knowledge of the Maya civilization and its cultures and a sympathy for its descendants which he reveals in this account of his early expeditions. Drawings, photographs, maps, a glossary, and key to pronunciation accompany the text.

147.   Villicana, Eugenio. **Viva Morelia.** Illustrated by Elisa Manriquez. New
j   York: M. Evans Co., 1972. 63p.
A Mexican boy describes the homes, holidays, schools, bullfights, markets, people, and other aspects of life in his country.

148.   Von Hagen, Victor. **Maya, Land of the Turkey and the Deer.** Illustrated
j   by Alberto Beltran. Cleveland, Ohio: World Publishing Company, 1960. 126p.
Ancient Mayan civilization which arose about 350 B.C. and lasted until the final Spanish Conquest in 1697 is described through the life of Ah Tok, a young boy. Chronological chart is included.

149.   Von Hagen, Victor. **The Sun Kingdom of the Aztecs.** Illustrated by
j   Alberto Beltran. Cleveland, Ohio: World Publishing Company, 1958. 126p.
Aztec customs, religion, culture and methods of warfare just before the coming of the Spaniards. A chronological chart of world events places the Aztecs in relation to European and Asian civilizations.

150.   Wilkie, James W. **The Mexican Revolution: Federal Expenditure and Social Change Since 1910.** 2nd ed. Berkeley, Calif.: University of California Press, 1967. 337p.
An original study as to how expenditures by the federal government relate to social changes covering a four-period basis: political revolution (1910-1930), social revolution (1930-1940), economic revolution (1940-1960) and balanced revolution (since 1960).

151.   Wolfe, Linda, ed. **McCall's Introduction to Mexican Cooking.** New York: McCall Publishing Company, 1971. 96p.

Many Americans think that Mexican food is no more than a bowl of chili and a big tortilla. But this book will show you that it is a colorful, tangy, and immensely varied cuisine—an exciting mixture of the Aztec and Spanish culinary traditions. An introduction gives a brief history of Mexican cooking.

152.   Zelayeta, Elena Emilia. **Elena's Secrets of Mexican Cooking.** New York: Prentice-Hall, Inc., 1958. 266p.

A popular group of recipes from the author's native Mexico, adapted to U.S. tastes and kitchens. Grouped in an appetizer-through-dessert arrangement.

153.   Zorita, Alfonso de. **Life and Labor in Ancient Mexico: The Brief and Summary Relations of the Lords of New Spain.** Translated by Benjamin Keen. New Brunswick, N.J.: Rutgers University Press, 1964. 328p.

Written in 1590, this work provides many informative details about ordinary life in ancient Mexico. Its purpose is to show how and why the Indians disappeared in such numbers from the Mexican scene in the middle of the sixteenth century.

GEOGRAPHY, DESCRIPTION AND TRAVEL

154.   Brand, Donald D. **Mexico, Land of Sunshine and Shadow.** New York: Van Nostrand-Reinhold Books, 1966. 159p.

The land, people, economics, politics, and foreign relations of Mexico are given, with emphasis on data rather than narrative. A useful reference book.

155.   Brasch, R. **Mexico: A Country of Contrasts.** New York: David McKay Company, Inc., 1967. 210p.

An Australian rabbi presents his impressions of Mexico. After a short sketch of the history of Mexico, Dr. Brasch gives descriptions, experiences, and enthusiasms in a popular and entertaining style. He gives a fascinating account of the "Jews of Mexico." A welcome addition in young adult collections.

156.   Calderon de la Barca, Frances Erskine (Inglis). **Life in Mexico: The Letters of Fanny Calderon de la Barca.** Edited and annotated by Howard T. Fisher and Marion Hall Fisher. Garden City, N.Y.: Doubleday & Company, Inc., 1966. 834p.

The journals and letters of this Scotswoman comprise a picture of nineteenth century Mexico. She married a Spanish diplomat and spent two years (1840-1841) in Mexico, mostly in the capital, though she traveled to other parts of the country as well. This memoir, published more than a century ago, is one of the most enduring, lighthearted and informative books ever written about Mexico.

157.   Caldwell, John C. **Let's Visit Mexico.** New York: John Day Company, j   1965. 96p.

Mexico's history and present-day living presented in easy reading with many photographs.

158. Camp, Andre. **The Mexico I Love.** Translated from the French by
      Ruth Whipple Fermaud. New York: Tudor Publishing Co., 1968. 140p.
The author covers the entire area of Mexico with good text and lively illustrations and photographs. A good book for browsing.

159. Carlson, Loraine. **Mexico: An Extraordinary Guide.** Chicago: Rand-
      McNally and Company, 1971. 416p.
A well-written comprehensive guidebook which includes attractive, strategically
placed maps. This work is sufficiently complete to serve as an introductory reference on Mexico. Part 1 includes brief accounts of the history, people, economy,
government, architecture, literature, art, traditions and customs. Part 2 is devoted
to particulars of the trip and contains useful and valuable advice for a visitor or
prospective resident. The principal section, Part 3, is seeing Mexico.

160. Cobbe, Annetta J. **Why, How & Where to Live in Mexico.** Philadelphia:
      Dorrance and Company, 1971. 165p.
The author has written a comprehensive guidebook for the individual desiring
to live in Mexico: the how and where to live in Mexico is ably covered. The
emigration and immigration problems are indicated, with solutions for the
problems.

161. Crow, John A. **Mexico Today.** Rev. ed. New York: Harper & Row
      Publishers, 1972. 369p.
A revised edition of a book which has become a standard on the background and
character of Mexico and its people. The historical background as well as the
current scene are presented and differences between Mexican and U.S. cultures
are noted.

162. Dodge, David. **Best of Mexico by Car: A Selective Guide to Motor
      Travel South of the Border.** Rev. ed. New York: Macmillan Company,
      1969. 230p. 1968 ed. was published under the title *Fly Down, Drive
      Mexico.*
A selective candid guide for the economy-minded motorist. Customs, rental
procedures and costs, automobile regulations, road maps, and accommodations
are covered thoroughly. Tours of varying length to remote areas as well as visits
to familiar cities are described in detail with Dodge's wry humor.

163. Drumm, Stella M., ed. **Down the Santa Fe Trail and Into Mexico: The
      Diary of Susan Shelby Magoffin, 1846-1847.** Rev. ed. New Haven,
      Conn.: Yale University Press, 1962. 294p.
An interesting journal kept by Susan Shelby Magoffin of her travels with her
husband along the Santa Fe Trail. Excellent descriptions of the country.

164. Egan, Ferol. **The El Dorado Trail: The Story of the Gold Rush Routes
      Across Mexico.** American Trail Series. New York: McGraw-Hill
      Book Company, 1970. 313p.
Journeys across northern, central, and southern Mexico to California during the
1848 gold rush. Includes maps of the routes.

165. Ferlinghetti, Lawrence. **The Mexican Night**: **Travel Journal**. New
York: New Directions Publishing Co., 1970. 58p.
The first of a series of travel journals by Ferlinghetti presents Mexican life in
the village and the city as the author sees it during his tour of Mexico.

166. Flandrau, Charles Macomb. **Viva Mexico!** Rev. ed. Harvey C. Gardiner,
ed. Chicago: University of Illinois Press, 1964. 320p.
Originally published in 1908, this work has become recognized as a classic of
travel literature and is still regarded as one of the best travel books ever written.
Its perceptive account of the Mexican people is invaluable as an eye-witness
description of Mexican life near the end of the Diaz regime.

167. Ford, Norman D. **All of Mexico at Low Cost**. 4th rev. and exp. ed.
Greenlawn, N.Y.: Harian's Publications, 1972. 188p.
Originally published under the title *Fiesta Lands, Mexico and Guatemala by Car*.
This guide to Mexico and Guatemala covers hotels, restaurants, travel routes,
currency, shopping and describes the exciting things to see along the roads, in
the towns, and on outstanding side trips.

168. Gardner, Erle Stanley. **Mexico's Magic Square**. New York: William
Morrow & Company, Inc., 1968. 205p.
One more in a sequence of Gardner's interpretive reports on his wanderings in
an assortment of vehicles over the peninsula of Baja, California. This time he
introduces his reading public to the colorful, contradictory aspects of a 130-mile
square area south of the border, most of which is virtually unknown to the U.S.
tourist. He makes known picturesque and prominent personalities he encountered.

169. Gilmore, Betty, and Don Gilmore. **A Guide to Living in Mexico**. New
York: G. P. Putnam's Sons, 1971. 256p.
U.S. writers who are residents of Mexico highlight selected facts and insights to
assist Americans contemplating a similar move as well as recent arrivals under-
going cultural shock. Part 1 informally blends theory and date—the cultural
differences, income requirements, business opportunities and customs. Part 2 is
on language differences between Castilian and Mexican Spanish; it lists words
and phrases useful in post office, market, and other common situations.

170. Hanf, Walter. **Mexico City and Its Surroundings**. Panorama Book
Series. Garden City, N.Y.: Doubleday & Company, 1968. 61p.
Hanf describes Mexico, tells of its people and their history and how they are
"discovering their way into the future."

171. Hedrick, Basil Calvin, et al., eds. **The North Mexican Frontier: Readings
in Archaeology, Ethnohistory, and Ethnography**. Carbondale, Ill.:
Southern Illinois University Press, 1971. 225p.
Addresses, essays and lectures on the ancient culture and geography of northern
Mexico; the Tepehuan, Uto-Aztec, Indian tribes, archaeological sites at La
Quemada, Zape, Durango and others.

172.   Helfritz, Hans. **Mexican Cities of the Gods: An Archaeological Guide.**
       New York: Frederick A. Praeger, Inc., 1970. 180p.
The title is misleading: the book is not an archaeological guide, it is a travel
guide and "picture book" devoted to a number of famous prehistoric sites in
Mexico. Includes photographs, line drawings, maps, and a chronological list.

173.   Herhard, Peter. **Guide to the Historical Geography of New Spain.**
       Cambridge Latin American Studies 14. New York: Cambridge Univer-
       sity Press, 1972. 476p.
A historical geography of New Spain (modern Central and Southern Mexico).
The author omits Yucatan, Chiapa, and Nueva Galicia from the study. Time
period covered is 1519-1821.

174.   Hobart, Lois. **Mexican Mural: The Story of Mexico, Past and Present.**
   j   New York: Harcourt, Brace & World, Inc., 1963. 224p.
This portrait of Mexico presents the land and the people with clarity, perception
and vividness. Photographs included.

175.   Johnson, William Weber. **Mexico.** Rev. ed. New York: Time-Life,
       Inc., 1966. 160p.
Illustrated with numerous photographs, many of them in color, this book presents a political, historical, economic, social, and cultural tour of Mexico.

176.   Lummis, Charles Fletcher. **The Land of Poco Tiempo.** Albuquerque,
       N.M.: University of New Mexico Press, 1966. 310p.
This is a reprint of a popularly written book first published in 1928. While
dated, it does provide glimpses of life in the American Southwest which are
revealing.

177.   Marett, Sir Robert Hugh Kirk. **Mexico.** Nations and Peoples Series.
       New York: Walker & Company, 1971. 208p.
A romantic and revolutionary chronicle which highlights the diversity and natural
beauty of Mexico is recounted by a British aficionado. Marett's engaging style
characterizes a colorful people and country. A Who's Who briefly identifies
personages of the nineteenth and twentieth centuries.

178.   Milne, Jean. **Fiesta Time in Latin America.** Los Angeles, Calif.:
       Ward Ritchie Press, 1965. 236p.
This work includes holidays and related customs of Mexico. The book is useful
to teachers and to those who want background material on Mexican-American
roots.

179.   Nevins, Albert J. **Away to Mexico.** New York: Dodd, Mead & Com-
   j   pany, Inc., 1966. 96p.
A good pictorial book on Mexico which covers past and present economics,
government and the arts. The writer gives his own observations during many
visits to Mexico in an anecdotal and friendly style. Excellent photographs and
maps.

180. Nicholson, Irene. **The X in Mexico: Growth Within Tradition.** Garden City, N.Y., Doubleday & Company, Inc., 1962. 286p.
Analysis of modern Mexico built on the background of centuries of pre-Spanish culture.

181. Peissel, Michel. **The Lost World of Quintana Roo: Alone on Foot in the Jungles of Yucatan.** New York: E. P. Dutton & Company, Inc., 1963. 306p.
A few hours by air from Cape Canaveral lies Quintana Roo, a territory of Mexico on the Yucatan Peninsula. The ancient Maya flourished in this jungle, now sparsely inhabited. The author describes the sites of ruined pyramids, temples, and other archaeological remains.

182. Record, Paul. **Tropical Frontier.** New York: Alfred A. Knopf, Inc., 1969. 325p.
A colorful account of the people and natural setting of the undeveloped area of Mexico.

183. Reich, Hanns, ed. **Mexico.** Text by Hans Levenberg. New York: Hill
  j   & Wang, Inc., 1968. 124p.
The photographs follow a short descriptive text of the history of Mexico from pre-Columbian times to the present. The photographs are representative of the people and their way of life. A highly entertaining book for travelers and the general reader.

184. Rodman, Selden. **The Mexico Traveler: A Concise History and Guide.** New York: Meredith Corporation, 1969. 264p.
The history of Mexican suffering from European and United States interference, the struggle to raise living standards, and the present sad state of education are reviewed. A chronology is appended.

185. Sannebeck, Norvelle. **Everything You Ever Wanted to Know About Living in Mexico.** Anderson, S.C.: Drake House Company, 1971. 250p.
Discusses climate, cost of living, language, recreational facilities, and other matters of concern to the permanent or semipermanent resident.

186. Simon, Kate. **Mexico: Places and Pleasures.** Cleveland, Ohio: World Publishing Company, 1963. 447p.
Kate Simon provides sensitive observations and beautiful sketches of the Mexican people in this unusual travel book.

187. Stephens, John L. **Incidents of Travel in Yucatan.** 2 vols. New York: Dover Publications, 1963. 642p. (New York, 1843)
The recounting of Stephens and Catherwood in the Maya country in 1840 and 1841. The books on American archaeology are widely read and enjoyed because of the vivid descriptions of the antiquities and the very fine drawings by Catherwood. Many of the later editions do credit to the original text but the fine illustrations of the original are not as well done.

188.   Sutton, Ann, and Myron Sutton. **Among the Maya Ruins: The Adven-tures of John Lloyd Stevens and Frederick Catherwood.** Chicago: Rand McNally & Company, 1967. 224p.
An excellent description of ancient Mayan culture.

189.   Trevino, Elizabeth Borton de. **Here Is Mexico.** New York: Farrar,
j   Straus, & Giroux, 1970. 198p.
Facts and impressions about Mexico, which illuminate one or another of the qualities of this country and its people.

190.   Trevino, Elizabeth Borton de. **Where the Heart Is.** Garden City, N.Y., Doubleday & Company, Inc., 1962. 286p.
Shows Mexican daily life as well as the thoughts, feelings, and traditions which mold it.

191.   Tylor, Sir Edward Burnett. **Anahuac: Or Mexico and the Mexicans, Ancient and Modern.** New York: Bergman Publishers, 1970. 344p. Reprint of 1861 edition.
Description and travel in Mexico, showing both the modern world and the ancient.

192.   Weeks, Morris. **Hello, Mexico.** New York: W. W. Norton & Company,
j   Inc., 1970. 226p.
A general introduction to Mexico covering geography, history, and other facets of life in the past and its influence on the country's development. Emphasis is on contemporary life.

193.   Wolf, Eric R. **Sons of the Shaking Earth.** Chicago: University of Chicago Press, 1959. 302p.
The geography of Middle America, the biology of its inhabitants, the variegated languages, the prehistoric expansion of its culture, and the altered rhythms of its growth after the impact of foreign conquest are all parts of an American anthropologist's synthesis of the Central American world, a general statement of what anthropologists have learned about one area of the world.

2. MEXICAN AMERICANS IN THE UNITED STATES

CONTEMPORARY CHICANO LIFE

194.   Acuna, Rudolph. **A Mexican American Chronicle**. New York: American Book Company, 1971. 210p.
The story of the Mexican Americans in the United States.

195.   Acuna, Rudolph. **Occupied America: The Chicano Struggle for Liberation**. New York: Harper & Row Publishers, 1972. 197p.
Documented analysis of the oppression of Mexicans in the United States and their endeavors to achieve liberation.

196.   Acuna, Rudolph. **The Story of the Mexican-American: The Men and**
  j   **the Land**. New York: American Book Company, 1969. 140p.
The author writes of the hardships of the Mexican-American migrant laborer, in education and others areas. Includes biographical sketches of prominent leaders.

197.   Alford, Harold A. **We Speak Spanish: The Heritage and Cultures of Spanish-Speaking People in the United States**. New York: David McKay Company, Inc., 1972.
The author tells, in vividly personal terms, the story of the Mexican American, ranging from early Spanish conquistadores to the contemporary scene. The book includes biographical sketches of outstanding Spanish-speaking figures, from the sixteenth century to today. A good book for high school libraries.

198.   Anda, Jose de. "Mexican Culture and the Mexican-American." **El Grito**, III (Fall 1969), 42-48.
The author states that the Mexican culture signifies the collective experiences of all these nations: Olmeca, Teotihuacanos, Zapotecs, Mixtecs, Chichimecs, Toltecs, Mayas, Aztecs, and a great many others, each of which contributed in some form—architecture, art, ceramics, sculpture, or literature—to modern Mexico and to Mexican Americans.

199.   Bongartz, Roy. "The Chicano Rebellion." **The Nation**, No. 208 (March 3, 1969), 271-274
A description of the thinking and of the attitudes of Chicano students today in their efforts to destroy the stereotype image of the Mexican. This informative article relates how the students are making themselves heard through Chicano newspapers and journals.

200.   Burma, John H., comp. **Mexican-Americans in the United States: A Reader**. New York: Harper & Row Publishers, Inc., 1970. 487p.
A compact anthology compiles writings by Mexican Americans and Anglo sociologists, anthropologists, historians, educators, journalists, and others in a story survey of basic elements of contemporary Mexican-American cultures in the United States.

201. Burma, John H. **Spanish-Speaking Groups in the United States.**
Durham, N.C.: Duke University Press, 1954. 214p. o.p.
Examines the underlying causes of the major problems of the Mexican Americans, Hispanos, Filipinos, and Puerto Ricans in the United States. The author provides insight into aspects of various areas of the time. The bibliography is varied and extensive, concentrating on articles from sociological journals.

202. Bustamante, Charles J. **The Mexican-American and the United States.**
j Mountain View, Calif.: Patty-LARC Publications, 1971. 60p.
A workbook designed to answer questions such as "What is a Chicano?"

203. Cabrera, Arturo. **Emerging Faces: The Mexican Americans.** Dubuque, Iowa: William C. Brown & Co., 1971. 99p.
The author speaks out on important issues in the hope of stimulating further inquiry.

204. Carranza, Eliu. **Pensamientos on Los Chicanos.** Berkeley, Calif.: California Book Company Ltd., 1969.
A collection of essays dealing with Mexican-Americans is presented as an aid to creating a national awareness of the Chicano demand for equal opportunity and justice. A definitive and outspoken treatise on what it is to be a Chicano.

205. Garcia, George J., ed. **Selected Reading Materials on the Mexican and Spanish American.** Denver, Colo.: Commission on Community Relations, City and County of Denver, Colorado, 1969. 103p.
A compilation of articles written by Mexican Americans on their own history and culture: articles are grouped under four general headings—History, Culture, Inter-Cultural Relations, and Attitude and Status of the Chicano. A bibliography of selected readings on Spanish culture is appended.

206. Gardner, Richard M. **Grito! The New Mexico Land Grant War of 1967.** Indianapolis, Ind.: Bobbs-Merrill Company, Inc., 1970. 292p.
Taped interviews and information from scholars, officials, social workers, and citizens. A vivid account of the happenings, background and aftermath of a June 1967 bloody raid on the Rio Arribo County Courthouse by 20 men of the clandestine organization Alianza and its leaders.

207. Helm, June, ed. **Spanish-Speaking People in the United States.** American Ethnological Society Proceedings, 1968. Seattle, Wash.: University of Washington Press, 1969. 215p.
The work explores the tenacity of the cultural heritage of the Spanish-speaking peoples of the United States and the dimensions of their relationship and responses to the total society. A valuable kaleidoscope which furnishes a comprehensive view of the Mexican-American community.

208. Hernandez, Deluvina. **Mexican American Challenge to a Sacred Cow.** Los Angeles, Calif.: Mexican American Cultural Center, University of California, 1970. 60p.

The first monograph in a series published under the auspices of the Mexican American Cultural Center at the University of California, Los Angeles. The monograph is a critical review and analysis of two recent studies on the Mexican American. The author does not limit her challenge to the two UCLA studies alone, and she has much critical comment on contemporary social science research in general.

209.   Jenkinson, Michael. **Tijerina: Land Grant Conflict in New Mexico.** Albuquerque, N.M.: Paisano Press, 1969. 103p.
A journalistic history of the events of June 1967, in Tierra Amarilla, New Mexico. This is the story not so much of a man's life as of his struggle in the land grant conflict.

210.   "Libraries and the Spanish Speaking." **Wilson Library Bulletin**, LXIV (March 1970), 714-67.
Contents include articles on the following: Bicultural Americans with a Hispanic Tradition, The Chicano Movement, How Mexican-Americans View Libraries, Reading Resources and Project LEER. There are also articles on particular libraries and services to the Spanish-speaking in California, Texas, Florida, Colorado, and New York.

211.   McWilliams, Carey. **Mexicans in America: A Student's Guide to Localized History.** New York: Teachers College Press, 1968. 31p.
This is an overview of the history and current situation of Mexican Americans. It discusses most of the questions usually encountered when dealing with the problems of Mexican-American and Anglo cultures.

212.   Meier, Matt S., and Feliciano Riveria. **The Chicanos: A History of Mexican Americans.** New York: Hill & Wang Books, 1972.
This is the great untold story of the cultural, economic and political impact of the Mexican Americans in the Southwestern part of the United States. The book discusses the Spanish, Mexican, and Indian backgrounds of the Chicanos, describes the early settlement of the Southwest (beginning about 1500) and the evolution of its unique culture and economy up to the present.

213.   Morin, Raul. **Among the Valiant: Mexican-Americans in World War II and Korea.** Alhambra, Calif.: Borden Publishing Co., 1963. 290p.
Accounts of courageous acts by many Mexican-American servicemen during World War II and Korea.

214.   Nabokov, Peter. **Tijerina and the Courthouse Raid.** Albuquerque, N.M.: University of New Mexico Press, 1969. 308p.
A first-hand account of an armed uprising by militant Spanish Americans in the Southwest in 1967. "A distinguished piece of contemporary reporting . . . an illuminating inquiry into the tangled roots of American nationality."

215.   Nava, Julian. **Mexican Americans: A Brief Look at Their History.** New York: Anti-Defamation League of B'nai B'rith, 1970. 56p.

This short work will introduce the general reader to the Mexican American. Sketching the major themes and issues encompassed in the historical development of this significant group in our society.

216.   Nava, Julian. **Mexican-Americans: Past, Present, and Future.** New York:
j   American Book Company, 1969. 120p.
A well-illustrated history of the Mexican American from Spanish exploration to the present. Includes short biographies of outstanding Mexican Americans.

217.   Navarro, Joseph. "The Condition of Mexican-American History." **The Journal of Mexican American History,** I (Fall 1970), 25-52.
The author discusses the problems involved in the definition and extent of Mexican American history. He also examines and analyzes the usefulness and limitations of several works which deal with Mexican-American history.

218.   Rendon, Armando B. **Chicano Manifesto.** New York: Macmillan Company, 1971. 337p.
An outspoken, wide-ranging account traces the emergence, states the ambitions, and analyzes the problems of the Chicano movement in the United States.

219.   Romano-V, Octavio Ignacio. "The Historical and Intellectual Presence of Mexican-Americans." **El Grito,** II (Winter 1969), 32-47.
The author discusses four principal historical philosophies or currents of thought brought into the United States by Mexicans. These four ideas are: Indianism, Historical Confrontation, Cultural Nationalism, and Immigrant Experience.

220.   Romano-V, Octavio Ignacio. "Minorities, History, and the Cultural Mystique." **El Grito,** I (Fall 1967), 5-11.
An explanation of the minority situation in the United States, with a history of the stereotypes of minorities.

221.   Samora, Julian, ed. **La Raza: Forgotten Americans.** Notre Dame, Ind.: University of Notre Dame Press, 1966. 218p.
Seven papers on the Spanish-speaking minority in the Southwest which survey the religious, political, social and economic influences on the emerging middle class.

222.   Samora, Julian, and Richard A. Lamanna. **Mexican-Americans in a Midwest Metropolis: A Study of East Chicago.** Mexican-American Study Project Advance Report No. 8. Los Angeles, Calif.: University of California Press, 1967. 140p.
This report points out that the problems of discrimination, education and employment, among others, are essentially the same in East Chicago as elsewhere.

223.   Schular, Antonia, Thomas Ybarra-Frausto, and Joseph Sommers, eds. **Chicano Literature: Text and Context.** Englewood Cliffs, N.J.: Prentice-Hall, Inc., 1972. 368p.
Illustrating the variety and richness of Chicano writing, this new book offers a

basically bilingual historical presentation of the main theme of Chicano literary expression. Covering a wide range of material from pre-Hispanic time to urban Los Angeles today, some of the areas included are: the tradition of social protest from Mayan and Aztec times to the present; the legend of La Llorona; the Mexican antecedents of Chicano literature; and contrast of Chicano literary expression with that of Hispano-America.

224.　Servin, Manuel Patricio, ed. **The Mexican-Americans: An Awakening Minority**. Beverley Hills, Calif.: Glencoe Press, 1970. 160p.
Useful and historical articles by a Mexican-American historian who is not afraid to criticize his people. An anthology of historical work treating in chronological order the racial, cultural, educational, economic and political development of this minority group.

225.　Servin, Manuel Patricio. "The Pre-World War II Mexican-American: An Interpretation." **California Historical Society Quarterly**, Vol. 45 (December 1966), 325-38.
Servin, a distinguished Mexican-American editor and historian, blames Mexican Americans for some of their backwardness.

226.　Steiner, Stan. **La Raza: The Mexican Americans**. New York: Harper & Row Publishers, Inc., 1970. 418p.
A readable authoritative series of sketches that offers information on Mexican-American history not generally found in textbooks, plus background data on many of the organizations and leaders which purport to represent La Causa. Valuable for its discussions of Chavez, Tijerina, and Corky Gonzalez. Good introductory volume on Chicanos.

227.　U.S. Cabinet Committee Hearings on Mexican-American Affairs, El Paso, Texas, October 26, 27 and 28, 1967. **The Mexican American: A New Focus on Opportunity**. Washington: U.S. Government Printing Office, 1968. 253p.
The reports of the various speakers attending the meeting give new insight into the Mexican-American problems and offer hope for improvement.

228.　U.S. Cabinet on Opportunities for Spanish-Speaking People. **The Spanish-Speaking People of the United States, a New Era**. Washington: U.S. Government Printing Office, 1970. 24p.
Describes the history and work of the Committee, which was established by law to serve the Spanish-speaking community. This Committee, which replaced the former Inter-Agency Committee on Mexican American Affairs, is concerned with the education, jobs, and economic welfare of this group and is also interested in research regarding their needs.

229.　U.S. Congress. Senate. **Establishment of an Inter-Agency Committee on Mexican American Affairs**. Hearing Before the Subcommittee on Executive Reorganization of the Committee on Governmental Operations, Senate, 91st Congress, First Session on S.740, June 11-12, 1969. 234p.

The purpose of this act is to assure that federal programs are reaching all Mexican Americans and providing the assistance they need, and to seek out new programs that may be necessary to handle problems that are unique to the Mexican-American community.

230. U.S. Department of Commerce. Bureau of the Census. **We, the Mexican Americans: Nosotros, los Mexico Americanos.** (English and Spanish) Washington: U.S. Government Printing Office, 1970. 16p.
The purpose of this work was to encourage Mexican Americans to turn in complete census questionnaires and to work as census takers. Explanations of the purposes of the census and the useful things that can come from it.

231. United States. Inter-Agency Committee on Mexican American Affairs. **The Mexican-Americans: A New Focus on Opportunity.** Washington: U.S. Government Printing Office, 1967. 186p.
Transcripts of the hearings held before the Cabinet members on the problems of Mexican Americans. Concrete proposals and suggestions are given for many areas.

232. United States. Inter-Agency Committee on Mexican American Affairs. **The Mexican-American, a New Focus on Opportunity, 1967-1968.** Washington: U.S. Government Printing Office, 1968. 32p.
A report on the successes and programs of the Inter-Agency Committee on Mexican-American affairs during its first year.

233. United States. Inter-Agency Committee on Mexican American Affairs. **The Mexican American, A New Focus on Opportunity: The President's Remarks at the Installation of Commissioner Vincente T. Ximenes and a Cabinet Report on the Mexican American Community.** Washington: U.S. Government Printing Office, 1967. 32p.
Remarks by President Johnson and a Cabinet report on the state of affairs of the Mexican-American people. The report deals with the advances made by the Johnson administration and future needs of the Mexican-American community.

THE MEXICAN IN THE SOUTHWEST

234. Alisky, Marvin. "The Mexican-Americans Make Themselves Heard." **The Reporter,** XXXVI (February 9, 1967), 45-46.
A walk-out from a regional conference of the Federal Equal Employment Opportunities Commission in Albuquerque, March 1966, is now known as the signal to all Mexican Americans of the Southwest for the need of increased involvement in political action. This article concerns the recent political mobilization by the Mexican Americans in the Southwest.

235. Ashford, Gerald. **Spanish Texas: Yesterday and Today.** Austin, Texas: Jenkins Book Publishers, Inc., 1971. 296p.
The Spanish influence and the Spanish Americans in Texas history to 1846.

236. Beck, Warren A. **New Mexico: A History of Four Centuries.** Norman, Okla.: University of Oklahoma Press, 1971. Reprint of 1962 ed. 363p.
The history of New Mexico beginning at the time of the Spanish conquistadores. It gives careful consideration to the cultural impact effected by the Spanish on the indigenous people as well as the impact of the Anglos on the Hispano. The author also presents New Mexico's economic and political development.

237. Bolton, Herbert Eugene. **Coronado, Knight of Pueblos and Plains.** Albuquerque, N.M.: University of New Mexico Press, 1964. 491p.
Originally published in 1949 by Whittlesey House, this work was also published under the title *Coronado on the Turquoise Trail.* It covers the history of the hardships and failures of Coronado's long and futile search. Entertainingly written, with full documentation.

238. Day, A. Grove. **Coronado's Quest: The Discovery of the Southwestern States.** Gloucester, Mass.: Peter Smith, 1964. 421p.
A thorough and reliable account, popular in tone and very readable. The author consulted all the known Spanish sources and retraced the greater part of his hero's march.

239. Faulk, Odie B. **Land of Many Frontiers: A History of the American Southwest.** New York: Oxford University Press, 1968. 358p.
This account of the development of a region of the United States begins in 1519. The author describes the Spanish explorers, the occupation of the Southwest by the Anglo, the effect of the gold rush to California, the small part the area played in the Civil War, and the conquest of the Indian. He then sketches state politics of the area.

240. Fogel, Walter. **Mexican-Americans in Southwest Labor Markets.** Advance Report 10. Mexican American Study Project. Los Angeles, Calif.: University of California, 1967. 198p.
An analysis of the Mexican American occupational status in the Southwest. The author makes comparisons between states and ethnic groups and notes differences in the Mexican-American situation across time and among generations. The final chapter offers a summary of the findings of the study and observes areas of continuing difficulty for the Mexican American.

241. Forbes, Jack D. **Apache, Navaho, and Spaniard.** Norman, Okla.: University of Oklahoma Press, 1963. 304p. Reprint of 1960 edition.
The author describes the Spanish thrust, north from Mexico and into New Mexico, Arizona, and Texas, between 1540 and 1700.

242. Galarza, Ernesto, Herman Gallegos, and Julian Samora. **Mexican Americans in the Southwest.** 2nd ed. Santa Barbara, Calif.: McNally and Loftin, 1970. 94p.
A comprehensive and up-to-date overview of the Mexican Americans in the Southwest. The report contains information on population distribution, immigration, current economic and employment profiles, and the political organization of Mexican Americans in the sixties.

243. Gonzales, Nancie L. **The Spanish-Americans of New Mexico: A Heritage of Pride.** Rev. ed. Albuquerque, N.M.: University of New Mexico Press, 1969. 270p.

Originally written as a Mexican American Study Project Advance Report (No. 9) at the Los Angeles Division of Research, Graduate School of Business, University of California, 1969. An excellent study of Spanish-Americans on a one-state level. Gonzales presents important social and historical material, giving the book a perception that is sometimes missing in minority studies. For both the student and the general reader.

244. Gregg, Andrew K. **New Mexico in the 19th Century: A Pictorial History.** Albuquerque, N.M.: University of New Mexico Press, 1968. 206p.

A valuable reference and teaching tool for all periods of New Mexican and Southwestern history. There is a good balance of Indian, Spanish, and Anglo heritages. Captions are well done. An impressive history.

245. Hinkle, Stacy C. **Wings Over the Border: The Army Air Service Armed Patrol of the United States-Mexico Border, 1919-1920.** Southwestern Studies Monograph, No. 26. El Paso, Texas: Texas Western Press, 1970. 67p.

The patrol of the border by the Army Air Service—problems and solutions.

246. Hollon, William Eugene. **The Southwest: Old and New.** New York: Alfred A. Knopf, Inc., 1961. 486p.

The author presents the full panorama of Southwestern life from the ancient cliff dweller's communities to modern Houston, Phoenix and Santa Fe.

247. Horgan, Paul. **Great River: The Rio Grande in North American History.** Rev. ed. 2 vols. in one. New York: Holt, Rinehart & Winston, Inc., 1960. 1020p.

This is a study of events, explorations, battles, and empire building in the lands along the Rio Grande, with emphasis placed on Texas. It treats the indigenous Indian population, the Spanish exploration, the settlement of the area, and the clashes between Mexico and the United States.

248. Horgan, Paul. **The Heroic Triad: Essays in the Social Energies of Three Southwest Cultures.** New York: Holt, Rinehart and Winston, 1970. 320p.

The history of the three Southwestern cultures, the Indians, the Latin and the Anglo-American, is told in a vivid imaginative way, presenting their clash and co-existence along the Rio Grande.

249. Hutchinson, C. Alan. **Frontier Settlement in Mexican California: The Hijar-Padres Colony and Its Origins, 1769-1835.** Western Americana Series No. 21. New Haven, Conn.: Yale University Press, 1969. 457p.

The author deals in depth with the persistent efforts of that far-seeing Mexican Vice-President, Gomez Farias, to strengthen his country's hold upon California

49

through reorganization of the missions and above all, the systematic planting of Mexican colonists. The whole story richly illumines not only the California history of the period but equally the political, ideological, and diplomatic forces shaping the early Mexican Republic.

250. Kostyu, Frank A. **Shadows in the Valley: The Story of One Man's Struggle for Justice.** Garden City, N.Y.: Doubleday & Company, Inc., 1970. 192p.

A brief account that gives a general picture of the plight of the Mexican-American migrant worker in the Rio Grande Valley.

251. Lamb, Ruth. **Mexican Americans: Sons of the Southwest.** Claremont, Calif.: Ocelot Press, 1970. 198p.

Brief narrative of La Raza including contemporary leaders. Includes the Treaty of Guadalupe Hidalgo, February 2, 1848, and the Gadsden Treaty of 1853. English and Spanish.

252. Landes, Ruth. **Latin Americans of the Southwest.** New York: McGraw-Hill Book Company, 1965. 100p.

A compact analysis of the Mexican American culture and how it evolved from Spanish exploration and settlement, Mexican history and the history of Anglo-Mexican rivalries. The author shows the development of Mexican-American leadership and the struggles for identity.

253. Lord, Walter. **A Time to Stand.** New York: Harper and Bros., 1961. 255p.

A well-documented historical account of the battle of the Alamo. Material has been taken from original Mexican and American manuscripts, official land office records, letters and journals. An objective account brings to life an important piece of history. The work differs from textbook accounts of the battle as it does not place the Mexican in a negative image.

254. McDonald, Archie, ed. **The Mexican War: Crisis for American Democracy.** Problems in American Civilization Series. Lexington, Mass.: D.C. Heath & Company, 1969. 112p.

This work presents the Mexican War as viewed by American diplomats.

255. Madsen, William. **The Mexican-Americans of South Texas.** Case Studies in Cultural Anthropology Series. New York: Holt, Rinehart & Winston, Inc., 1964. 112p.

A study in cultural anthropology which deals with the Mexican Americans in South Texas. Their backgrounds, present attitudes, sentiments, and prospects are discussed. Madsen's study, financed by the Hogg Foundation for Mental Health at the University of Texas, is based on field research conducted in four communities in South Texas from 1957 to 1961. The volume includes many case histories to illustrate generalizations.

256. Manuel, Hershel T. **Spanish-Speaking Children of the Southwest: Their Education and the Public Welfare.** Austin, Texas: University of Texas Press, 1970. 222p.

This reprint of a 1965 edition shows the background analysis of the culture, occupational characteristics, and solutions to the problems encountered by the children in U.S. public schools. One of the basic educational studies on the education of Mexican-American children in the Southwest, with emphasis on Texas.

257. Mittelbach, Frank G., and Grace Marshall. **The Burden of Poverty.** Advance Report No. 5, Mexican-American Study Project. Los Angeles, Calif.: University of California, 1966. 48p.

The Mexican American and family income, a study of poverty in the Southwestern United States, is based on data from the 1960 census. The focus is on the Spanish-surnamed population, but the Anglo and non-white groups are also studied. The authors conclude that a number of approaches are needed to fight poverty because of the low level of education, low family income, broken homes, and the relatively large families of the Mexican American.

258. Moore, Joan W. "Colonialism: The Case of the Mexican American." **Social Problems**, XVII (Spring 1970), 463-72.

The author specifies three distinct types of colonialism in three regions of the Southwest: "Classic Colonialism" in New Mexico, "Conflict Colonialism" in Texas, and "Economic Colonialism" in California. These models are then applied to explain a traditional stereotype—the supposed low degree of formal voluntary organization—among Mexican Americans.

259. Moore, Joan W., and Alfredo B. Cuellar. **Mexican Americans.** Rev. ed. Ethnic Groups in American Life Series. Englewood Cliffs, N.J.: Prentice-Hall, Inc., 1970. 172p.

A well-documented study of Mexican Americans, particularly in the Southwestern United States, in which the authors examine their history and the social, economic, educational, and occupational disparities.

260. Moore, Joan W., and Frank G. Mittelbach. **Residential Segregation in the Urban Southwest.** Advance Report 4, Mexican-American Study Project. Los Angeles, Calif.: University of California, 1966. Various paging.

This study used data from the 1960 census to derive indices of residential segregation for 35 cities in the American Southwest concerning the two largest minority groups in the country. Cultural, economic, and demographic-ecological factors are examined.

261. Norquest, Carrol. **Rio Grande Wetbacks: Migrant Mexican Workers.** Albuquerque, N.M.: University of New Mexico Press, 1972. 159p.

Presents an accurate and descriptive picture of the migrant Mexican workers in the Rio Grande Valley.

262.   Perkins, William. **Three Years in California: Journal of Life at Sonora, 1849-1852**. Edited by Dale L. Morgan and James R. Scobie. Berkeley, Calif.: University of California Press, 1964. 424p.

A first-hand account by a man who lived in Sonora. He describes his experiences from 1849 to 1852, including descriptions of Mexican Americans of that period.

263.   Perrigo, Lynn, ed. **American Southwest: Its People and Cultures**. New York: Holt, Rinehart & Winston, Inc., 1971. 469p.

A new informative and readable history of the people of the Southwest. Extensive bibliography.

264.   Perrigo, Lynn. **Our Spanish Southwest**. Dallas, Texas: Banks Upshaw and Company, 1960. 518p.

The best survey on the Southwest up to the Mexican War, this work also contains an exhaustive bibliography.

265.   Rojas, Arnold R. **The Vaquero**. Charlotte, N.C.: McNally and Loftin, 1964. 194p.

Reminiscences of the cattle herds, cowboys and Indios on the ranchos of old California. A work of popular nature. Illustrated.

266.   Samora, Julian. "The General Status of the Spanish-Speaking People in the Southwest," in **Summary of Proceedings of the Southwest Conference** on "Social and Educational Problems of Rural and Urban Mexican-American Youth," sponsored by the Rosenberg Foundation at Occidental College, April 6, 1963.

Disucsses the educational, social, political, and working status of the Mexican American in the Southwest, and compares his status in these areas with that of the Anglo.

267.   Sanchez, George I. **Forgotten People: A Study of New Mexicans**. Albuquerque, N.M.: Calvin Horn Publisher, Inc., 1967. Reprint of 1940 edition. 98p.

The problems of education, labor, and integration into the wider society remain to be solved. Although done in 1940, this study of the Spanish-speaking in northern New Mexico (Taos County) is still valid. The author presents a scholarly analysis of the diversity of factors that created the problems facing the people today.

268.   Taylor, Paul. **An American-Mexican Frontier: Nueces County, Texas**. New York: Russell & Russell, 1971. Reprint of 1934 ed. 337p.

The author concentrates on the problems of employment, education, race question, and labor. He describes the history of the Nueces region, especially the armed clashes that led to hate and fear between South Texas ethnic groups.

269.   Tebbel, John. **South by Southwest: The Mexican American and His Heritage**. Garden City, N.Y.: Doubleday and Company, 1969. 120p.

Some 2.5 million Mexican Americans (the second largest minority group in the

United States) live in the Southwest. Here is the history of the Mexican American, and the problems he faces in becoming truly accepted as an American.

270. Tuck, Ruth D. **Not With the Fist: Mexican-Americans in a Southwest City.** New York: Harcourt, Brace and Company, Inc., 1956. 234p. o.p.
An account of the Mexican-American problems in a typical city. The author traces the origins of Mexican-American immigration, the attitudes of indifference assumed by the United States, and the lack of any plan for Mexican education and assimilation.

271. United States Commission on Civil Rights. **Concentration of Spanish Surnames in the Five Southwestern States.** Washington: U.S. Government Printing Office, 1962.
Statistical approach using census reports of Spanish-surnamed people in the Southwestern states of Texas, California, Arizona, New Mexico, and Colorado.

272. United States Commission on Civil Rights. **Hearings in San Antonio, Texas, December 9-15, 1968.** Washington: U.S. Government Printing Office, 1969. 21p.
Hearings on the civil rights of Mexican Americans in Texas; included along with testimony are 64 exhibits and three additional documents entered into the hearing record.

273. United States Commission on Civil Rights. **Mexican Americans and the Administration of Justice in the Southwest.** Washington: U.S. Government Printing Office, 1970. 135p.
An appraisal of allegations that American citizens of Mexican descent in five Southwestern states are being denied equal protection of the law in the administration of justice.

274. Vigil, Antonio S. **The Coming of the Gringo and the Mexican American Revolt.** New York: Vantage Press, 1970. 156p.
The history of the Mexican-American revolt in the Southwest.

275. Webb, Walter Prescott. **The Texas Rangers.** Rev. ed. Austin, Texas: University of Texas Press, 1965. 583p.
Webb traces the Texas Rangers from their organization in 1835 to 1915. Because of fire, records prior to the Civil War are scant, therefore the author sought veterans and listened to their accounts, thus catching "something of the spirit of an institution." He recounts individual episodes, always emphasizing that the Rangers were human. Dr. Webb describes three races the Rangers were forced to contend with in their work: Indians, Mexican bandits, and American desperados.

276. Wellman, Paul I. **Glory, God and Gold.** Garden City, N.Y.: Doubleday & Company, Inc., 1956. 402p.
A history of the American Southwest, beginning when Coronado marched north from Mexico in 1540, and ending with the atom bomb. The main story of

Spanish activities is told with realism, vividness, and clarity. This is a well-researched history for the general reader.

277.   Zermeno, Andy, and the Staff of El Malcriado. **Don Sotaco**. Delano, Calif.: Farm Workers Press, 1966.
Cartoons from the Delano Grape Strike in which the farmworker, grower, foreman-henchman characters are easily recognized. A strong message is presented.

SOCIAL ISSUES AND CUSTOMS

278.   Allen, Steve. **The Ground Is Our Table**. Garden City, N.Y.: Doubleday & Company, 1966. 141p.
This noted entertainer takes a personal view of the life of migrant workers. Photographs and a chapter on Delano are included in the work.

279.   American Ethnological Society. **Spanish-Speaking People in the United States**. Seattle, Wash.: University of Washington Press, 1969. 215p.
A wide range of subjects concerning Mexican Americans and other Spanish-speaking groups is examined in this work which represents papers given at the annual spring meeting of the American Ethnological Society.

280.   Bakke, Edward Wight, and Mary S. Bakke. **Campus Challenge: Student Activism in Perspective**. Hamden, Conn.: Archon Books, 1971. 573p.
The causes for student activism in Mexico, Colombia, Japan, India, and the United States are defined and interpreted in a dispassionate sociological study conducted by means of extensive interviews from 1962 to 1968. The characteristics of students protesting in the four foreign countries are explored in the first section, with an examination of the rites of coming of age in each nation. The third area of inquiry concerns methods by which Japanese, Indian, Mexican, and Colombian young people become recognized as citizens of their nations, eligible to participate in government. The interaction of groups is shown.

281.   Ballis, George. **Basta!** Delano, Calif.: Farm Workers Press, 1966. unpaged.
A photographic essay on the issues of Delano.

282.   Blawis, Patricia Bell. **Reies Lopez Tijerina and the Chicano Movement in the Southwest: The Fight to Save the Mexican American Heritage**. New York: International Publishers, 1971. 191p.
The leader of the Alianza and of the Mexican Americans' struggle for the return of their traditional lands.

283.   Briegel, Kaye. **The History of Political Organizations Among Mexican-Americans in Los Angeles Since the Second World War**. Los Angeles, Calif.: University of Southern California, 1967. Master's thesis.
A well-documented account of the Mexican-American organizations.

284. Burma, John. "The Civil Rights Situation of Mexican-Americans and Spanish-Americans," in Jitsuichi Masuoka and Preston Valien, editors, **Race Relations: Problems and Theory.** Chapel Hill, N.C.: University of North Carolina Press, 1961. pp. 155-67.

This chapter surveys the status of Mexican Americans' and Hispanos' civil rights in the schools, politics, public facilities, economic and social relations in the Southwest.

285. Coles, Robert. **Uprooted Children: The Early Life of Migrant Farm Workers.** Pittsburgh, Pa.: University of Pittsburgh Press, 1970. 176p.

Written with directness and power by the author of the outstanding *Children of Crisis*, this book is a psychiatric study of migrant farm children in Florida and along the eastern seaboard. It describes how white, black, and Mexican-American children of migrant families grow up in rural America under conditions of extreme hardship and stress and how they come to terms with the world and with themselves.

286. Cosio Villegas, Daniel. **American Extremes.** Translated by Americo Paredes. Austin, Texas: University of Texas Press, 1964. 227p.

The work compares our two Americas and contains valuable insights into Mexican and Latin American character and culture. Daniel Cosio Villegas is one of Mexico's best historians.

287. D'Antonio, William V., and William H. Form, editors. **Influentials in Two Border Cities: A Study in Community Decision-Making.** Notre Dame, Ind.: University of Notre Dame Press, 1965. 273p.

A comparative study of two cities—El Paso, Texas, and Ciudad Juarez, Mexico. The work examines the elements that govern local policymaking and the resulting influence on the people.

288. Day, Mark. **Forty Acres: Cesar Chavez and the Farm Workers.** New York: Praeger Publishers, Inc., 1971. 222p.

Admittedly biased in favor of the farm workers, the author describes his three-year involvement beginning in 1967 as a priest and volunteer with Cesar Chavez and his movement. Along with his vivid chronicle of the grape strike and boycott, Father Day offers insight into California's agribusiness, early attempts to organize farm workers, and the role of the Church in alleviating social injustice. Appended is a copy of the first major contract signed with the grape industry, and a list of suggested readings.

289. Dobrin, Arnold. **La Vida Nueva: The Mexican Americans Today.** New York: Dodd, Mead & Company, 1971. 128p.

La Vida Nueva (the new life) will open a path for understanding between Anglos and Mexican Americans. Dobrin focuses on present-day Chicanos and their communities and through a series of interviews reveals how many Mexican Americans feel about prejudice, education, and political action.

290.   Dunne, John Gregory. **Delano: The Story of the California Grape Strike.** Rev. ed. New York: Farrar, Straus and Giroux, 1971. 176p.
The story of Chavez, his organization, and his leadership of the Mexican migrant grape pickers.

291.   Fergusson, Erna. **New Mexico: A Pageant of Three Peoples.** 2nd ed. New York: Alfred A. Knopf, 1964. 408p.
The author relates the history of New Mexico, the cultures, and the tribes of Indians, using portraits, maps, and illustrations.

292.   Galarza, Ernesto. **Merchants of Labor: The Mexican Bracero Story.** Santa Barbara, Calif.: McNally & Loftin Publishers, 1966. 206p.
In this study of the managed migration of farm workers, Dr. Galarza presents the complete background of one of the most important social and economic features of California history.

293.   Galarza, Ernesto. **Spiders in the House and Workers in the Field.** Notre Dame, Ind.: University of Notre Dame Press, 1970. 320p.
A description of the efforts to organize farm labor in the period just before Cesar Chavez. A documented historical and a critical study revealing the role of several congressional leaders and the Di Giorgio Fruit Corporation in the demise of the union which made earlier attempts to organize these farm workers.

294.   Gamio, Manuel. **The Mexican Immigrant, His Life Story, Autobiographic Documents.** New York: Arno Press, 1969. Reprint of 1931 edition. 288p.
The collected statements of 57 immigrants from Mexico during the 1920s, telling why they left Mexico and how they lived in the United States.

295.   Gamio, Manuel. **Mexican Immigration to the United States.** New York: Arno Press, 1969. Reprint of 1930 edition. 196p.
This study treats the different economic and social forces tending to produce immigration from Mexico. Gamio also deals with the reception of the immigrants in the United States in terms of wages, prejudice, and acceptance. This book and the above by Gamio, along with Paul Taylor's *Mexican Labor in the United States*, are among the classic studies of the Mexican immigration into the American Southwest.

296.   Goodman, Mary Ellen. **The Mexican-American Population of Houston: A Survey in the Field, 1965-1970.** Houston, Texas: Rice University, 1971. 125p.
This work contains a demographic sketch of Houstonians with Spanish surnames, the setting and personnel with life styles in the barrio. Interviews with Mexican Americans of high school age and after high school, the middle class, and the many traditional organizations are covered in the study.

297.   Grebler, Leo, ed. **Mexican Immigration to the United States: The Record and Its Implications.** Advance Report 2, Mexican-American

Study Project. Los Angeles, Calif.: University of California, 1966.
106p.
A general survey of Mexican immigration to the United States focuses on temporary population movements. The author also studies the immigrants themselves, their demographic and social characteristics, their geographic origins in Mexico, their distribution in the United States, and the characteristics which distinguish them from the general population of Mexico. The work is both descriptive and analytical.

298.   Griffith, Beatrice W. **American Me.** Boston: Houghton Mifflin Co.,
       1948. 309p. o.p.
A collection of stories told by Mexican-American adolescents illustrating their problems and the discriminatory tactics used to perpetuate the inferior position of the "Mexican community." The glossary includes information and definitions of pachuco and barrio slang.

299.   Guzman, Ralph. "Politics and Policies of the Mexican-American
       Community," in Eugene P. Dvorin and Arthur I. Misner, editors,
       California Politics and Policies. Palo Alto, Calif.: Addison-Wesley,
       1966. pp. 350-84.
This chapter gives a history of Mexican American political action groups, including a sketch of the Chicano's social history in California, his current economic position, his heritage of Mexican loyalty and his strife with Anglos, the Order of the Sons of America and the League of United Latin American Citizens (LULAC), the Community Service Organization, the American GI Forum, and the Political Association of Spanish-Speaking Organizations, which is identified with the Kennedy family in politics.

300.   Heaps, Willard A. **Wandering Workers: The Story of American Migrant
       Farm Workers and Their Problems.** New York: Crown Publishers, Inc.,
       1968. 192p.
This book consists of taped interviews of workers obtained by the author in migrant camps in New Jersey, Maryland, Virginia, Indiana, Illinois, Texas, and California. The migrants describe who they are, where they are from, where they travel, their work, their lives, and the problems of housing, health, community acceptance, and their children's welfare and education.

301.   Heller, Celia S. **Mexican American Youth: Forgotten Youth at the
       Crossroads.** New York: Random House, 1966. 113p.
The conflicts and opportunity expectations of Mexican American youth in Los Angeles. Contains materials on educational relationships and juvenile delinquency. The author concludes her study by stating that prejudice and lack of education hold back young Mexican Americans, but she also suggests that the traditional culture of the Mexican American hampers success.

302.   Heller, Celia S. **New Converts to the American Dream? Mobility
       Aspirations of Young Mexican Americans.** New Haven, Conn.: College
       & University Press, 1971. 287p.

A sociological investigation of the educational and occupational aspirations of young Mexican Americans which attempts to determine whether or not Mexican-American youth are pursuing the "American dream." The research focusing on the goals and skills of the Mexican Americans was conducted in the Los Angeles area, based on 1957-1958 surveys and 1965 interviews. The author's conclusions are that Mexican Americans will no longer be an exception to the American ethnic pattern of generational advancement.

303.   Hill, Gladwin. "The Political Role of Mexican-Americans," in Arnold M. Rose and Caroline B. Rose, editors, **Minority Problems.** New York: Harper & Row Publishers, Inc., 1965. pp. 202-204.
A report from the *New York Times* concerning Americans of Mexican descent exemplifies the practical importance to minority groups of having and exercising the franchise. When Mexican Americans were in political charge of a town, the government was better, yet the Anglos reacted with hostility. This incident provides many clues to the nature of prejudice.

304.   Kramer, Judith R. **The American Minority Community.** New York: Thomas Y. Crowell Company, 1970. 293p.
This book explores the social and psychological consequences of the minority situation, a situation that is premised on coercion.

305.   Liebman, Arthur, Kenneth N. Walker, and Myron Glazer. **Latin American University Students: A Six Nation Study.** Cambridge, Mass.: Harvard University Press, 1972. 296p.
A six-nation study of the political activities of college and university students.

306.   Lopez, Arthur, and Kenneth G. Richards. **El Rancho de Muchachos.**
  j   Open Door Books. Chicago: Childrens Press, 1970. 64p.
Arthur Lopez, son of Mexican migrant workers, runs the Natividad Ranch for boys in trouble and tries to direct them back into society.

307.   Lopez, Richard Emilio. **Anxiety, Acculturation and the Urban Chicano.** Berkeley, Calif.: California Book Co., Ltd., 1970. 41p.
This study explores the relationship between acculturation and anxiety, in a sample of Mexican-American college students.

308.   McWilliams, Carey. **Brothers Under the Skin.** Rev. ed. Boston: Little, Brown & Company, 1951. 364p.
Discussions of the status of the non-white minorities in the United States.

309.   McWilliams, Carey. **Factories in the Field: The Story of the Migratory Farm Labor in California.** Boston: Little, Brown & Company, 1939. 325p.
A work on California-agriculture and agricultural workers before World War II. The central thesis is that land in California was monopolized from the beginning by a few men, through fraudulent Spanish grants, illegal speculation in state and federal land grants, and force. Agriculture was also based on the exploitation

of a series of minority group immigrants as a cheap labor force. The author concludes with an account of unionization attempts and suggests the conditions advantageous and disadvantageous to union formation.

310.   McWilliams, Carey. **Ill Fares the Land: Migrants and Migratory Labor in the United States.** Boston: Little, Brown & Company, 1942. 390p.
This survey discusses migrant labor, agricultural regional history, the ethnic group involved, physical conditions and racial strife in the different geographical regions. The Mexican American status in each region is treated and the chapter on Texas focuses on the Mexican American.

311.   Marden, Charles F., and Gladys Meyer. **Minorities in American Society.** 3rd ed. New York: American Book Co., 1968. 486p.
Each numerically significant minority group, including the Mexican American, is considered in relation to the dominant group. The current situation is discussed in terms of problem areas and social policy.

312.   Matthiessen, Peter. **Sal si Puedes: Escape If You Can; Cesar Chavez and the New American Revolution.** New York: Random House, 1970. 372p.
A sympathetic portrait of California labor organizer Cesar Chavez and a full retracing of the long-drawn-out farm strike. The book's title—Spanish for "escape if you can"—is the ironic name given to San Jose's Mexican American community in which Chavez grew up.

313.   Mittelbach, Frank G., Joan W. Moore, and Ronald McDaniel. **Intermarriage of Mexican Americans.** Advance Report 6, Mexican American Study Project. Los Angeles, Calif.: University of California, 1966. 47p.
An effort is made to measure the degree of assimilation of Mexican Americans into Anglo society, using the extent of intermarriage between the two groups as an indicator. The work is based on data from the Los Angeles County Marriage Licenses Bureau for 1963. The conclusion of the study shows that some 75 percent of the Mexican Americans in Los Angeles marry within their own group, although the number marrying outside the group has increased in recent years.

314.   Molnar, Jose. **Graciela: A Mexican American Child Tells Her Story.**
j   New York: Franklin Watts, Inc., 1972. 48p.
A young Mexican-American girl describes her home, family, school, amusements, and daily life in a Texas border town. "The text of this book is based on tape recordings of conversations with Graciela."

315.   Montiel, Miguel. "The Social Science Myth of the Mexican American Family," **El Grito**, III (Summer 1970), 56-63.
A criticism of many studies on the Mexican-American family, in the author's opinion, is that they lack both methodological sophistication and empirical verification. He discusses three examples of studies of the Mexican family, by Bermudez, Diaz-Guerrero, and G. M. Gilbert.

316.   Moore, Truman E. **The Slaves We Rent.** New York: Random House, 1965. 171p.
Compassionate portrait of migratory workers throughout the United States, with an explanation of the economic system that holds them in thrall. The work contains reading notes, maps, and bibliographic references for additional research.

317.   Munoz, Carlos. **Toward a Chicano Perspective of Political Analysis.** Unpublished paper delivered at the 66th annual meeting of the American Political Science Association, Los Angeles, California, September 1970.
The author contends that, due to the present status of the social sciences, no relevant research which can contribute toward the understanding and solution of Mexican American problems can be hoped for in the near future.

318.   Nelson, Eugene. **Huelga, the First Hundred Days of the Great Delano Grape Strike.** Delano, Calif.: Farm Workers Press, 1966. 122p.
A day-by-day account of the issues and actions involved in the strike.

319.   Pitrone, Jean Maddern. **Chavez, Man of the Migrants.** New York:
j   Pyramid Publications, Inc., 1971. 169p.
A picture of Cesar Chavez aiding the agricultural and migrant laborers in his successful efforts in organizing a union.

320.   Pitt, Leonard Marvin. **The Decline of the Californios: A Social History of the Spanish-Speaking Californians, 1846-1890.** Berkeley, Calif.: University of California Press, 1966. 296p.
The author captures the flavor of nineteenth century life and the struggle of Mexican Americans in California. He describes the Anglo settlers as illegally seizing the land, the mines, and reforming the old political order, with many accounts of greed, malice, and bigotry. The work includes portraits of famous California Mexican Americans and their families.

321.   Pozas, Ricardo. **Juan the Chamula: An Ethnological Re-Creation of the Life of a Mexican Indian.** Translated by Lysander Kemp. Berkeley, Calif.: University of California Press, 1962. 115p.
The study of a modern-day Mexican Indian—his habits and his relationships with life.

322.   Romano-V, Octavio Ignacio. "The Anthropology and Sociology of the Mexican Americans." **El Grito**, II (Fall 1968), 13-26.
In this review article, Romano states that observations and conclusions of prominent social scientists (Ruth Tuck, Lyle Saunders, Munro S. Edmonson, Florence R. Kluckhorn, Celia S. Heller, Julian Samors, and others) totally ignore such things as the pluralistic nature of the Mexican American people and only present a stereotyped picture.

323.   Romano-V, Octavio Ignacio, ed. **Voices: Readings from El Grito.** Berkeley, Calif.: Quinto Sol Publications, Inc., 1971. 211p.
This publication contains 16 addresses, essays, and lectures by Chicanos on the current scene.

324. Rose, Peter Isaac, comp. **Nation of Nations: The Ethnic Experience and the Racial Crisis**. New York: Random House, 1972. 351p.

A collection of readings on the minority groups and their problems in the United States, and papers on the racial issues of today. Topics include the various types of discrimination, explanations of the cures of discrimination, and some techniques which might be used to change the situation.

325. Rosenquist, Carl M., and Edwin I. Megargee. **Delinquency in Three Cultures**. Hogg Foundation for Mental Health. Austin, Texas: University of Texas Press, 1969. 554p.

A presentation of a cross-cultural, cross-national study of the sociological, psychological, and medical differences between delinquents and comparison groups of nondelinquents in three cultures. Delinquent and non-delinquent boys from Anglo and Latin cultures in San Antonio and from Mexican culture in Monterrey.

326. Samora, Julian. **Los Mojados: The Wetback Story**. Notre Dame, Ind.: University of Notre Dame, 1971. 205p.

An examination of the illegal mass movement of people from Mexico to the United States.

327. Sandage, Shirley M., and Jo M. Stewart. **Child of Hope**. Cranbury, N.J.: A. S. Barnes and Company, 1968. 135p.

The text describes the life of a Mexican-American migrant family and furnishes statistics on income, mortality, injuries, and number of migrants. The main body of the book is a pictorial essay which eloquently illustrates the poverty of the family.

328. Shalkop, Robert L. **Wooden Saints: The Santos of New Mexico**. Buchcim Verlag: Feldafing, 1967. 63p.

This remarkable folk art came into being when New Mexico was a remote outpost of Spain. This little guide presents a brief historical sketch of the cultural background, followed by a discussion of the art itself. Colored plates have explanatory text.

329. Simmen, Edward, ed. **The Chicano: From Caricature to Self Portrait**. New York: New American Library, 1971. 318p.

A series of short stories by or about Mexican Americans. The author's approach is chronological, and he has gathered for the first time in one volume some of the more representative short stories. In his introduction, he provides a useful outline of the history of the short story by or about Mexican Americans or Chicanos.

330. Taylor, Paul Schuster. **Mexican Labor in the United States**. 2 vols. New York: Arno Press, 1970. Reprint. 575p.

These separate monographs are detailed comparative studies of selected regions or topics, showing characteristics common to the progress of Mexican migration in the U.S. Includes such areas as Bethlehem, Pa., Chicago, and the Calumet Region.

331. Tobias, Henry J., and Charles E. Woodhouse, eds. **Minorities and Politics.** Albuquerque, N.M.: University of New Mexico Press, 1969. 131p.

A survey of how minorities see politics and their attempts to use political factors for their own interests. The movements covered are: the Jews in Tsarist Russia, the Separatist movement of the French Canadians in Quebec, the Pueblo Indians, the Negro in Albuquerque, New Mexico, and the Alianza movement of New Mexico. One section dealing with the Alianza movement gives the history, actions, and sources on Mexican action as to the Alianza group.

332. United States Cabinet Committee on Opportunity for the Spanish Speaking. **Spanish Surnamed American College Graduates: 1970.** Washington: U.S. Government Printing Office, 1970. 331p.

This publication is prepared annually and is an actual listing of prospective college graduates. Information included provides the recruiter with the names, addresses, date of graduate, and degree or majors of the individual students.

333. United States Commission on Civil Rights. **The Mexican American.** A paper prepared for the U.S. Commission on Civil Rights by Helen Rowan. Washington: U.S. Government Printing Office, 1968. 70p.

The purpose of this paper is to indicate the type and range of problems facing the Mexican American community and to suggest ways in which some of these problems are peculiar to this community, or have distinctive features with respect to it.

334. Valdez, Armando. "Insurrection in New Mexico—The Land of Enchantment." **El Grito,** I (Fall 1967), 15-24.

The author discusses the history, the ethnic denominator, the insurrection, the Anglo law, and taxes relating to the Mexican in New Mexico.

335. Wald, Richard A. **The Effect of Cultural Influences on Mexican American Consumers.** Monograph. Institute for Business and Economic Research, San Jose State College, 1970.

The author attempts to provide factual information about Mexican-American families in an urban environment.

336. Weiner, Sandra. **Small Hands, Big Hands: Seven Stories of Mexican
j   American Migrant Workers and Their Families.** New York: Pantheon Books, Inc., 1970. 55p.

Seven migrant workers, ranging in age from 11 to 67, tell what it is like to live in an agricultural labor camp.

337. Weiss, Karel. **Under the Mask: An Anthology About Prejudice.** New York: Delacorte Press, 1972. 311p.

Major writings about our oppressed minorities, perceptively selected and arranged. Presenting over 120 excerpts by 89 contributors, including Kenneth Clark, Archibald MacLeish, Robert Coles, Gordon Parks, and others.

338.   Williams, Robin M., Jr. **Strangers Next Door: Ethnic Relations in American Communities**. Englewood Cliffs, N.J.: Prentice-Hall, Inc., 1964. 391p.

This book is based on the Cornell Studies in Intergroup Relations. They analyzed not only racial and ethnic prejudices but actual pathways of interaction and avoidance among the people. Research for the book was done in 17 small cities, including several in the Southwest. Mexican Americans are among the ethnic groups specifically treated in the numerous tables as well as in the general discussion.

339.   Wollenberg, Charles. "Huelga: 1928 Style." **Pacific Historical Review**, XXXVIII (February 1969), 45-68.

Excellent background reading of Huelga prior to World War II.

340.   Young, Jan. **The Migrant Workers and Cesar Chavez**. New York:
  j   Julian Messner, 1972. 189p.

After a century of struggle, oppressed migrant farm workers achieved their first real triumph, led by the charismatic Chavez.

EDUCATION

341.   Beals, Ralph, and Norman D. Humphrey. **No Frontier in Learning: The Mexican Student in the United States**. Minneapolis, Minn.: University of Minnesota Press, 1957. 148p. o.p.

The author studied the partial acculturation of the Mexican student in U.S. universities. He discusses the changes in the Mexican's opinions about the United States and in his basic attitudes and values as a result of contact with its culture. The study was based on interviews conducted primarily with Mexican students at the University of California at Los Angeles in 1952-1953.

342.   Brussell, Charles B. **Disadvantaged Mexican American Children and Early Educational Experience**. Austin, Texas: Southwest Educational Development Corporation, 1968.

The work describes educational deprivation of the school children and resulting low scores and high dropout rates.

343.   Carter, Thomas P. **Mexican Americans in School: A History of Educational Neglect**. Princeton, N.J.: College Entrance Examination Board, 1970. 235p.

Field research data, based on interviews conducted primarily in California and Texas, serve to identify needed areas of empirical research and to expose the perceptions of school personnel concerning Mexican Americans: why they fail in school, what their culture entails, and curricular patterns used. A brief history of the educational plight of Mexican Americans begins the book, and in the final chapter, "Where Do We Go from Here?" possible areas of curricular change which may provide Mexican Americans with the skills, knowledge, and credentials essential for entrance to higher levels of society are presented.

344. Davidson, Walter Craig. **The Mexican American High School Graduate of Laredo.** Laredo, Texas: Laredo Independent School District, 1971. 76p.
"The study concerns itself with the identification and interpretation of those factors that are germane to a Mexican-American high school graduate's perception of himself, his school and community, his home, and the interrelationship of these areas and from which he extracts those factors that, to him, are pertinent in his attempts to relate himself effectively to the rest of the world and upon which he attempts to construct the matrix of his life after graduation from high school." The study contains many graphs, charts and the questionnaire used in the interviews.

345. "Education for the Spanish Speaking." **The National Elementary Principal**, L (November 1970), 15-122.
The entire issue is devoted to a discussion of education for Spanish-speaking people. These articles will help bring into clear perspective the educational needs of this minority group.

346. Ericksen, Charles A. "Uprising in the Barrios," **American Education**, IV (November 1968), 29-31.
A call for a more comprehensive education for Mexican-American citizens. "The goal: to educate the total Mexican-American, not just parts of him." Lists Mexican-American activists in California.

347. Fedder, Ruth, et al. **No Longer Deprived: Using Minority Cultures and Languages in Educating Disadvantaged Children and Their Teachers.** New York: Teachers College Press, Columbia University, 1969. 223p.
A realistic presentation of teachers discussing the personal methods and relationships they have developed through working with children from Indian and Mexican-American backgrounds.

348. Fogel, Walter. **Education and Income of Mexican Americans in the Southwest.** Mexican-American Study Project Advance Report 1. Los Angeles, Division of Research, Graduate School of Business, University of California, 1965. 28p.
This study, based on census data, reports the relation between educational attainment and income among Anglos, Spanish-surnamed people, Negroes, and Orientals in the Southwest.

349. Forbes, Jack D. **Mexican-Americans: A Handbook for Educators.** Berkeley, Calif.: West Laboratory for Educational Research and Development, 1967. 34p.
A manual treating Mexican-American cultures with practical application for teachers and administrators.

350. Grebler, Leo. **The Schooling Gap: Signs of Progress.** Mexican-American Study Project Advance Report 7. Los Angeles, Calif.: University of California, 1967. 48p.

This is an analysis of 1960 census data on educational attainment among Anglos, Negroes and Spanish-surnamed people in the American Southwest. The author devotes a final chapter to the differences in educational attainment between native and foreign-born Spanish-surnamed people.

351. Halliburton, Warren J., and William Loren Katz. **American Minorities and Majorities: A Syllabus of United States History for Secondary Schools.** New York: Arno Press, 1970. 219p.

This work is a syllabus for teachers in secondary schools of United States history. Patterned after traditional curricula currently used in our nation's schools, it integrates into the course of study the contributions of Afro-Americans and other minorities to our common heritage. Its aim, like that of any school course in social studies, is the preparation of good citizens. The solution of our racial problem has in part been hindered by the lack of accurate information and the prevalence of misinformation. This syllabus is a contribution toward remedying our miseducation.

352. Heath, G. Louis. **Red, Brown, and Black Demands for Better Education.** Philadelphia: Westminster Press, 1972. 216p.

Examining the educational structure across the country, this works argues for the justified educational demands of Indians, Blacks, and Chicanos.

353. Hernandez, Luis F. **A Forgotten American: A Resource Unit for Teachers on the Mexican American.** New York: Anti-Defamation League of B'nai B'rith, 1969. 56p.

The introduction is by Robert Finch, Secretary of Health, Education and Walfare. The work outlines the contemporary life styles of Mexican Americans and relates these to the Mexican-American student and everyday classroom situations. Includes numerous suggestions for the teacher, a survey of Mexican history, and useful bibliographical material.

354. Johnson, Henry S. **Educating the Mexican American.** Valley Forge, Pa.: Judson Press, 1970. 384p.

The author speaks with enduring timeliness on specific educational issues. Major sections are devoted to guidance, curriculum, bi-lingual education and the role of educational institutions. Although the Chicano child may be culturally different, he should not be treated as deprived.

355. Landes, Ruth. **Culture in American Education: Anthropological Approaches to Minority and Dominant Groups in the Schools.** New York: John Wiley & Sons, Inc., 1965. 330p.

The teacher-training experiment described in this book rested on years of studying culture as a research anthropologist and of applying the knowledge acquired. Appendixes discuss the Mexican-American family. Bibliography and index included.

356. Moreno, Steve. "Problems Related to Present Testing Instruments." **El Grito**, III (Spring 1970), 25-29.

A discussion of the problems related to the use and effectiveness of traditional tests of intelligence, aptitude, and achievement of Mexican-American children. The author includes several recommendations to measure Mexican-American children.

357.   National NEA-PR & R Conference on Civil and Human Rights in Education. 3rd Conference. Tucson, Arizona, 1966. **Los Voces Nueva del Sudoeste.** Washington: National Education Association, 1967. 20p.
This report is a blueprint for action in six areas ranging from the individual classroom to the federal government. It is made up of the facts, ideas, suggestions, and proposals that were presented during this conference.

358.   National Education Association. Department of Rural Education. **The Invisible Minority: Pero no Vencibles.** Washington: National Education Association, 1966. 39p.
A report of the NEA-Tucson survey on the teaching of Spanish to the Spanish-speaking people.

359.   Ortega, Phillip D. "Montezuma's Children." **El Grito,** III (Spring 1968), 38-50.
The author discusses educational problems facing the Mexican Americans in the Southwest areas, such as: 1) the failure of existing educational programs, 2) intelligence testing, 3) the high dropout rate among Mexican Americans, 4) college and university enrollment, and 5) bilingual educational programs.

360.   Parr, Eunice Elvira. **A Comparative Study of Mexican and American Children in the Schools of San Antonio, Texas.** San Antonio, Texas: R & E Research Associates, 1971. 52p.
A study originally done for the author's thesis at the University of Chicago reveals the areas of difficulty for the Mexican-American children because of cultural differences and makes comparisons with Anglo children.

361.   Pitt, Leonard. **Plan de Santa Barbara.** Santa Barbara, Calif.: La Causa Publications, 1970.
A guideline designed to help in the establishment of Chicano studies departments and classes.

362.   Rodriguez, Armando M. "Speak Up, Chicano," **American Education,** IV (May 1968), 25-27.
The director of the Office of Education's Mexican-American Affairs Unit describes the problems involved in the education of Spanish-speaking children.

363.   United States Commission on Civil Rights. **Education and the Mexican American Community in Los Angeles County.** A Report of the California State Advisory Committee to the U.S. Commission on Civil Rights. Washington: United States Government Printing Office, 1968. 28p.
A report evaluating and recommending the materials received at two days of open

meetings held in East Los Angeles on June 8-9, 1967. This report concentrates on the issue of education, which has recently been the cause of disruptions in the East Los Angeles schools and communities.

364. United States Commission on Civil Rights. **Equal Educational Opportunities for the Spanish-Speaking Child: Bilingual and Bicultural Programs.** Washington: U.S. Government Printing Office, 1970.

The purpose of this booklet is to provide a brief and concise outline of those federal education programs which are of most interest to the Spanish-speaking community.

365. United States Commission on Civil Rights. **Mexican-Americans: Ethnic Isolation of Mexican-Americans in the Public Schools of the Southwest.** Mexican-American Education Study, Report No. 1. Washington: U.S. Government Printing Office, 1971. 103p.

The first of a series of reports which discuss education problems of Mexican Americans. Contains detailed data on school enrollment, sutdent distribution within school districts, and ethnic background of the teachers, administrators, and members of boards of education. The questionnaire used in the conduct of the study has been included as Appendix A.

366. United States Commission on Civil Rights. **The Unfinished Education.** Mexican-American Educational Study, Report No. 2. Washington: U.S. Government Printing Office, 1971. 101p.

In this second report investigating the nature and scope of education opportunities for Mexican Americans in the public schools of the states of Arizona, California, Colorado, New Mexico, and Texas, attention is focused on the performance of the schools as reflected in the achievements of their pupils.

367. United States Department of Health, Education and Welfare. Office of Education. **Mexican-American Education.** A Special Report. Washington: U.S. Government Printing Office, 1968. 31p.

This field survey by the Mexican-American Affairs Unit of the Office of Education through Arizona, California, New Mexico, Colorado, and Texas revealed a lack of coordination among all government levels and a lack of creativity in the schools. The report contains specific recommendations for improving education for Mexican Americans.

368. United States Office of Education. **National Conference on Bilingual Education: Language Skills.** Washington: U.S. Government Printing Office, 1969. 4p.

The report of a conference on bilingual education held at the University of Maryland in June 1969. The objectives of bilingual education were defined and specific goals listed. In the conference report seven papers by specialists in bilingual education were presented; they are included here.

369. United States Office of Education. **Programs Under Bilingual Education Act: Manual for Project Applicants and Grantees.** Washington:

U.S. Government Printing Office, 1971. 30p.
The purpose and objectives of the Bilingual Education Act are given, and procedures for planning a bilingual program are outlined. The procedure for submitting a plan, procedures for reporting, and requirements are given in the manual.

HEALTH AND PSYCHOLOGY

370.   Anderson, Henry P. **The Bracero Program in California, with Particular Reference to Health Status, Attitudes and Practices.** Berkeley, Calif.: School of Public Health, University of California, 1961. 294p.
This work, based on interviews with Mexican nationals, was confidential and limited as to circulation. Primarily the study relates to the health and medical care of the bracero program, but it does report on other aspects of the program such as labor camps, housing, and border processing.

371.   Clark, Margaret. **Health in the Mexican-American Culture: A Community Study.** 2nd ed. Berkeley, Calif.: University of California, 1970. 253p.
A study of Sal si Puedes, an unincorporated community on the eastern edge of San Jose, in Santa Clara County. A study focusing on the "culture of health," but covering many other areas of the community life.

372.   Crawford, Fred R. **The Forgotten Egg: A Study of the Mental Health Problems of Mexican-American Residents in the Neighborhood of the Good Samaritan Center, San Antonio, Texas.** San Antonio, Texas: Good Samaritan Center, 1961. 43p.
A survey and study of mental health problems among the first-grade school children, conducted by Spanish-speaking nurses. The research found that the local medical center was accepted and used by a large percent of the inhabitants and that a decrease had been noted in the treatment of Mexican Americans by folk healers in the area of mental problems. A comparison of attitudes in child behavior of Mexican Americans and Anglos noted similar patterns.

373.   Dworkin, Anthony Gary. "Stereotypes and Self-Images Held by Native-Born and Foreign-Born Mexican-Americans." **Sociology and Social Research**, LXIX (January 1965), 214-24.
"Stereotypes of the Anglo and self-images were obtained from two hundred eighty native-born (U.S. born) and foreign-born (Mexican-born) and Mexican-American students and community residents. Statistical comparisons indicate that significantly more foreign-born subjects hold favorable stereotypes and self-images than do native-born subjects. Findings were attributed to differences in the groups' definition of their present social situation as influenced by whether they employed their prior socioeconomic situation or the socioeconomic situation of the dominant society as a standard of evaluation."

374.   Fabrega, Horacio, Jr., and Carole Ann Wallace. "Value Identification and Psychiatric Disability: An Analysis Involving Americans of Mexican Descent." **Behavioral Science**, XII (1968), 362-71.

A research project conducted with two groups of Mexican Americans living in South Texas. The two groups were 1) psychiatric outpatients and 2) nonpatients. The results of the study report the nonpatients showed higher measures of stability, social competence and self-sufficiency in economic life. Scalogram analysis indicated that persons allowed to act within a pattern or framework of fewer basic premises showed improved social conditions.

375. Finney, Joseph C., ed. **Culture Change, Mental Health, and Poverty.**
      Lexington, Ky.: University Press of Kentucky, 1969. 344p.
Conference reports of a meeting on thenopsychology and crosscultural psychiatry held at the University of Kentucky in 1965. The essays concern the possibility of judging objectively a particular way of life as to whether it is a malfunctioning way to the group; the extent change should be directed toward persons or institutions; and the right to take measures to intervene in an attempt to change the way of life for a group of people.

376. Johnson, Dale L., and Melvin P. Sikes. "Rorschach and TAT Responses of Negro, Mexican-American, and Anglo Psychiatric Patients." **Journal of Projective Techniques and Personality Assessment**, XXIX (March 1965), 183-88.
Three groups of 25 Negro, Mexican-American, and Anglo psychiatric patients in a veterans' hospital in Houston, Texas, were studied for this report. The Rorschach and Thematic Apperception Test projective techniques were used to study the differences of personality among the culture of the Negro, Mexican American and Anglo. Differences were shown in themes of family unity and family relationships and in the measure of hostility.

377. Karno, Marvin, and Robert B. Edgerton. "Perception of Mental Illness in a Mexican-American Community." **Archives of General Psychiatry**, XX (February 1969), 233-38.
The authors endeavor to show that mental illness is much higher among Mexican Americans than that reported. This is an introductory report to a larger study covering five years of research on mental illness among the Mexican Americans in East Los Angeles.

378. Kelly, Isabel. **Folk Practices in North Mexico: Birth Customs, Folk Medicine, and Spiritualism in the Laguna Zone.** Latin American Monograph No. 2. Austin, Texas: University of Texas Press, 1965. 166p.
Folk customs and habits, a list of ailments and their local cures, magic, witchcraft and spiritualism, and the incipient lodestone cult are presented in a scientific work of special interest to anthropologists, yet fascinating to the layman.

379. Kiev, Ari. **Curanderismo: Mexian-American Folk Psychiatry.** New York: Free Press, 1968. 207p.
An account of actual practices, the therapeutic value of Mexican-American folk medicine, its role in resolving tensions, and its limitations. The author believes

that curanderismo is superior in some areas to modern practice because it relates to the Mexican Americans' belief and culture, although this would not apply to mental disturbance caused by organic origin.

380. McLemore, S. Dale. "Ethnic Attitudes Toward Hospitalization: An Illustrative Comparison of Anglos and Mexican-Americans." **Southwestern Social Science Quarterly**, LXIII (March 1963), 341-46.

An illustrative comparison of Mexican Americans and Anglos in their approach to and use of hospital facilities. The attitudes and cultural patterns influencing both Anglos and Mexican Americans are discussed in this study.

381. Madsen, William. "The Alcoholic Agringado." **American Anthropologist**, LXVI (April 1964), 355-61.

Madsen discusses the psychological stresses on Agringado (defining the term Agringados as a Mexican American who has rejected his own culture and has adopted the outward patterns of the Anglo) and the ways and means he uses to resolve the stresses. The turning to alcohol is too often the means of escape for the Agringado. The author also notes the fact that therapy for the Mexican American is not as successful as it should be because the therapists do not understand Mexican-American culture.

382. Meadow, Arnold, and Louise Bronson. "Religious Affiliation and Psychopathology in a Mexican-American Population." **Journal of Abnormal Psychology**, LXXIV (April 1969), 177-80.

Protestant and Catholic Mexican Americans of similar levels of acculturation, education, and socioeconomic background were studied with a variety of instruments for this report. Evaluations of psychopathology, reported here, were derived from the L-R sections of the Cornell Medical Index and behavioral observations. "The lower rate of pathological responses by Protestant Ss was attributed to the social support offered by the small, intimate congregations with their strong, paternal leadership and the Protestant doctrine of asceticism and individual responsibility which contribute to impulse control."

383. Moustafa, A. Taher, and Gertrud Weiss. **Health Status and Practices of Mexican Americans**. Mexican-American Study Project Advance Report 11. Division of Research, Graduate School of Business, University of California. Los Angeles, Calif.: University of California, 1968. 47p.

A report of contemporary literature on Mexican-American mortality rates, morbidity characteristics, mental illness, and health attitudes and practices.

384. Nall, Frank C., and Joseph Speilberg. "Social and Cultural Factors in the Responses of Mexican-Americans to Medical Treatment." **Journal of Health and Social Behavior**, VIII (December 1967), 299-308.

The authors point out factors and attitudes of both cultural and social natures influencing Mexican Americans regarding medical treatment. The article indicates the need for reconciling modern medical practice with folk beliefs and the need to understand Mexican-American culture in order to treat the Mexican American properly.

385.   Romano-V, Octavio Ignacio. "Charismatic Medicine, Folk-Healing, and Folk-Sainthood." **American Anthropologist,** LXVII (October 1965), 1151-73.

This paper utilizes findings drawn from a study of charismatic medicine among the Mexican Americans in three communities in South Texas. The specific case of Don Pedrito Jaramillo is presented as an example of a healer who rose in the healing hierarchy from a relatively unknown healer to, ultimately, the status of folk-sainthood.

386.   Rubel, Arthur J. **Across the Tracks: Mexican-Americans in a Texas City.** Austin, Texas: University of Texas Press, 1966. 266p.

The dilemma of the young Mexican-American man caught between conflicting goals and values of Anglo and Chicano culture. This anthropological study is a product of the Hidalgo County Project directed by William Madsen under the Hogg Foundation for Mental Health at the University of Texas. A good community study of a South Texas border town. Similar to Clark's book in focusing on health, but the coverage is broad.

387.   Saunders, Lyle. **Cultural Differences and Medical Care: The Case of the Spanish-Speaking People of the Southwest.** New York: Russell Sage Foundation, 1954. 245p. o.p.

The author presents information about the Mexican-American people in the Southwest and the relationship between medicine and culture. The study shows how difficult it is for the Mexican American to accept Anglo medical practices because of his cultural patterns.

388.   Wagner, Nathaniel N., and Marsha J. Haug, eds. **Chicanos: Social and Psychological Perspectives.** St. Louis, Mo.: Mosby, 1971. 303p.

Available in English or Spanish, this book is a collection of current psychological studies and writings on the social life and customs of the Mexican American, with photographs by Irwin Nash interspersed throughout the volume.

3: THE ARTS

ART AND ARCHITECTURE

389. Anton, Ferdinand. **Ancient Mexican Art.** Translated by Betty and
      Peter Rose. New York: G. P. Putnam's Sons, 1969. 309p.
A well-documented and superbly illustrated history of the arts of ancient Mexico.

390. Anton, Ferdinand. **Art of the Maya.** New York: G. P. Putnam's Sons,
      1970. 304p.
The famous art treasures of the mysterious Mayan culture. Many important
examples are reproduced here for the first time.

391. Bernal, Ignacio. **Ancient Mexico in Colour.** New York: McGraw-Hill
      Book Company, 1968. 159p. o.p.
Colorful illustrations and text present the magnificence of ancient Mexico.

392. Bernal, Ignacio. **Mexican Wall Paintings of the Maya and Aztec Periods.**
      New York: New American Library, 1963. 30p.
Text on Mexican wall paintings, followed by color plates.

393. Bernal, Ignacio, and Jacques Soustelle. **Mexico: Pre-Hispanic Paintings.**
      Greenwich, Conn.: New York Graphic Society, 1958. 92p.
Reproductions of paintings with informative text.

394. Bernal, Ignacio, and others. **3,000 Years of Art and Life as Seen in the
      National Museum of Anthropology, Mexico City.** New York: Harry
      N. Abrams, Inc., 1969. 216p.
Summarizes the museum's origins, aims, achievements, and the cultures represented in its archaeological and ethnographic sections.

395. Boos, Frank H. **The Ceramic Sculptures of Ancient Oaxaca.** Cranbury,
      N.J.: A. S. Barnes & Company, Inc., 1965. 488p.
This book presents a representative selection of the figures carved on funerary
urns and ceremonial braziers, whistles, and plaques by sculptors in the pre-
Columbian Oaxacan culture of South Mexico.

396. Brenner, Anita. **Idols Behind Altars.** Boston: Beacon Press, 1970.
      359p.
Reprint of a 1929 edition. Mexican art, closely related as it is to native history,
customs, and religion, is the subject of this book. Early chapters are devoted to
products of the Aztec civilization, and the Spanish invasion of Mexico under
Cortez. Art of the Colonial Period is next described. Part 3 is concerned chiefly
with modern art and the works of such artists as Siqueiros, Orozco, Goitia, and
Charlot.

397.   Burchwood, Katherine Tyler. **The Origin and Legacy of Mexican Art.** Cranbury, N.J.: A. S. Barnes & Company, Inc., 1972. 159p.
Mexican history presented through the history of art.

398.   Cali, Francois. **The Spanish Arts of Latin America.** New York: The Viking Press, 1961. 300p. o.p.
Photographs illustrate the study of the baroque art developed by the Aztecs, Mayas, and Incas during the age of the conquistadors in Latin America—a religious art, for the most part, blending Catholic and pagan elements.

399.   Charlot, Jean. **Mexican Art and the Academy of San Carlos, 1785-1915.** Austin, Texas, University of Texas Press, 1962. 177p.
Examines the art of the neo-classic period through a study of the curricula, drawings and finances of the academy which dominated the movement.

400.   Charlot, Jean. **Mexican Mural Renaissance 1920-1925.** New Haven, Conn.: Yale University Press, 1963. 328p.
This book records the beginning of the contemporary Mexican mural renaissance, when Siqueiros, Orozco, Rivera, and others groped through their first mural tasks, not yet knowing where they would emerge.

401.   "Chicano Art." **El Grito,** II (Spring 1969).
The complete issue is devoted to the art of the following: Portfolio 1, Malaquios Montoya; Portfolio 2, Esteban Villa; Portfolio 3, Manuel Hernandez Trujillo; Portfolio 4, Rene Yanez; and Portfolio 5, Jose Ernesto Montoya.

402.   Coe, Michael D. **The Jaguar's Children: Pre-Classical Central Mexico.** Greenwich, Conn.: New York Graphic Society, 1965. 126p.
The rich arts of the people of Central Mexico who lived from 1500 B.C. to 250 A.D. Photographs and line drawings.

403.   Cordry, Donald, and Dorothy Cordry. **Mexican Indian Costumes.** Texas Pan American Series. Austin, Texas: University of Texas, 1968. 373p.
The authors spent 30 years collecting, photographing, and recording details of the costumes of the Indians of Mexico who are slowly disappearing. The book contains 276 plates, 16 in color, and is an authoritative work on the making of textiles and the wearing of the costumes. The Cordrys examine the development of the textile art from pre-historic times to the present.

404.   Covarrubias, Miguel. **Indian Art of Mexico and Central America.** New York: Alfred A. Knopf, Inc., 1957. 360p.
The chronological period of Indian art from the pre-classic to and including the Aztec period. A magnificently illustrated book that has also been published in Mexico (1961) as *Arte Indigena de Mexico y Centro-America.*

405.   Davis, Mary L., and Greta Pack. **Mexican Jewelry.** Austin, Texas: University of Texas Press, 1963. 262p.

Illustrations of Mexican jewelry are so well done that they will serve as an excellent guide to the aspiring artist and craftsman.

406. Dockstader, Frederick J. **Indian Art in Middle America: Pre-Columbian and Contemporary Arts and Crafts of Mexico, Central America and the Caribbean.** Greenwich, Conn.: New York Graphic Society, 1964. 221p.

A text with excellent color photographs of pre-Columbian Indian arts and crafts makes delightful browsing; the book is also well documented.

407. Dorner, Gerd. **Folk Art of Mexico.** Cranbury, N.J.: A. S. Barnes & Company, 1963. 67p.

A brief and colorful introduction to many areas of Mexican folk art.

408. Edwards, Emily, and Manuel Alvarez Bravo. **Painted Walls of Mexico: From Pre-historic Times Until Today.** Austin, Texas: University of Texas Press, 1966. 306p.

An instructive visual and textual chronological survey of Mexican mural painting.

409. Emmerich, Andre. **Art Before Columbus: The Art of Ancient Mexico.** New York: Simon & Schuster, Inc., 1963. 256p.

Descriptions of early village cultures as well as better known groups. Black and white photographs illustrate the text.

410. Enciso, Jorge. **Design Motifs of Ancient Mexico.** New York: Dover Publications, Inc., 1947. 153p.

A collection for artists and designers of Mexican art work.

411. Fernandez, Justino. **A Guide to Mexican Art from Its Beginnings to the Present.** Translated by Joshua C. Taylor. Chicago: University of Chicago Press, 1969. 378p.

Arranged in four time periods: ancient indigenous art done prior to the sixteenth century; art of New Spain created during 300 years of the viceregal period; modern art executed in the nineteenty century; and contemporary art exemplified in the post-revolutionary period. Murals by Rivera, Orozco, and Siqueiros since 1910.

412. Gay, Carlo T. E., and Frances Pratt. **Xochipala: The Beginning of Olmec Art.** Princeton, N.J.: Princeton University Press, 1972. 61p.

Published in connection with the exhibition held January 11 to February 13, 1972, at the Art Museum of Princeton University. The text is taken from a work in progress on preclassic ceramic figures from Central and Midwestern Mexico.

413. Glubok, Shirley. **The Art of Ancient Mexico.** Designed by Gerard Nook.
j Special photography by Alfred H. Tamarin. New York: Harper & Row, Publishers, 1968. 41p.

The author examines the Aztec, Mixtec, Toltec, Olmec, Zapotec cultures through their art.

414.	Gual, Enrique. **Siqueiros**. New York: Tudor Publishing Co., 1966. 46p. o.p.
Reproductions of David Siqueiros' paintings.

415.	**Image of Mexico I: The General Motors of Mexico Collection of Mexican Graphic Art (A-K)**. Edited by Thomas Mabry Cranfill. A special issue of the *Texas Quarterly*. Austin, Texas: University of Texas Press, 1970. 338p.
Includes an introduction by the editor describing the collection; an essay by John L. Brown; photographs of artists; reproductions of drawings and prints; and artists' biographical data.

416.	**Image of Mexico II: The General Motors of Mexico Collection of Mexican Graphic Art (L-Z)**. Edited by Thomas Mabry Cranfill. A special issue of the *Texas Quarterly*. Austin, Texas: University of Texas Press, 1970. 340p.
Photographs, reproductions of drawings and prints. Biographical information about artists.

417.	Jones, Edward H., Jr., and Margaret S. Jones. **Arts and Crafts of the**
j	**Mexican People**. Los Angeles, Calif.: Ward Ritchie Press, 1971. 64p.
Here are the history, tradition, and influences of the Mexican people: pottery, weaving, metalcrafts, woodworking, leathercrafts, glassware, and lacquerwork. Here is also a discussion of the minor crafts: toys, fireworks, paperworks, yarnwork, and the now-extinct featherwork.

418.	Jones, Julie. **Bibliography for Olmec Sculpture**. New York: New York Library Museum of Primitive Art, 1963. 8p.
This bibliography is an introduction to Olmec sculpture, written for the Institute of Fine Arts, New York University.

419.	Los Angeles County Museum. **Masterworks of Mexican Art from Pre-Columbian Times to the Present**. Los Angeles, Calif.: Los Angeles County Museum, 1963. unpaged.
A most informative exhibition catalog, with an extensive bibliography. There are many illustrations of fine and folk art.

420.	Merida, Carlos. **Modern Mexican Artists**. Freeport, N.Y.: Books for Libraries Press, 1968. 202p. Reprint of 1937 edition.
A collection of essays about renowned Mexican artists.

421.	Myers, Bernard Samuel. **Mexican Painting in Our Time**. New York: Oxford University Press, Inc., 1956. 283p.
Modern Mexican art surveyed in relation to the social and historical background of the country.

422.	**National Museum of Anthropology, Mexico City**. Great Museums of the World Series. Newsweek. New York: Simon & Schuster, Inc., 1970. 171p.
The treasures of pre-Hispanic Mexico.

423. Payne, Robert, and Dick Davis. **Mexico City.** New York: Harcourt, Brace & World, Inc., 1968. 212p.

One of the most beautiful of the descriptive volumes available. Text and photographs describe the beauties of the old and the new in Mexico City.

424. Ramirez, Vasquez Pedro. **The National Museum of Anthropology: Art, Architecture, Archaeology, Anthropology.** New York: Harry N. Abrams, Inc., 1968. 257p.

Describes the museum and its large collection in text and photographs. Many beautiful colored plates are included.

425. Reed, Alma M. **The Mexican Muralists.** New York: Crown Publishers, Inc., 1960. 191p. o.p.

An excellent presentation of Mexican mural painters since 1920, with discussions of each muralist and his art.

426. Rodriquez, Antonio. **A History of Mexican Mural Painting.** Translated from Spanish and German by Marina Corby. New York: G. P. Putnam's Sons, 1969. 517p.

A comprehensive, well-illustrated, and authoritative history of Mexico's typical art expression. It is an in-depth study of the muralists and their world. Luxuriously illustrated with both reproductions and photographs of the artists and their workshops.

427. Rojas Rodriquez, Pedro. **Art and Architecture of Mexico: From 10,000 B.C. to the Present Day.** Translated by J. M. Cohen. New York: Tudor Publishing Co., 1968. 71p.

An excellent introduction to the art and architecture of Mexico.

428. Ross, Patricia Fent. **Made in Mexico.** Illustrated by Carlos Merida.
    j   New York: Alfred A. Knopf, Inc., 1952. 329p.

An interesting and informative survey of Mexican fine arts and scientific contributions. Beautiful illustrations by one of Mexico's foremost painters. Glossary.

429. Sanford, Trent Elwood. **The Architecture of the Southwest: Indian, Spanish, American.** New York: W. W. Norton Co., Inc., 1971. Reprint of 1950 edition. 312p.

In the Southwest are blended three cultures: Indian, Spanish, and Anglo-American. This study tells of the builders of the Southwest, what and how they built. It shows that the work of Americans today is influenced by earlier cultures.

430. Shipway, Verna, and Warren Shipway. **Mexican Homes of Today.** New York: Hastings House Publishers, Inc., 1964. 272p.

Photographs and plans of six homes are followed by a collection of interior and exterior design details.

431. Shipway, Verna, and Warren Shipway. **The Mexican House: Old and New.** New York: Hastings House Publishers, Inc., 1960. 208p.

A record of a way of life in which architecture, climate, and tradition combine to reproduce the gracious, leisurely charms of the past. Photographs, measured drawings.

432. Shipway, Verna, and Warren Shipway. **Mexican Interiors.** New York: Hastings House Publishers, 1962. 272p.
A collection of photographs showing a wide variety of furnishings, ceramics, fabrics and metalwork representative of all periods.

433. Smith, Bradley. **Mexico: A History in Art.** New York: Harper & Row Publishers, Inc., 1968. 296p.
A history of ancient and modern Mexico as shown in sculpture and painting. Chronologies introduce each important era and result in an excellent melding of text and pictures.

434. Smith, Clive Bamford. **Builders in the Sun: Five Mexican Architects.** New York: Hastings House Publishers, Inc., 1966. 224p.
Juan O'Gorman, Luis Barragan, Felix Candela, Mathias Goeritz, and Mario Pani are the five architects whose work is analyzed. Photographs.

435. Soustelle, Jacques. **Arts of Ancient Mexico.** New York: Viking Press, Inc., 1967. 100p.
An outstanding book on ancient Mexican art. Contains photographs, maps with archaeological sites indicated, text describing Olmec, Teotihuacan, Maya, Zopotec, Toltec, Mixtec, and Aztec cultures.

436. Strand, Paul. **The Mexican Portfolio.** 2nd ed. Text by Leo Hurwitz. New York: Da Capo Press, 1967. unpaged.
Twenty plates of outstanding photography of Mexico. Brief descriptive text. Included in Fifty Books of the Year 1967, Exhibition Year 1968, by the American Institute of Graphic Arts.

437. Tamayo, Rufino. **Tamayo.** Translated by Emma Gutierrez Saurez. Folio. New York: Tudor Publishing Co., 1967. 50p.
Reproductions of the beautiful paintings of Rufino Tamayo.

438. Thompson, J. Eric. **Ancient Maya Relief Sculpture.** New York: Museum of Primitive Art, 1967. unpaged.
This book of rubbings of Maya low relief sculpture done by Merle Greene is the result of four summers spent in the jungles of Mexico. The rubbings are rich in detail and illustrate the great ceremonial centers, the altars, tombs and monuments.

439. Toor, Frances. **Mexican Popular Arts.** Detroit, Mich.: Blaine Ethridge, 1971. 107p.
The varied and beautiful Indian arts of weaving, needlework, jewelry and pottery making, leather and metal work, and other native handicrafts are described in this reprint of a 1939 work.

440.   Toussaint, Manuel. **Colonial Art in Mexico.** Translated by Elizabeth
            Welder Weismann. Austin, Texas: University of Texas Press, 1968. 489p.
The first attempt to consider the panorama of one of the most interesting,
varied, and significant of the American cultures in its colonial phase, the 300
years between conquest by Spain and the winning of independence. Reprint
of 1949 edition.

441.   Velazquez Chavez, Agustin. **Contemporary Mexican Artists.** Freeport,
            N.Y.: Books for Libraries Press, 1969. 304p.
The author has included artists born around 1880 who were responsible for the
art movement in Mexico, and the younger artists who contributed to its more
recent development. A brief outline is given of the period during which the
Mexican cultural movement first gave birth to what has come to be contemporary
Mexican art.

442.   Wicke, Charles R. **Olmec: An Early Art Style of Pre-Columbian Mexico.**
            Tucson, Ariz.: University of Arizona Press, 1971. 188p.
Discusses who created the spectacular, massive sculpture complex found from
northern Veracruz to El Salvador—when was it made and why.

443.   Wilcox, Ruth Turner. **Folk and Festival Costumes of the World.** New
            York: Scribner Publications, 1965. unpaged.
A survey of traditional dress including the countries who preserve their traditional garb for festive occasions. More than 150 countries and ethnic groups are
included; 600 drawings and accompanying text describe the costumes. Tells
where and how the costume is worn, and indicates typical colors.

DRAMA AND THE THEATER

444.   "Actos; Teatro Campesino, A Theatrical Part of the United Farmworkers
            Organizing Committee." **The New Yorker,** XLIII, No. 25 (August 19,
            1967), 23-25.
Reporters in New York view and analyze the plays performed by the Teatro
Campesino and report the interesting interview held following the performance.

445.   Bailey, Clay. "Guanajuatos Teatro Juarez." **Opera News,** XXXI
            (February 18, 1967), 6-7.
Description of the theatre and its historical background, including plays given there.

446.   Campa, Arthur L. **Spanish Religious Folk Theater in the Southwest.**
            Albuquerque, N.M.: University of New Mexico Press, 1934. 157p. o.p.
Folk and religious drama of the Spanish Americans in the Southwest.

447.   Carballido, Emilio. **"The Golden Thread" and Other Plays.** Translated
            by Margaret Sayers Peden. Texas Pan American Series. Austin, Texas:
            University of Texas Press, 1970. 224p.
A selection of the fantastic plays of Emilio Carballido, the most inventive and
the most accomplished of Mexico's playwrights. The plays range from surreal-
ist farce in "The Intermediate Zone" to the grotesqueries of "The Time and

the Place," from tragicomedy to "Theseus" to the dreamlike permutations of "The Golden Thread."

448.   Carballido, Emilio. **Medusa**. Englewood Cliffs, N.J.: Prentice-Hall, Inc., 1971. unpaged.

The play is a modern rendering of the classical myth of Perseus and the Gorgon, but Carballido's treatment of the fable is very much his own. He has preserved only the most essential elements of the myth. "Medusa" is a play about man's quest for moral autonomy in life and politics.

449.   Deuel, Pauline. **Mexican Serenade: The Story of the Mexican Players and the Padua Hills Theater.** Claremont, Calif.: Padua Institute, 1961. 80p.

A description of the Padua Hills Theater, the plays and the actors.

450.   Gillmor, Frances. **The Dance Dramas of Mexican Villages.** Arizona University Humanities Bulletin, No. 5. Tucson, Ariz.: University of Arizona, 1943. 28p.

An interesting article relating to the folk plays in existence in Mexico.

451.   Holzapfel, Tamar. "A Mexican Medusa." **Modern Drama**, XII, No. 3 (December 1969), 231-37.

"Medusa," a play written by Emilio Carballido, was written in 1958 but was first made available to the public in 1960. This major work remains unproduced in Mexico. It was staged at Cornell University in April 1966. This article provides a synopsis of the play, which is a modern rendering of the classical myth of Perseus and the Gorgon.

452.   Jones, Willis Knapp. **Behind Spanish American Footlights.** Austin, Texas: University of Texas Press, 1966. 609p.

This clearly documented account of the drama and stage not only covers the Spanish-speaking countries but even extends to the West Indies. A comprehensive study in English covering the theatrical efforts of 19 countries over 475 years.

453.   Niggli, Josephine. **Mexican Folkplays.** Chapel Hill, N.C.: University of North Carolina Press, 1938. 220p. o.p.

The plays, representing certain folk attitudes of northern Mexico, were written for American audiences. The plays make one aware of such things as the lot of the woman in the Mexican Revolution.

454.   Oliver, William I., ed. **Voices of Change in the Spanish American Theater: An Anthology.** Austin, Texas: University of Texas Press, 1971. 302p.

The aim of this anthology is to present a selection of plays that are representative of a new spirit in Spanish American culture and of societal pressures and changes below the border. The plays reflect the tenor of the dramatic imagination of today—an imagination that is seeking new forms and ways of expressing a new awareness of the Spanish American dilemma. Included are "The Day They

Let the Lions Loose," by Emilio Carballido; "The Mulatto's Orgy," by Luisa Josefina Hernandez; and others.

455. Peden, Margaret Sayers. "Greek Myth in Contemporary Mexican Theater." **Modern Drama**, XII, No. 3 (December 1969), 221-30.
The author explains many of the Greek myths now incorporated in Mexican drama.

456. Peden, Margaret Sayers. "Emilio Carballido." **Latin American Theater Review**, I, No. 1 (Fall 1967), 38-39.
A discourse on the most accomplished Mexican playwright and his plays.

457. Theater in the Streets Presents "My People—My Life" starring Spanish American residents of Santa Fe, New Mexico. **Vista Volunteer**, IV (September 1968), 16-25.
Original play depicting the life of the Spanish-American people in New Mexico.

458. Thompson, Lawrence S. **A Bibliography of Spanish Plays on Microcards**. Hamden, Conn.: Shoe String Press, 1968. 498p.
This bibliography records over 6,000 Spanish and Spanish-American plays from the sixteenth century to the present, all published in microcard editions from 1957 through 1966.

459. Trifilo, S. Samuel. "Contemporary Theater in Mexico." **Modern Language Journal**, XLVI, No. 4 (April 1962), 153-57.
The author gives a brief historical background of the theater and explains the increase of interest in recent years. Current playwrights are given with a discussion of several of their plays.

460. Usigli, Rodolfo. **Two Plays: Crown of Light and One of These Days.** Translated from the Spanish by Thomas Bledsoe. Contemporary Latin American Classics Series. Carbondale, Ill.: Southern Illinois University Press, 1971. 224p.
The first English translation of two plays by Rodolfo Usigli, a renowned Latin American dramatist.

461. Valdez, Luis. **Actos: El Teatro Campesino.** Los Angeles, California: Cucaracha Press, 1971.
Short one-act plays produced by the Teatro Campesino.

MUSIC AND DANCE

462. Borrows, Frank. **Theory and Techniques of Latin-American Dancing.** London: Muller Publishers, 1961. 276p.
Latin-American dances are presented here for the amateur, the student, and the teacher. The dance descriptions include the name or figure, general description, number of steps, footwork, alignment, details of movement, following figures, and notes.

463. Chase, Gilbert. **A Guide to the Music of Latin-America.** 2nd ed. Washington: Pan American Union, 1962. 274p.

This guide provides a means of orientation in the field of Latin American music. An annotated bibliography with introductory comments on each country, it gives the main outline of the developments of music in each country, the nomenclature of the most typical songs, dances and musical instruments, and basic data on the principal composers.

464. Harrison, Frank, and Joan Harrison. **Spanish Elements in the Music of Two Maya Groups in Chiapas.** (Selected Reports of the Institute of Ethnomusicology.) Los Angeles, Calif.: University of California at Los Angeles, 1968. 44p.

An attempt at identifying old musical practices of Spanish art music still in use in some Mexican Indian communities of Chiapas. Includes nine musical examples.

465. Hecht, Paul. **The Wind Cried: An American's Discovery of the World of Flamenco.** New York: Dial Press, Inc., 1967. 186p.

A sensitive exploration of the world of flamenco. Emphasis is on the music, a highly emotional and tragic type of song, accompanied by a guitar, in which spontaneity and depth of feeling are more important than the actual singing voice. Many songs are listed, including a hundred coplas with literal translations and discography of a few choice long-playing records.

466. Johnston, Edith. **Regional Dances of Mexico.** Skokie, Ill.: National Textbook Corporation, 1935. 78p. o.p.

Music and dance instructions for authentic Mexican folk dances.

467. Marti, Samuel, and Gertrude P. Kurath. **Dances of Anahuac.** Chicago: Aldine Publishing Company, 1964. 251p.

The choreography and music of pre-Cortesian dances. Historical investigation and reconstruction of obsolete dances and music.

468. Paz, Elena, ed. **Favorite Spanish Folksongs.** New York: Oak Publications, Inc., 1965. 96p.

Traditional folksongs from Spain and Latin America. Includes English translations of the text.

469. Robb, John Donald. **Hispanic Folk Songs of New Mexico.** Albuquerque, N.M.: University of New Mexico Press, 1954. 83p.

A discussion of Spanish folk song survivals, along with a collection of the songs themselves.

470. Simmons, Merle Edwin. **The Mexican Corrido as a Source for Interpretive Study of Modern Mexico, 1870-1950.** Bloomington, Ind.: Indiana University Press, 1957. 619p.

Interprets certain important aspects of modern Mexico using the corrido or ballads sung by the Mexican. Includes a history of the corrido.

471.   Slight, Charlotte Frances. **A Survey of Musical Background and an Analysis of Mexican Piano Music, 1928 to 1956**. Thesis. North Texas State University, Denton, Texas. 1957. 102p.
A well-documented survey of music and piano music in Mexico.

472.   Stevenson, Robert. **Music in Aztec and Inca Territory**. Berkeley, Calif.: University of California Press, 1968. 378p.
A two-fold study, the study of Aztec music and the study of Inca music. A well-documented study containing many footnotes, a 30-page bibliography, and an index.

473.   Stevenson, Robert. **Music in Mexico: A Historical Survey**. New York: Thomas Y. Crowell Company, 1970. 300p.
A reprint of a 1952 edition, valuable for the historical survey from the time of the Aztecs through the years of Spanish influence, and up to the music of today.

474.   Tinker, Edward Larocque. **Corridos and Calaveras**. Translated by Americo Paredes. Austin, Texas: University of Texas Press, 1961. 60p.
Reproduces Mexican broadsides and gives the songs sung by the Mexican counterparts of the ancient troubadors. Beautifully printed, of interest to students of Mexican culture.

475.   Van Stone, Mary R. **Spanish Folk Songs of the Southwest**. Sausalito, Calif.: Academy Guild Press, 1963. 96p.
Songs ranging from a seventeenth century New Mexico lullabye to a bootlegger's ballad from the prohibition era.

4: LITERATURE

GENERAL LITERATURE

476.   Alurista. "The Poetry of Alurista." **El Grito**, VII (Fall 1968), 5-12.
A collection of short poems in both Spanish and English, by Alurista (Alberto Balta Urista Heredia).

477.   Anderson-Imbert, Enrique. **Spanish American Literature: A History.**
        2nd edition, rev., enl., and updated. 2 vols. Translated from the
        Spanish by John V. Falconieri. Detroit, Mich.: Wayne State University
        Press, 1969. 844p.
This is by far the best and most complete work on Spanish American literature
to appear in English. Vol. 1 covers the period 1492 to 1910; Vol. II, 1910 to
1963. Arranged chronologically, the work treats all literary genres and writers
collectively, with clear evaluations in a narrative form.

478.   Arias-Larreta, Abraham. **Pre-Columbian Literatures.** Kansas City, Mo.,
        New World Library, 1964. 118p.
History and criticism of pre-Columbian literature: Aztec, Inca, and Maya-Quiche.

479.   **Aztlan: An Anthology of Mexican American Literature.** Edited by
        Stan Steiner and Luis Valdez. New York: Alfred A. Knopf, Inc.,
        1972. 410p.
One of the first anthologies of Mexican American literature to be published.
The work contains poetry, short stories, and essays.

480.   Boyd, Lola Elizabeth. **The Image of Emiliano Zapata in the Art and
        Literature of the Mexican Revolution.** New York: Columbia Univer-
        sity, 1965. 450p. University Microfilm No. 68-5639.
Unpublished doctoral dissertation on Emiliano Zapata as reflected in the art
and literature of the time.

481.   Brushwood, John Stubbs. **Mexico in Its Novel: A Nation's Search for
        Identity.** Austin, Texas: University of Texas Press, 1970. Reprint of
        1966 edition. 292p. The Texas Pan American Series.
A perceptive examination of the Mexican reality as revealed through the nation's
novel. The Mexican novel is presented as a cultural phenomenon, a manifestation
of the impact of history upon the nation, an attempt by a people to come to
grips with and understand what has happened and is happening to them. Deals
with the period between 1521 and 1963.

482.   Brushwood, John Stubbs. **The Romantic Novel in Mexico.** Columbia,
        Mo.: University of Missouri Press, 1969. 131p.
Describes and evaluates those novels of the Romantic Period in Mexico which
are not historical. The Romantic Period is the span from 1820 to the end of
the period of the struggle for independence. The first part of the book is a study
of the development of the Mexican novel; the second part is an annotated bibliography of the Romantic novels in Mexico.

483.   Brushwood, John Stubbs. **Enrique Gonzalez Martinez.** New York: Twayne Publishers, Inc., 1969. 166p.
This work covers the life and works of Martinez, "one of the masters of twentieth century Hispanic poetry." An extensive chronology is included.

484.   Carballido, Emilio. **The Norther.** Translated by Margaret Sayers Peden. Illustrated by Jose Trevino. Austin, Texas: University of Texas Press, 1968. 102p.
Skillful characterization of a triangle of slightly unsavory characters.

485.   Carpentier, Hortense, and Janet Brof, eds. **Doors and Mirrors: Contemporary Writing from Spanish America, 1920-1970.** New York: Grossman Publishers, Inc., 1971. 454p.
An anthology of poetry and prose by nearly 50 writers from the last half century. The original language accompanies the included poetry. The introduction defines the influential themes and scans the literary history of the period. Biographical notes and an index of translators are appended.

486.   Cranfill, Thomas M., ed. **The Muse in Mexico: A Mid-Century Miscellany.** Austin, Texas: University of Texas Press, 1959. 117p.
This book offers a welcome selection of fiction, poetry, and graphic art, in which are admirably displayed various stylistic approaches and moods.

487.   Delgado, Avelardo. **Chicano: 25 Pieces of a Chicano Mind.** 2nd printing. Santa Barbara, California: La Causa Publications, 1971.
A collection of bilingual poetry revealing various themes on the Chicano.

488.   Gonzalez, Rodolfo. **I Am Joaquin, An Epic Poem.** Denver, Colorado: Crusade of Justice, 1967. 20p.
The author utilizes a historical perspective to portray the Chicano and his heritage. The historical approach begins with the pre-Columbian heritage and skillfully includes the Aztec era, the invasion of the Anglo, and the struggle of the immigrants. The conclusion of the work emphasizes the plight of the Chicano.

489.   Gonzalez Pena, Carlos. **History of Mexican Literature.** 3rd ed. rev. and enl. Translated by Gusta Barfield Nance and Florence Johnson Dunstan. Dallas, Texas: Southern Methodist University Press, 1968. 540p. Revision of English translation 1943. First published in 1928.
The history of Mexican literature has been, like that of the country itself, one of conflict and creation. Covering the sixteenth to the twentieth centuries, this volume portrays the inner life of a people through their struggles and achievements, and through the lives and works of the historians, poets, novelists, playwrights, critics and orators of these tumultuous centuries.

490.   Gorostiza, Jose. **Death Without End.** Translated by Laura Villasenor. Humanities Research Center. Austin, Texas: University of Texas Press, 1969. 38p.

Original title: *Muerte Sin Fin*. A handsomely printed and illustrated translation of the masterpiece of an important Mexican poet. Text in both English and Spanish.

491. Harss, Luis, and Barbara Dohman. **Into the Mainstream: Conversations with Latin-American Writers.** New York: Harper & Row Publishers, 1967. 385p.

A collection of essay interviews with Latin American authors. Mexican authors whose backgrounds and works are discussed are Juan Rulfo and Carlos Fuentes.

492. Haslam, Gerald W. **Forgotten Pages of American Literature.** Boston: Houghton Mifflin Co., 1970. 398p.

This work contains material written by Indian, Oriental, Negro, and Latin American authors.

493. Hulet, Claude L., ed. **Latin American Poetry in English Translation: A Bibliography.** Washington, D.C.: Pan American Union, 1965. 192p. Basic Bibliographies, 2.

This bibliography lists titles translated into English from colonial times to the present (1963). An appendix lists titles omitted from the text. Author index.

494. Hulet, Claude L., ed. **Latin American Prose in English Translation: A Bibliography.** Washington, D.C.: Pan American Union, 1964. 191p. Basic Bibliographies, 1.

A bibliography listing Latin American prose titles translated into English from the sixteenth century to the present time (August 1, 1962). Published by the Division of Philosophy and Letters of the Pan American Union.

495. Jones, Willis Knapp, ed. **Spanish-American Literature in Translation.** 2 vols. New York: Frederick Ungar Publishing Co., 1963-1966. 825p.

Volume 1 contains a selection of prose, poetry, and drama before 1888. Volume 2, a selection of poetry, fiction, and drama since 1888.

496. Langford, Walter M. **The Mexican Novel Comes of Age.** Notre Dame, Indiana: University of Notre Dame, 1971. 224p.

This work blends the literary history and criticism of twentieth century novelists and their works after a brief mention of nineteenth century novels. The lives and novels of Azuela, B. Traven, Yanez, Rulfo, Spota, Fuentes, Lenero, and Galindo are discussed, with brief mention of a dozen lesser-known authors.

497. Leon-Portilla, Miguel. **Aztec Thought and Culture: A Study of the Ancient Nahuatl Mind.** Norman, Oklahoma: University of Oklahoma, Press, 1963. 241p. Repr. 1970. Originally published in 1959.

Philosophy of the Aztec taken from original documents. A companion work to *Pre-Columbian Literature of Mexico*, which stresses textual analysis and interpretation. Translated by Jack E. Davis.

498. Leon-Portilla, Miguel. **Pre-Columbian Literatures of Mexico.** Norman, Oklahoma: University of Oklahoma Press, 1969. 191p.
A selection of myths, sacred hymns, lyric poetry, rituals, drama, and various forms of prose from Aztec, Mayan and other cultures.

499. Ludwig, Edward W., and James Santibanez, eds. **The Chicanos: Mexican American Voices.** New York: Penguin Books, Inc., 1971. 286p.
An anthology of short stories, poems, and prose selections, all written by Chicanos or by those who have worked closely with the Chicano community.

500. Maass, Henry Eugene Lester. **Mexico and Mexicana in the Fiction of Steinbeck, Morris, Traven, and Porter.** Denton, Texas: North Texas State University, 1966. Thesis.
The author discusses and compares the Mexican culture and Mexican characters in the works of fiction by Steinbeck, Morris, Traven, and Porter.

501. Martinez, Jose Luis, ed. **The Modern Mexican Essay.** Translated by H. W. Hilborn. Toronto, Canada: University of Toronto Press, 1965. 524p.
An excellent translation of a first-rate collection of essays; a must for anyone wishing to become better acquainted with a representative of the emerging nations to our south.

502. Mondragon, Sergio, ed. **Anthology of Contemporary Mexican Poetry.** Translated by Tim Reynolds. New York: Unicorn Press, Inc., 1970. 150p.
A collection of bilingual poems—each by a different poet. Bibliographical notes are included.

503. Nicholson, Irene. **Firefly in the Night: A Study of Ancient Mexican Poetry and Symbolism.** London: Faber and Faber, 1959. 231p. o.p.
Poems quoted are taken from original compositions in Nahua and translated by the Friars phonetically into Spanish.

504. Nicholson, Irene. **Guide to Mexican Poetry, Ancient and Modern.** New York: International Publications Services, 1968. 96p.
History and criticism of Mexican poetry, both ancient and modern.

505. Ortega, Phillip D. "Mexican American Literature." **Nation,** CCIX (September 15, 1969), 258-59.
A discussion of Mexican-American literature. The work *El Espejo* is given as the first fruit of a "new wave" of literary Mexican Americans.

506. Paredes, Americo, and Raymond Paredes, eds. **Mexican-American Authors.** Boston: Houghton Mifflin Company, 1972. 152p.
A collection of literature by outstanding Mexican-American writers such as Josephine Niggli, J. Gonzalez, A. Paredes, L. O. Salinas, A. D. Trejo, and others.

507.	Paz, Octavio. **Anthology of Mexican Poetry.** Translated by Samuel
Beckett. Bloomington, Indiana: Indiana University Press, 1958. 213p.
Good representative collection of poetry beginning with the sixteenth century.

508.	Paz, Octavio. **Configurations.** Translated from the Spanish by G.
Aroul and others. Norfolk, Conn.: New Directions, 1971. 198p.
An anthology of the author's poetry containing works written since 1957.
This collection includes two long works, *Sun Stone* and *Blanco.*

509.	Paz, Octavio. **Selected Poems of Octavio Paz: A Bilingual Edition.**
Translated by Muriel Rukeyser. Bloomington, Indiana: Indiana
University Press, 1964. 171p.
The Mexican poet has selected 49 of his poems for this volume. The original
text of each poem appears on the page facing the translation.

510.	Resnick, Seymour. **Spanish-American Poetry: A Bilingual Selection.**
New York: Harvey House, Inc., 1964. 96p.
This companion to the author's *Selections from Spanish Poetry* includes a range
of poems from the times of the conquistadors through the nineteenth and
twentieth centuries. Included are short biographies of the authors and notes
about the circumstances under which the poems were written.

511.	Reyes, Alfonso. **Mexico in a Nutshell and Other Essays.** Berkeley,
Calif.: University of California Press, 1966. 145p.
A collection of informative essays by one of the great Mexican writers of the
twentieth century. The essays describe a wide range of topics: films, painting,
Diego Rivera, Mexican history, and the author himself.

512.	Rios, Francisco Armando. "The Mexican in Fact, Fiction, and Folk-
lore." **El Grito,** II (Summer 1969), 3-28.
The Mexican characters in Steinbeck's *Tortilla Flat*, Mangan's *Bordertown*,
Clark's *Ox-Bow Incident*, Parkman's *The Oregon Trail*, Dobie's *The Voice of
the Coyote*, and others are discussed. Includes the popular image and the
stereotype presentation.

513.	Robinson, Cecil. "Spring Water with a Taste of the Land." **American
West,** III (Summer 1966), 6-15, 95.
The author uses the literature of the Southwest to describe the difference in
cultures between the Americans and the Mexicans in that region.

514.	Robinson, Cecil. **With the Ears of Strangers: The Mexican in American
Literature.** Tucson, Arizona: University of Arizona Press, 1963. 338p.
A better understanding of Southwest borderland relations is unfolded in this
exploration of the North American literary record of the contact between
Mexican and Anglo, from the early nineteenth century to the 1930s.

515.	Romano-V, Octavio I., ed. **El Espejo—The Mirror: Selected Mexican-
American Literature.** Berkeley, Calif.: Quinto Sol Publications, Inc.,
1969. 241p.

A bilingual collection of current writing from both sides of the border. The 11 contemporary authors represented deal with such themes as barrio and migrant life, poverty, alienation, repression, and cultural and historical heritage.

516.   Rutherford, John. **Annotated Bibliography of the Novels of the Mexican Revolution of 1910-1917.** Troy, N.Y.: Whitston Publishing Company, Inc., 1972. 180p.
A good representative bibliography from a sepcified period of time. Well-annotated work.

517.   Rutherford, John. **Mexican Society During the Revolution: A Literary Approach.** New York: Oxford University Press, 1971. 347p.
Mexican society during the Mexican Revolution of 1910-1946, as seen in historical fiction.

518.   Salinas, Luis Omar. **Crazy Gypsy.** Fresno, Calif.: Ornia: Origenes Publications, La Raza Studies, F.S.C., 1970. 87p.
A collection of poems portraying the dreams, aspirations, and nightmares of the Chicanos. It is a first of its kind in that it was published by La Raza Studies Program.

519.   Schwartz, Kessel. **A New History of Spanish American Fiction.** 2 vols. Coral Gables, Fla.: University of Miami Press, 1971. 827p.
Spanish American fiction, history and criticism. Volume 1 is a study from colonial times to the Mexican Revolution and beyond. Volume 2 relates to social concern, universalism, and the new novel.

520.   Sommers, Joseph. **After the Storm**: Landmarks of the Modern Mexican Novel. Albuquerque, N.M.: University of New Mexico Press, 1968. 208p.
This is the first study in English devoted exclusively to the work of Agustin Yanez, Juan Rulfo, and Carlos Fuentes, three novelists who won worldwide recognition for contemporary Mexican fiction. Sommers' balanced critical assessments show the remarkable diversity in each author's structure, craft, technique and world view.

521.   Sonnichsen, Charles Leland, ed. **The Southwest in Life and Literature, a Pageant in Seven Parts.** Old Greenwich, Conn.: Devin-Adair Co., 1962. 554p.
This anthology, selected from the literature of the Southwest ranging in date from 1849 to 1960, covers folklore, anthropology, history, and geography of Texas, Arizona, New Mexico, and Oklahoma. Among the 43 writers represented are J. Frank Dobie, Edna Ferber, Paul Horgan, Oliver LaFarge, Conrad Richter, Paul Wellman, and Stewart Edward White.

522.   Strand, Mark, ed. **New Poetry of Mexico, 1915-1966.** New York: E. P. Dutton & Company, 1970. 224p.
This is a bilingual edition of a work previously published in Spanish. The selec-

tions from various poets reveal the various themes within twentieth century Mexican poetry. Included are works by such poets as Octavio Paz, Salvador Nova, Jose Emilio, and others.

523.   Torres Bodet, Jaime. **Selected Poems of Jaime Torres Bodet.** Translated by Sonja Karsen. Bloomington, Indiana: Indiana University Press, 1964. 155p.
A selection of 44 poems written by the former Director General of UNESCO. The poems are lucid and penetrating, and cover a variety of romantic and search-for-identity themes.

524.   Torres-Rioseco, Arturo. **Aspects of Spanish-American Literature.** Seattle, Wash.: University of Washington Press, 1963. 95p.
Humor in Hispanic literature and notes on the literary influence of the United States in Spanish American letters and Spanish American novelists of today.

525.   Zieman, Irving Pergament. **Mexican Mosaic.** Boston: Forum Publishing Co., 1964. 231p.
Mexican poetry of places, description, and travel.

FOLKLORE AND MYTHOLOGY

526.   Aiken, Riley. "Fifteen Mexican Tales." **Texas Folklore Society Publications,** 32 (1964), 3-56.
This collection contains 15 Mexican folk tales and folklore of various areas and subjects.

527.   Boatright, Mody C., ed. **Mexican Border Ballads and Other Lore.** Dallas, Texas: Southern Methodist University Press, 1967.
A reprint of the 1946 edition. Includes history and stories of Mexican balladry.

528.   Boggs, Ralph Steele. **Bibliography of Latin American Folklore.** Detroit, Mich.: Blaine Ethridge Books, 1971. 109p. Reprint of 1940 ed.
Tales, myths, festivals, customs, arts, music, and magic titles are included in this extensive bibliography.

529.   Braddy, Haldeen. **Mexico and the Old Southwest: People, Palaver, Places.** Port Washington, N.Y.: Kennikat Press, 1971. 229p.
A selection of previously published papers written by a leading authority on Southwest border history and lore.

530.   Braddy, Haldeen. **The Pachucos and the Argot.** Reprint from *Southern Folklore Quarterly*, 1960. unpaged. o.p.
A short article dealing with the Pachuco subculture and the vocabularly used by these people.

531.   Burland, Cottie A. **The Gods of Mexico.** New York: G. P. Putnam's Sons, 1967. 219p.

Ancient religions of Mexico are discussed. Includes the cultures of the Olmec, Maya, Toltec, and Aztec.

532. Campa, Arthur L. **Treasures of the Sangre De Cristos: Tales and Traditions of the Spanish Southwest.** Norman, Okla.: University of Oklahoma Press, 1963. 210p.

A book of folk legends from an author who is heir to both the Spanish and the Anglo cultures. It is filled with the tales of lost mines, hidden gold, and legends of the people of the Southwest. The author heard some of them from the story-tellers of his childhood, as family and guests gathered on the patio to visit.

533. Campbell, Camilla. **Star Mountain and Other Legends of Mexico.**
j Illustrated by Frederic Marvin. 2nd ed. New York: McGraw-Hill Book Company, 1968. 92p.

Short legends which give the stories behind such Indian names as Mexico, Popocatepetl, and Quetzalcoatl, as well as telling of stories passed down from the time of the Spanish Conquest.

534. de Gerez, Toni. **2-Rabbit, 7-Wind: Poems from Ancient Mexico Retold from Nahuatl Texts.** New York: Viking Press, 1971. 56p.

From the wealth of Nahuatl texts Toni de Gerez has selected, retold, and re-shaped songs and other writings that reflect the lives of the ancient people of Mexico. Color decorations from ancient design motifs.

535. Dobie, J. Frank. **Coronado's Children: Tales of Lost Mines and Buried Treasures of the Southwest.** New York: Grosset & Dunlap, Inc., 1939. 367p.

Tales and legends of the treasure-hunters, including the story of Coronado's famous expedition in search of the lost Seven Cities of Cibola, the lost San Saba Mine and the Padre Mine, the subject of the secrets of the Guadalupes, the treasure of the Wichitas, and others.

536. Dobie, J. Frank. **I'll Tell You a Tale.** Boston: Little, Brown and Co., 1960. 362p.

These notable stories come from the folklore of the Southwest.

537. Dobie, J. Frank. **Puro Mexicano.** Dallas, Texas: Southern Methodist University Press, 1935. 261p.

A book of pure Mexican folklore containing tales, legends, songs, sayings, and Mexican usages in English and Spanish.

538. Dobie, J. Frank. **Southwestern Lore.** Dallas, Texas: Southern Methodist University, 1965, Reprint of 1931 ed. 198p.

A miscellany of legends of the Southwest, Mexican folklore, Indians of Mexico and superstitions, cowboys both Mexican and gringo, songs, plant life, etc.

539. Dobie, J. Frank. **Tongues of the Monte.** Boston: Little, Brown and Company, 1947. 301p.

This is a collection of Mexican folk beliefs presented in the format of a wanderer's journey across northern Mexico. Sayings, magic formulas, foods, medicines, and legends are included in the work. There is an emphasis on ghost stories and uncanny happenings.

540. Dolch, Edward W., and M. P. Dolch. **Stories from Mexico.** Folklore
j   of the World Series. Champaign, Ill.: Garrard Publishing Company, 1960.
         168p.
A collection of folk tales from Mexico for the young reader.

541. Dorson, Richard M. **American Folklore.** Chicago: The University of
         Chicago Press, 1959. 328p.
This volume deals with the history of varied and significant aspects of American folklore. Included in the regional folk cultures is a section on Spanish New Mexico, which relates the regional variations and the conditions of folk culture within the state. The folk culture of New Mexico is a rich, old-world legacy.

542. Dorson, Richard M. **Buying the Wind.** Chicago: The University of
         Chicago Press, 1964. 574p.
The present volume is intended as a supplement to *American Folklore*. Five regions are discussed, including Southwestern Mexicans. Within each regional section the texts are divided according to the genus of folk material—folk narrative, proverbs, riddles, beliefs, folk-drama, and folksongs.

543. Espinosa, Jose E. **Saints in the Valleys: Christian Sacred Images in the
         History, Life, and Folk Art of Spanish New Mexico.** Albuquerque,
         N.M.: University of New Mexico Press, 1966. 210p.
A study of the forms, artistic, religious, and social meanings of New Mexican Santos, the painted and carved saints which are one of America's finest examples of true folk art.

544. Espinosa, Jose Manuel. **Spanish Folk-Tales from New Mexico.** New
         York: American Folk-lore Society. G. E. Stechert & Company,
         agents. Kraus repr. of 1937 edition.
Folklore material from New Mexico, collected among the Spanish-speaking inhabitants of the Rio Grande region of northern New Mexico in the summer of 1931.

545. Giffords, Gloria. **Miniature Masterpieces: A Study of Mexican Folk
         Retablos.** Tucson, Arizona: University of Arizona Press, 1971. unp.
A look at the origins, authorship, and identification of a disappearing art. Paintings on tin of the holy figures which became household icons in the transference of folk worship from pagan images to the Catholic hierarchy of saints.

546. Goss, Robert C. **The Principal Retablo of San Xavier del Bac.**
         Tucson, Arizona: University of Arizona Press, 1971. unp.
This work focuses on the altarpiece of the famed mission Church of San Xavier in southern Arizona. The author approaches the retablo in its entirety, as a

complete work of art, through analysis of the history and iconography of the statuary, the architectural detail and the decorative motifs that comprise it.

547.	Hudson, Wilson M., ed. **Healer of Los Olmos and Other Mexican Lore.** Dallas, Texas: Southern Methodist University, 1951. 139p.
A curandero (healer) whose fame and feats have spread widely through South Texas and entered into local tradition is Pedro Jaramillo, known as the healer of Los Olmos.

548.	Jagendorf, Moritz Adolph. **The King of the Mountains: A Treasury of Latin American Folk Stories.** New York: Vanguard Press, 1960. 313p.
Folk tales from all the Latin American countries including Mexico.

549.	Lea, Aurora, ed. **Literary Folklore of the Hispanic Southwest.** San Antonio, Texas: The Naylor Co., 1953. 247p. o.p.
A collection of folk dramas, ballads, stories, and folk-ways from New Mexico, written in both Spanish and English. Includes sayings, proverbs, maxims, and a bibliography.

550.	Miller, Elaine Kay. **Mexican Folk Narrative from the Los Angeles Area.** Los Angeles, Calif.: University of California, 1967. Unpublished doctoral dissertation. Order No. 68-7476. Microfilm. $8.95.
Folklore as told by the Mexican Americans to the author and others.

551.	Nicholson, Irene. **Mexican and Central American Mythology.** New York: Tudor Publishing Company, 1967. 141p.
A revelation of the tales of adventure and love, the creation stories and religious beliefs of the ancient Mayans, Toltecs, Aztecs, and other mid-American cultures that spanned a period of some 2,000 years.

552.	Paredes, Americo. **Folktales of Mexico.** Richard M. Dorson, editor. Folktales of the World Series. Chicago: University of Chicago Press, 1970. 282p.
A collection of folktales of Mexico with an excellent foreword and introduction giving the historical background and the many folk tellers of Mexico. Notes, glossary, bibliography, and an index of motifs are included.

553.	Paredes, Americo. **With His Pistol in His Hands: A Border Ballad and Its Hero.** Austin, Texas: University of Texas Press, 1971. 247p.
Based on a famous ballad, this study attempts to illuminate the attitudes and life styles of the Mexicans living along the Texas-Mexico Rio Grande border in the early twentieth century.

554.	Pillsbury, Dorothy L. **Star Over Adobe.** Albuquerque, N.M.: University of New Mexico Press, 1963. 208p.
This collection of essays deals with the celebration of Christmas by the Indians, the Spanish Americans, and the Anglos of northern New Mexico.

555. Romano-V, Octavio Ignacio. **Don Pedrito Jaramillo: The Emergence of a Mexican American Folk Saint.** Berkeley, Calif.: University of California, 1964. Doctoral dissertation. Order No. 64-9078. Microfilm. $2.75.
Folk-healing in Mexican-American rural life in South Texas presented as an anthropological case study. The ascension of Don Pedro Jaramillo from a simple folk healer to a healer of international fame approaching sainthood. Romano's chapter on the "Ideal Culture of La Raza" presents an illustration of a working definition of culture.

556. Ross, Patricia Fent. **In Mexico They Say.** New York: Alfred A. Knopf,
j   Inc., 1942. 211p.
Stories based on legends and folklore of Mexico.

557. Roy, Cal. **The Serpent and the Sun: Myths of the Mexican World.** Retold and with decorations by Cal Roy. New York: Farrar, Straus and Giroux, 1972. 96p.
In *The Serpent and the Sun*, Cal Roy has retold in beautiful lyric cadences 12 myths of the Aztecs, the Mayans, and the Mexican Indians of today. "They are tales of violence, yet all of them contain seeds of a profound spiritual philosophy."

558. Sayles, E. B., and Joan A. Henley. **Fantasies of Gold: Tales of Treasures and How They Grew.** Tucson, Arizona: University of Arizona Press, 1968. 135p.
A telling of the legends encountered during archaeological expeditions begun in the 1920s. Many of the legends go back to Spanish and even pre-historic days and range from Mexico through Texas, New Mexico, and Arizona. The book is divided between "people," "places," and "peculiar things."

559. Tinkle, Lon. **Miracle in Mexico.** New York: Hawthorne Books, 1965. 188p. o.p.
A description of the miracle of the vision of the Virgin Mary which led to the building of the Shrine of Our Lady of Guadalupe. The account is based on Aztec and Spanish records of the period; other miracles and tributes to the shrine are also given.

560. Toor, Frances. **A Treasury of Mexican Folkways.** Illustrated by Carlos Merida. New York: Crown Publishers, Inc., 1947. 566p.
Includes fiestas, dances and songs, customs, myth and folklore of the Mexican people. Music is included for many of the songs and dances.

561. Traven, B. **The Creation of the Sun and the Moon.** New York: Hill
j   & Wang, Inc., 1968. 65p.
The Aztec version of the creation.

562. Waugh, Julia (Nott). **The Silver Cradle.** Austin, Texas: University of Texas Press, 1955. 160p.
Describes religious folk customs of Mexican Americans in San Antonio, with detailed descriptions of the fiestas and their religious significance.

5: BIOGRAPHY

563.   Almaraz, Felix D., Jr. **Tragic Cavalier: Governor Manuel Salcedo of Texas, 1808-1813.** Austin, Texas: University of Texas Press, 1971. 216p.
An historical account of the Mexican independence movement from the Spanish point of view through the biography of Governor Manuel Salcedo of Texas.

564.   Arquin, Florence. **Diego Rivera: The Shaping of an Artist, 1889-1921.** Norman, Okla.: University of Oklahoma Press, 1971. 150p.
Diego Rivera is one of the giants among twentieth century painters. In reviving mural painting and fresco techniques, he led the renaissance of Mexican art and gave it an authentic national character. The text is illustrated with many of Rivera's earlier works and examples of the styles that influenced him.

565.   Atwater, James D., and Ramon E. Ruiz. **Out from Under: Benito Juarez and Mexico's Struggle for Independence.** Garden City, N.Y.: Doubleday & Company, 1969. 118pp.
Presents a history of 300 years of Spanish rule over Mexico, of its cruelties and hardships, of the rebellion of the people against it, and of the man who helped solve the problems that came with independence—Benito Juarez.

566.   Baez, Joan. **Daybreak.** New York: Dial Press, Inc., 1968. 159p.
Autobiographical account by a folksinger-pacifist. Focuses on her philosophies of nonviolence and of life.

567.   Baker, Nina Brown. **Juarez, Hero of Mexico.** Illustrated by Marion
j   Greenwood. New York: Vanguard Press, Inc., 1942. 316p.
This biography of Benito Juarez presents Mexican culture in the nineteenth century from the political, social, religious, and economic angles.

568.   Beteta, Ramon. **Jarano.** Translated by John Upton. Illustrated by Mario Perez-O. Austin, Texas: University of Texas Press, 1970. 163p.
The reminiscences, in short form, of Ramon Beteta, an important figure in contemporary Mexican life: politician, cabinet member, diplomat, economist, professor, and journalist.

569.   Buchanan, Rosemary. **Don Diego de Vargas: The Peaceful Conquistador.**
j   New York: P. J. Kenedy & Sons, 1963. 189p. o.p.
The author recounts Don Diego's exciting adventures and includes other experiences of his life in Old Mexico and in Santa Fe. She tells of the jealous plots of his Spanish rivals, of his resettlement of New Mexico, and of his wise rule as governor of the province.

570.   Caruso, John Anthony. **The Liberators of Mexico.** Magnolia, Mass.: Peter Smith Publisher, Inc., 1967. 342p.

A brief biography of each of the three men who helped to free Mexico from Spanish rule—Hidalgo, Morelos, and Iturbide.

571. Cintron, Conchita. **Memoirs of a Bullfighter.** New York: Holt, Rinehart & Winston, Inc., 1968. 272p. o.p.
Autobiography of the famous bullfighter, Conchita Cintron.

572. Galarza, Ernesto. **Barrio Boy.** Notre Dame, Indiana: University of
j   Notre Dame Press, 1971. 275p.
In this autobiographical story the author tells what he remembers from his childhood days. It begins in the small Mexican village of Jalcocotan, where he was born, and terminates when as a teenager he is about to enter high school in his adopted home town of Sacramento. In skillfully chosen language Galarza recounts the way of life of the poor in Mexico and his experiences during the Mexican Revolution of 1910 that led to his being brought to America.

573. Gillmor, Frances. **Flute of the Smoking Mirror.** Albuquerque, N.M.: University of New Mexico Press, 1968. Repr. of 1949 ed. 183p.
A portrait of Nezhualcoyotl, poet king of the Aztecs from 1400 to 1470.

574. Gillmor, Frances. **The King Danced in the Market Place.** Tucson, Ariz.: University of Arizona Press, 1964. 271p.
A biography of Huehue Montezuma Ilhuicamina, grandfather of the famous Montezuma II and the leader who first made the Aztecs into a formidable power extending their domain over neighboring peoples. The book admirably conveys to the reader the color and tone of Aztec society and the psychology of the people.

575. Gomara, Francisco Lopez de. **Cortes: The Life of the Conqueror of Mexico by His Secretary.** Los Angeles, Calif.: University of Southern California Press, 1964. 425p.
The first translation in English in 400 years of a sixteenth century chronicle of Cortes.

576. Guzman, Daniel de. **Carlos Fuentes.** New York: Twayne Publishers, 1972. 171p.
The author relates the life of the famed writer of Mexico with history and criticism of his works.

577. Guzman, Martin Luis. **Memoirs of Pancho Villa.** Translated by Virginia H. Taylor. Austin, Texas: University of Texas Press, 1965. 512p.
The story of the 16-year-old outlaw who became the scourge of the Mexican Revolution and the hero of the masses. The author provides a sympathetic insight into the life of Villa to 1915, in a valuable and skillfully translated version of the original memoirs, which were based on the author's recollections of his participation in the movement and other documentary materials. The atmosphere of the Revolution is well depicted and the book makes interesting history.

578.   Haddox, John H. **Antonio Caso: Philosopher of Mexico.** Austin, Texas: University of Texas Press, 1971. 156p.
A patriot of his beloved Mexico, who sought to deliver his humanitarian message to his countrymen.

579.   Haddox, John H. **Vasconcelos of Mexico, Philosopher and Prophet.** Austin, Texas: University of Texas Press, 1967. 103p.
A unified, inclusive, and occasionally critical presentation of Vasconcelos' thought, from his metaphysics and theory of knowledge through his aesthetics and ethics to his social and political philosophy. Jose Vasconcelos died in 1959 and was "without question the most inspiring intellectual and human figure that Mexico has produced."

580.   Harmon, Mary. **Efren Hernandez: A Mexican Writer and Philosopher.** Hattiesburg, Miss.: University and College Press of Mississippi, 1972. 128p.
The author covers the life of Hernandez as a writer and as a philosopher, discussing some of his outstanding works.

581.   Haslip, Joan. **The Crown of Mexico: Maximilian of Mexico and His Empress Carlota.** New York: Holt Rinehart & Winston, 1972. 531p.
Denied participation in the government of his native country, Maximilian of Austria succumbed to the blandishments of Napoleon III, embarking upon his tragic career in Mexico with his empress Carlota.

582.   Iduarte, Andres. **Nino, Child of the Mexican Revolution.** Translated
j   and adapted by James F. Shearer. New York: Praeger Publishers, Inc., 1971. 156p.
The boyhood and youth of a Mexican of Tabasco born into a much respected family, some of whom held positions under the dictator, Porfirio Diaz. When Andres' father, a professor of philosophy and a magistrate of unquestioned integrity, lost his job during the Mexican Revolution, the family moved often and was desperately poor. The author recalls his deep feeling for his father and their close relationship and tells of the schools he attended, and his perplexity about the Revolution. Eventually he decided the Revolution was not bad for Mexico in spite of atrocities committed by some rebels. Although it is well written and presents a clear picture of Mexican life, the book will have limited appeal.

583.   Iglesia, Ramon. **Columbus, Cortes and Other Essays.** Translated and edited by Lesley Byrd Simpson. Berkeley, California: University of California Press, 1969. 286p.
Distinctive interpretations of the personalities and drives of the men of the Spanish Conquest.

584.   Jones, Oakah L. **Santa Anna.** New York: Twayne Publishers, 1968. 211p.
An analysis of Santa Anna against the background of his time.

585.   Lieberman, Mark. **Hidalgo: Mexican Revolutionary.** New York:
j   Frederick A. Praeger, Inc., 1970. 168p.
Portrays Hidalgo as a man of fascinating contradictions—aristocrat, parish
priest, teacher, military tactician, condemned traitor, and a national hero.

586.   Lovelace, Maud Hart. **What Cabrillo Found: The Story of Juan**
j   **Rodriquez Cabrillo.** New York: Thomas Y. Crowell Company, 1958.
         180p.
Biography of the first discoverer of California.

587.   McKittrick, Myrtle M. **Vallejo, Son of California.** Portland, Oregon:
         Binfords and Mort, 1944. 377p.
A biography, with some illustrations, of the great Californian who was the most
influential Spanish American of his time.

588.   Matthiessen, Peter. "Organizer: Profile of Cesar Chavez." **The New**
         Yorker, Part I (June 21,1969), 42ff; Part II (June 28, 1969), 43ff.
Through informal interviews, the author has obtained many personal notes about
Chavez, such as his conversations with the late Senator Robert Kennedy, information regarding the Chavez family, and the relations between his career and
his family.

589.   Meyer, Michael C. **Huerta: A Political Portrait.** Lincoln, Neb.: Univer-
         sity of Nebraska Press, 1972. 272p.
A political biography of a self-made general in Mexico. The author describes
the formative years of Huerta in military academy, his early army career,
marriage and family, and his portrait as a dictator of Mexico from February
1913 to July 1914. Included are appendixes and an excellent bibliography.

590.   Meyer, Michael C. **Mexican Rebel: Pascual Orozco and the Mexican**
         Revolution, 1910-1915. Lincoln, Neb.: University of Nebraska Press,
         1967. 172p.
Orozco's revolutionary career and the course of the 1910 Revolution in
Chihuahua are traced in this first full-length biography to appear in either
Spanish or English. Well-documented study.

591.   Millon, Robert Paul. **Zapata: The Ideology of a Peasant Revolutionary.**
         New York: International Publishers Co., Inc., 1969. 159p.
The role of the Zapatistas in the Mexican Revolution; complements Womack's
Zapata and the Mexican Revolution.

592.   Moises, Rosalio. **The Tall Candle: The Personal Chronicle of a Yaqui**
         Indian. Lincoln, Neb.: University of Nebraska Press, 1971. 251p.
The narrative of a man whose people were based in the Sierra Villages of north-
west Mexico. The story begins during the Yaqui revolutionary period and continues through the last uprising in 1926, then covers the Yaqui on a Texas farm
from 1952 to 1969. The introduction, by Professor Jane Holden Kelly, adds
scholarly analysis to the poignant autobiographical narrative.

593.   Newlon, Clarke. **Famous Mexican-Americans.** New York: Dodd,
j   Mead & Co., 1972. 187p.
Brief biographies of 20 Mexican Americans who have made significant contributions in government, sports, entertainment, education, and other fields.

594.   Norman, James. **The Navy That Crossed Mountains.** Illustrated by
j   Dirk Gringhuis. New York: G. P. Putnam's Sons, 1963. 152p. o.p.
The story of Martin Lopez, whose sword and saw played large parts in Cortes'
conquest of Mexico.

595.   O'Connor, Richard. **The Cactus Throne: The Tragedy of Maximilian
       and Carlota.** New York: G. P. Putnam's Sons, 1971. 375p.
An absorbing narrative of Archduke Maximilian of Austria and Princess
Charlotte of Belgium and their pathetic roles as rulers of Mexico. The account
describes mid-1860 intrigues concerning the fate of the young rulers. Maximilian
is portrayed as a dedicated but ineffectual ruler tragically but understandably
executed by Mexican insurgents in 1867.

596.   Robinson, Fayette. **Mexico and Her Military Chieftains: From the
       Revolution to the Present Time.** Glorieta, N.M.: Rio Grande Press,
       Inc., 1970. 353p.
Comprising sketches of the lives of Hidalgo, Morelos, Iturbide, Santa Anna,
Gomez, Farias, Bustamente, Paredes, Almonte, Arista, Aleman, Ampudia,
Herrera, and De La Vega.

597.   Rosenblum, Morris. **Heroes of Mexico.** New York: Fleet Press Corp.,
j   1969. 144p.
Seventeen heroic men and women—from Quetzalcoatl to Chavez—are portrayed
in this work. A good presentation of the Mexican-American heritage.

598.   Ross, Stanley Robert. **Francisco I. Madero, Apostle of Mexican
       Democracy.** New York: AMS Press, Inc., 1970. Reprint of 1955 ed.
       378p.
The life of Francisco I. Madero, President of Mexico from 1873 to 1913, based
on extensive documentary material. Spanish edition appeared in 1959.

599.   Ruiz, Ramon Edwardo. "New Mexican-Americans: Rodolfo Gonzalez
       and His Band in Denver." **New Republic,** CLIX, No. 4 (July 27, 1968),
       11.
Brief biographical background of Gonzalez with a statement of his interests,
plans and organization with respect to Mexican Americans.

600.   Smart, Charles Allen. **Viva Juarez.** Philadelphia: J. B. Lippincott
       Company, 1963. 444p. o.p.
An excellent biography of the Abraham Lincoln of Mexico.

601.   Sterne, Emma Gelders. **Benito Juarez: Builder of a Nation.** Illustrated
j   by Ray Cruz. New York: Alfred A. Knopf, Inc., 1967. 208p.

Good primary sources and an objective viewpoint of Benito Juarez are presented in this biography.

602. Syme, Ronald. **Cortes of Mexico.** Illustrated by William Stobbs. New
 j York: William Morrow & Co., Inc., 1951. 191p.
Accurate historical material presented in an interesting manner.

603. Syme, Ronald. **Francisco Coronado and the Seven Cities of Gold.**
 New York: William Morrow & Co., Inc., 1965. 188p.
An interesting and personal account of Coronado's hopeless quest for gold in North America.

604. Tebbel, John. **Men of the Revolution.** Garden City, N.Y.: Doubleday
 & Company, Inc., 1969. 125p.
The lives of five great Mexican leaders.

605. Terrell, John U. **Estevanico the Black.** Los Angeles, Calif.: Western-
 lore Press, 1968. 155p.
An excellent piece on the "Black Mexican," a Negro slave said to have preceded Fray Marcos of Nice in his exploration of the American Southwest in 1539.
A carefully written study of Estevanico and his achievements.

606. Terzian, James P., and Kathryn Cramer. **Mighty Hard Road: The**
 j **Story of Cesar Chavez.** Garden City, N.Y.: Doubleday & Company,
 1970. 136p.
This narrative biography of Cesar Chavez conveys the character of the man and the nature of the movement he is leading, in a sympathetic but balanced account.

607. Timmons, Wilbert H. **Morelos of Mexico: Priest, Soldier, Statesman.**
 El Paso, Texas: Texas Western College Press, 1970. 184p.
A biography of an inspired warrior and statesman, and a recreation of the era of the Mexican Revolution for independence and of the colorful men who dominated the scene.

608. Trevino, Elizabeth Borton de. **My Heart Lies South: The Story of My**
 Mexican Marriage. New York: Thomas Y. Crowell Company, 1953.
 248p.
An account of an American ex-newspaperwoman's marriage and life in Mexico.

609. Vance, Marguerite. **Ashes of Empire: Carlota and Maximilian of**
 Mexico. Illustrated by J. Luis Pellicer. New York: E. P. Dutton &
 Company, 1959. 160p. o.p.
The tragic struggle and end of Carlota and Maximilian of Mexico.

610. Vasconcelos, Jose. **Mexican Ulysses: The Autobiography of Jose**
 Vasconcelos. Bloomington, Indiana: Indiana University Press, 1963.
 288p.
The autobiography of one of Mexico's great men of the twentieth century:

lawyer, politician, writer, educator, philosopher, prophet and mystic. An excellent translation by W. R. Crawford.

611.   White, Jon E. Manchip. **Cortes and the Downfall of the Aztec Empire: A Study in a Conflict of Cultures.** New York: St. Martin's Press, Inc., 1971. 352p.

The subtitle strikes the theme of this biography which sympathetically portrays the Mexican and Spanish cultures and their leaders, never minimizing the barbarities of either but also recognizing their good qualities.

612.   Wolfe, Bertram. **The Fabulous Life of Diego Rivera.** Chicago: Stein and Day Publishers, 1969. Reprint of 1963 ed. 457p.

Diego Rivera, Mexican painter whose influence led to the formation of a purely national school of painting, is best known for his vast historical murals.

613.   Womack, John. **Zapata and the Mexican Revolution.** New York: Alfred A. Knopf, Inc., 1969. 435p.

Depicts the tragic figures of Zapata and his followers in their roles in the revolution of the state of Morelos, south of Mexico City, between 1911 and the end of the decade. Treatment is scholarly but sympathetic.

614.   Worcester, Donald E. **Makers of Latin America.** New York: E. P.
   j   Dutton and Company, Inc., 1966. 222p.

The biographies of 20 men and one woman who especially influenced the course of Mexican, Central American, and South American history from the conquest to the twentieth century.

615.   Young, Bob, and Jan Young. **Anza: Hard-Riding Captain.** San Carlos,
   j   Calif.: Golden Gate Junior Books, 1967. 197p.

A detailed biography of Anza, the famous Spanish explorer.

616.   Young, Bob, and Jan Young. **Liberators of Latin America.** New York:
   j   Lothrop, Lee and Shepard Co., 1970. 244p.

Accounts of Haiti's Toussaint, of San Martin, Bolivar, Pedro, of the Mexicans Hidalgo, Morelos, Iturbide, and Juarez.

617.   Young, Bob, and Jan Young. **Seven Faces West.** New York: Julian
   j   Messner, Inc., 1969. 191p.

Biographical sketches of Spanish Indians, Orientals, and blacks who played important roles in the westward expansion of America in building railroads and establishing missions and townsites.

6: FICTION

618.   Andrews, Matthew. **The Black Palace.** New York: Delacorte, 1972.
        184p.
Simon Grant goes to Mexico for a quick divorce but is caught with "pot" and
sent to prison. The letters he writes from prison attempting to gain his freedom
comprise the story. A weak story, but entertaining and humorous letters.

619.   Appel, Benjamin. **We Were There with Cortez and Montezuma.** New
   j   York: Grossett & Dunlap, Inc., 1959. 179p.
An easy-to-read fictionalized story of the conquest of Mexico by Cortez.

620.   Arnold, Elliot. **The Time of the Gringo.** New York: Alfred A. Knopf,
        Inc., 1953. 612p.
An historical novel of the Southwest in the 1830s. Tells of the rise to power of
Manuel Armejo, who became the Mexican governor of New Mexico, in the
years preceding the conquest of the country by the Americans.

621.   Azuela, Mariano. **Two Novels of Mexico: The Flies; The Bosses.**
        Berkeley, Calif.: University of California Press, 1956. 194p.
Two novellas, for mature readers, about the Mexican Revolution.

622.   Azuela, Mariano. **The Underdogs.** Translated by E. Munguia, Jr.
        Preface by Carleton Beals. Illustrated by J. Clemente Orozco. New
        York: The New American Library, Inc., 1963. 151p.
Originally published in Spanish in 1916. This work provides excellent insight
to the character and motivation of the peasant bands that fought during the
Mexican Revolution. Portrays the rise of Demetrio Macias from poverty in
rural Mexico to the rank of general in the forces of Pancho Villa.

623.   Bagley, Desmond. **The Vivero Letter.** Garden City, N.Y.: Doubleday
        & Company, Inc., 1968. 278p.
A fascinating historical jigsaw puzzle which moves from the present-day English
countryside to Yucatan. The solution involves Cortes and the conquest of
Mexico, and the discovery of a lost city of the Mayas.

624.   Baker, Betty. **The Blood of the Brave.** New York: Harper & Row
   j   Publishers, Inc., 1966. 165p.
A sixteenth century adventure with Cortez in Mexico.

625.   Baker, Betty. **The Dunderhead War: A Novel.** New York: Harper &
   J   Row Publishers, Inc., 1967. 216p.
The adventures of 17-year-old Quincy Heffendorf. Eager to enlist in the U.S.
Army in the Mexican War but still too young, he joins a wagon train to follow
the same route as the soldiers.

626.   Baron, Alexander. **The Golden Princess**. New York: Ives Washburn,
         Inc., 1954. 378p. o.p.
Princess Marina was an Aztec of noble descent who became attached to the camp
of Cortez when he was conquering Mexico. She served as interpreter and guide
for Cortez when he was dealing with Montezuma.

627.   Barrio, Raymond. **The Plum Plum Pickers**. New York: Canfield Press
         Books, 1971. 201p. Reprint of 1969 edition.
A novel protesting the exploitation of Mexican-American migrant farm workers.
A series of vignettes in Santa Clara County, California, depict various representative characters: a Mexican migrant family, the migrant camp foreman, the
grower, and the young unmarried pickers. The aspects of the migrants' lives
are well portrayed.

628.   Barry, Jane. **A Shadow of Eagles**. Garden City, N.Y.: Doubleday &
         Company, Inc., 1964. 424p. o.p.
An 1875 story during the last of the free wild days of Texan and Mexican
cattle barons.

629.   Beckett, Hilary. **My Brother, Angel**. New York: Dodd, Mead &
  j   Company, 1971. 196p.
Left in charge of his five-year-old brother, Angel, Carlos has mixed feelings.
However, he manages to cope—but not without some tense moments as mysterious happenings occur in the neighborhood on Halloween and Carlos discovers
some insights into being Mexican American in a predominantly Anglo world.

630.   Behn, Harry. **Two Uncles of Pablo**. New York: Harcourt, Brace &
  j   World, Inc., 1959. 96p.
The story of Pablo, a Mexican boy, who discovers the worth of two uncles.

631.   Bishop, Curtis. **Fast Break**. Philadelphia: J. B. Lippincott Company,
  j   1967. 192p.
Sam realizes that his selection to the varsity squad at Riverside High is due to
his new friend, a Mexican boy, with whom he worked well on the court. The
team's chance for the championship dims when his friend suddenly returns to
Mexico.

632.   Bonham, Frank. **The Vagabundos**. New York: E. P. Dutton & Com-
  j   pany, Inc., 1969. 222p.
When his father leaves home without explanation Eric tracks him for one
thousand miles along the Baja coast. By the time the two finally confront one
another, they both know what they want.

633.   Bonham, Frank. **Viva Chicano**. New York: E. P. Dutton & Company,
         Inc., 1970. 180p.
Keeny, a Mexican American on parole, feels he must not return to the
atmosphere of his home and neighborhood and devises a solution to the problem.
This is the story of a real boy as told by the parole officer to Frank Bonham.

634. Bourjaily, Vance Nye. **Brill Among the Ruins: A Novel.** New York: Dial Press, Inc., 1970. 354p.

A penetrating characterization introduces Robert Brill, a small-town lawyer in Illinois. His law practice involves him in the troubles of his fellow towns-people, whom he observes with a candid liberal humor that completely avoids cliche and stereotype. Sparked by the interest of a friend in the archaeology and anthropology of Mexico, Brill first goes on a vacation to visit some of the digging sites, then returns to pry more deeply into a subject now enthralling him with the prospect of reclaiming lost civilizations. A fantasy concerning an ancient Mexican tribal community.

635. Bradford, Richard. **Red Sky at Morning.** Philadelphia: J. B. Lippincott Company, 1968. 256p.

The cultural traditions of the Indians, the Mexican Americans, and the Anglos meet, but do not always mix. Josh, a young seventeen-year-old boy, is caught in the middle.

636. Breck, Vivian. **Maggie.** Garden City, N.Y.: Doubleday & Company, Inc., 1954. 249p.

Maggie Duncan, high-spirited San Francisco debutante, marries an adventurous English gold miner and accompanies him into the wilds of Mexico. Building upon the real life of her mother, with authentic details recollected from her own childhood, the author has produced a vivid, realistic, and mature novel.

637. Brenner, Anita. **Timid Ghost: Or, What Would You Do with a Sackful**
j **of Gold?** New York: Addison-Wesley Publishing Co., 1966. unp.

A humorous story about a Mexican ghost who searches for someone who can give the right answer to his question.

638. Bristow, Gwen. **Jubilee Trail.** New York: Thomas Y. Crowell Company, 1950. 564p.

A romantic novel of the Spanish Trail from Santa Fe before the discovery of gold in California.

639. Bruckner, Karl. **Viva Mexico!** Translated from the German by Stella
j Humphries. Illustrated by Adalbert Pilch. New York: Roy Publishers, Inc., 1960. 190p.

Juanita, a laborer on the Hacienda La Rica, aids the revolutionary leader, Miguel, to escape imprisonment on the hacienda; both then join the revolutionaries. The story is valuable for its clear view of the revolutionary causes and movements.

640. Cannon, Cornelia James. **Pueblo Boy: A Story of Coronado's Search**
j **for the Seven Cities of Cibola.** Boston: Garrett Press, Inc., 1926. 197p.

A study of Coronado's search for the seven cities of Cibola, 1535-1542. Tyami, the Eagle, a 12-year-old boy, wins the friendship of Coronado's men and saves his tribe.

641.   Carr, Harriett H. **Mystery of the Aztec Idol.** New York: Macmillan
  j   Company, 1967. 193p.
An American boy and a Mexican boy become involved in an adventure concerning some archaeological diggings in Mexico.

642.   Carruth, Estelle. **Three Sides to the River.** San Antonio, Texas: The
       Naylor Company, 1968. 167p.
Presents the Anglo's prejudice against the Chicano as well as the Chicano's
against the Anglo.

643.   Castellanos, Rosario. **The Nine Guardians: A Novel.** Translated by
       Irene Nicholson. New York: Vanguard Press, 1959. 272p.
The scene is a remote province of southern Mexico during the presidency of
Lazaro Cardenas. Cardenas' reforms reach the province in only a desultory
fashion, but enough to upset the precarious balance of society. The novel
shows the disintegration of a Mexican ranch family under the impact of the
land reforms. The book was voted the best fiction of the year in Mexico.

644.   Cather, Willa. **Death Comes for the Archbishop.** New York: Alfred
       A. Knopf, 1927. 303p.
The first missionary bishop of New Mexico and his devoted vicar are the central
characters of this early history of the Southwest.

645.   Chandler, David. **Huelga!** New York: Simon & Schuster, Inc., 1970.
       284p.
A tractlike novel portrays the early years of the Mexican-American farm
workers' strike against the California table-grape growers. The narrative illustrates the issues involved as interpreted by persons on all sides of the dispute,
emphasizing the rise of the charismatic leader Daniel Garcia.

646.   Clark, Ann Nolan. **Summer Is for Growing.** Illustrated by Agnes Tait.
  j   New York: Farrar, Straus & Giroux, Inc., 1968. 192p.
This story of hacienda life treats the mixing of two cultures. The setting is
New Mexico in 1851.

647.   Coleman, Eleanor S. **The Cross and the Sword of Cortes.** New York:
  j   Simon & Schuster, Inc., 1968. 191p.
The fantastic and tragic story of the conquest of Mexico is told through the eyes
and voice of a young padre who accompanied Cortes to the Mexican capital.
This historical novel colorfully depicts sixteenth century Mexico.

648.   Covin, Kelly. **Many Broken Hammers.** New York: Delacorte, 1971.
       288p.
Set in an imaginary state in the Southwest and confined to the events of a
single day, this novel is about a conflict between the poor and the power structure. The poor are Chicanos organized under Carlos Dominguin to protect themselves from land swindlers. A forceful, timely novel, written with insight and a
flair for suspense.

649. Cox, William R. **Third and Goal**. New York: Dodd, Mead & Company,
j   Inc., 1971. 182p.
Rafael Cortez wanted to join the Bombers' football team. Several obstacles
blocked his way. The Cortez family were Mexican Americans and there was
still racial prejudice against Chicanos. Then mamma opposed having her son
hurt playing football, as his brother had been. It took mamma's aching back,
plus the tolerance of the Cortez family, and Rafe's willingness to serve only as
an occasional substitute to prove that he was a true Anglo and a good football
player.

650. Cox, William R. **Trouble at Second Base**. New York: Dodd, Mead &
j   Company, Inc., 1966. 181p. o.p.
As always in stories by this author, the game is of prime importance. In addition to genuine baseball action, we have interest and depth added by a valiant
Mexican and a Japanese boy who play on the Studio City High team, in spite of
the ignorant opposition of a few. A great friendly Saint Bernard and a very
independent school cat provide fun and added appeal.

651. Crary, Margaret. **Mexican Whirlwind**. New York: Ives Washburn, Inc.,
j   1969. 149p.
What happens when a very attractive Mexican schoolgirl, an exchange student,
comes to spend a year with popular basketball enthusiast Taffy Webster and
her Midwestern family.

652. De Cesco, Frederica. **The Prince of Mexico**. New York: John Day
j   Company, 1970. 224p.
The love between young Prince Cuauhtemac, the last of the Aztec rulers, and
Tecuichop, daughter of Emperor Montezuma.

653. Dunne, Mary Collins. **Reach Out, Ricardo**. New York: Abelard-
j   Schuman, 1971. 192p.
In this absorbing story, the author depicts the results of a strike: the tensions,
the shattered friendships, and the plight of a boy torn between his alliances
and his principles.

654. Du Soe, Robert C. **Three Without Fear**. New York: David McKay
j   Company, Inc., 1947. 185p.
A young boy is shipwrecked off Baja California. Two Indian children find him,
and he accompanies them on their journey to Santo Thomas.

655. Edmondson, G. C. **Chapayeca**. Garden City, N.Y.: Doubleday &
j   Company, Inc., 1971. 192p.
An American Anthropologist becomes the protector of an alien from outer
space who is living among the Yaqui Indians of Mexico.

656. Erdman, Loula Grace. **My Sky Is Blue**. New York: David McKay
j   Company, Inc., 1953. 218p.
Jinny, seeking a change in her life, leaves a promising teaching career in a large

city school to teach in a rural school in New Mexico. Here in a one-room school she encounters prejudice against a Mexican-American family. Rosie, a white girl, torments the Garcia children, creating a disturbing situation in the school and in the village. Jinny is able to help Rosie change her attitude and at the same time instill cultural pride in the Garcia family. This good junior novel of romance develops interest in teaching and also shows a way of combating prejudice.

657. Evarts, Hal G. **Smugglers' Road.** New York: Charles S. Scribner's
j   Sons, 1968. 192p.
A teacher's offer to assume responsibility for Kern's good conduct during a working summer in Mexico prevents the boy's being sent to a juvenile home. How he justifies that faith leads him into adventure, involves him in solving a mystery, and wins the approval of his sponsor and a community.

658. Fiedler, Jean. **Call Me Juanita.** Illustrated by Ursula Koering. New
j   York: David McKay Company, Inc., 1968. 152p.
When an American girl's father accepts a job in Mexico, Johanna is sure she will be unhappy, but the fascination of the food, language, and sights soon change her attitude.

659. Fuentes, Carlos. **The Death of Artemio Cruz.** New York: Farrar,
    Straus and Giroux, Inc., 1964. 306p.
Artemio Cruz, a wealthy but hypocritical newspaper publisher and false revolutionary, reviews his life while lying on his deathbed. For mature readers.

660. Fuentes, Carlos. **The Good Conscience.** New York: Farrar, Straus
    and Giroux, Inc., 1968. 148p.
In Guanajuato the Ceballo family had acquired wealth, only to lose it in the Revolution. Jaime at one time considered the priesthood, but decided that religion is meant for the righteous, not the sinner.

661. Galindo, Sergio. **The Precipice.** Translated by John and Carolyn
    Brushwood. Austin, Texas: University of Texas Press, 1969. 185p.
The complexity of the thoughts and behavior of a contemporary Mexican family come across vividly in this moving novel by one of Mexico's finest young writers. Original title was *El Bordo*.

662. Gallen, A. A. **The Wetback.** Boston: Bruce Humphries, 1961. 243p.
    o.p.
A novel showing social stereotypes of the wetback in Texas.

663. Garro, Elena. **Recollections of Things to Come.** Translated by Ruth
    L. C. Simms. Austin, Texas: University of Texas Press, 1969. 289p.
A fine example of the modern Mexican novel written by a young gifted writer whose prose shows great skill, taste, and sensitivity. The novel recreates the inner life, the conflicts and many facets of the people of the small town of Ixtepec during turbulent times of the Cristero Rebellion.

664.	Garthwaite, Marion Hook. **Mario: A Mexican Boy's Adventure.**
j	Garden City, N.Y.: Doubleday & Company, Inc., 1960. 167p. o.p.
Mario, who has put his faith in a trader in wetbacks, is hijacked to California
and blackmailed into picking cotton.

665.	Gault, William C. **Wheels of Fortune.** New York: E. P. Dutton &
	Company, 1963. 157p.
A Mexican boy seeks equality at the race track.

666.	Gavin, Catherine. **The Cactus and the Crown.** Garden City, N.Y.:
	Doubleday & Company, 1962. 472p.
An historical novel in Mexico during the days of Maximilian and Carlota.

667.	Gordon, Alvin. **Inherit the Earth: Stories from Mexican Ranch Life.**
	Tucson, Ariz.: University of Arizona Press, 1963. 79p.
A collection of two- to three-page short stories of Mexican ranch life.

668.	Greene, Graham. **The Power and the Glory.** New York: Viking Press,
	Inc., 1946. 301p.
The suspenseful story of a priest who must flee the police in strife-ridden
Mexico. A reflection on the meaning of religion in Mexican culture. For
mature readers.

669.	Guzman, Martin Luis. **The Eagle and the Serpent.** Gloucester, Mass.:
	Peter Smith Publishers, Inc., 1930.
A novel of the Mexican revolution of 1910, based on the author's own experiences. Original title was *Labyrinthine Ways.*

670.	Hart, Carolyn G. **Rendezvous in Veracruz.** New York: M. Evans and
	Co., Inc., 1970. 224p.
Maura Kelley and Linda Prescott, students in Mexico City, are involved in a
plot more dangerous for them—and perhaps for a nation than they ever
dreamed. Good suspense.

671.	Hazelton, Elizabeth Baldwin. **Tides of Danger.** New York: Charles
j	Scribner's Sons, 1967. 266p.
A suspenseful tale of the quest of a 14-year-old boy for a valuable pearl.

672.	Henderson, LeGrand. **Tomb of the Mayan King.** New York: Holt,
	Rinehart & Winston, Inc., 1958. 192p. o.p.
A young boy wished to be rich but instead found his own identity.

673.	Heuman, William. **City High Five.** New York: Dodd, Mead & Com-
j	pany, Inc., 1964. 176p.
A fast-moving story about Mike Harrigan and his friend Pedro Martinez on the
high school basketball team. When Pedro has to spend time on an extra job,
the game suffers, and the squad thinks he is quitting. Mike enlists the coach's aid
because he feels the team can go on to win the city championship with Pedro.

674.   Hobart, Alice Tisdale. **The Peacock Sheds His Tail**. New York: Bobbs-Merrill Company, 1945. 360p. o.p.
In the midst of social change for the aristocratic Navarro family of Mexico City, Concha marries Jim Buchanan, who is in the American diplomatic service. Problems for the Navarro family arise from the inter-ethnic marriage.

675.   Jackson, Helen Hunt. **Ramona**. Boston: Little, Brown & Company, 1939. 249p.
Ramona is brought up in an aristocratic Mexican family in California not knowing of her part-Indian ancestry. She falls in love and runs away with an Indian.

676.   Kalnay, Francis. **It Happened in Chichipica**. New York: Harcourt
j   Brace Jovanovich, Inc., 1971. 127p.
Chuco was one of the busiest boys in Chichipica, a bustling Mexican village. He was the top student in the school and he wanted very much to win a scholarship to the new school in the capital, but his hopes were nearly wrecked by a neighbor's malicious attempt to spoil his good name. In this warm and lively story, told with humor, Chucho and his friends overcome the forces of mischief.

677.   Keith, Harold. **Komantica**. New York: Thomas Y. Crowell Company,
j   1965. 299p.
Pedro Pavon, during a raid on his uncle's Mexican rancho, is abducted by the barbaric Comanche warrior who killed his mother.

678.   Kidwell, Carl. **The Angry Earth**. New York: Viking Press, Inc., 1964.
j   224p. o.p.
Recreation of a pre-Columbian civilization in the Valley of Mexico. An exciting story of the life of the young slave is climaxed by the eruption of a volcano amid earthquakes and upheaval. The author has based his story on modern archaeological discoveries.

679.   Kidwell, Carl. **Arrow in the Sun**. New York: Viking Press, Inc., 1961. 256p. o.p.
The Indian prince Netzah avenges the death of his father and recaptures their lost kingdom in this authentic story of pre-Aztec Mexico.

680.   Knott, Bill. **The Secret of the Old Brownstone**. Austin, Texas:
j   Steck-Vaughn Co., 1969. 210p.
Twelve-year-old Bobby Sanchez, snooping through an old evacuated building, is lured into a series of adventures.

681.   Krumgold, Joseph. **. . . And Now Miguel**. Illustrated by Jean Charlot.
j   New York: Thomas Y. Crowell Co., 1953. 245p.
Mexican-American and Indian-American values are subtly conveyed in this heartwarming story of a young shepherd's coming to manhood.

682. Laklan, Carli. **Migrant Girl.** New York: McGraw-Hill Book Company,
j   1970. 142p.
The 16-year-old migrant worker and her family follow the crops from Florida
to Maine with Juan, a Mexican-American worker—the only migrant making any
effort to improve their lot.

683. Lampman, Evelyn Sibley. **The Tilted Sombrero.** Illustrated by Ray
j   Cruz. Garden City, N.Y.: Doubleday & Company, Inc., 1966. 260p.
A story set in 1810 (the time of Hidalgo) which is sympathetic to the problems
of the Creoles and to the revolutionary figure Hidalgo. This is consistent with
Hidalgo's belief that Mexico needed a ruler from the Creole class.

684. Lansford, William Douglas. **Pancho Villa.** Los Angeles, Calif.:
        Shelbourne Press, 1965. 129p.
The author utilizes the romantic novel style to explore the legend of Pancho
Villa. Although many of the incidents described in the novel are historically
accurate, the book should not be used as a historical reference text. Lansford
provides interesting insights into the involvement of the Wilson administration
and the Republic of Germany in the internal affairs of Mexico during the 1910
revolution.

685. Laughlin, Florence. **The Horse from Topolo.** Illustrated by Barbara
j   Werner. Philadelphia: Macrae Smith, 1966. 191p. o.p.
A mystery about the theft of Toltec artifacts. Archaeology and Mexican history
are interwoven into this adventure story.

686. Lawrence, D. H. **The Plumed Serpent.** New York: Alfred A. Knopf,
        1951. 445p.
"The plumed serpent" is the English name of one of the old Aztec gods,
Quetzalcoatl, and the action of the story is based upon a semi-mystical, semi-
political movement to revive the cult of the ancient deities. A remarkable
attempt to penetrate to the essential spirit of modern Mexico as it reveals
itself to a lovely, world-weary Irishwoman resident there.

687. Lawrence, Mildred. **Gateway to the Sun.** New York: Harcourt Brace
j   Jovanovich, Inc., 1970. 190p.
Val is shipped off to New Mexico to live with her father, his Spanish American
wife and her daughter, Rosita. Cultural adjustments are made by both Val
and Rosita.

688. Lawrence, Mildred. **Good Morning, My Heart.** New York: Harcourt,
j   Brace & World, Inc., 1957. 190p.
Jan is roused to action by discrimination against a Mexican girl.

689. Lea, Tom. **The Brave Bulls: A Novel.** Boston: Little, Brown & Co.,
j   1949. 270p.
Realistic rendition of the bullfighters in Mexico.

690.	Lea, Tom. **The Hands of Cantu.** Boston: Little, Brown & Company,
j	1964. 244p.
In 1580 Toribio de Ibarra was sent to Don Cito Cantu as a courier and servant.
The two made an eventful 83-day journey into the unknown north to recover
stolen horses.

691.	Lea, Tom. **The Wonderful Country.** Boston: Little, Brown & Com-
pany, 1952. 387p.
The many people who helped build the frontier town of Puerto in Texas during
the 1880s are pictured in this novel.

692.	Lopez Y Fuentes, Gregorio. **El Indio.** Translated by Anita Brenner.
New York: Frederick Ungar Publishing Company, Inc., 1961. 256p.
An outstanding novel of Indian life, set in a small rancheria in Mexico where the
Indians live in submission to white men and to mestizos. Originally published
in 1937.

693.	Lowry, Malcolm. **Dark As the Grave Wherein My Friend Is Laid.**
New York: New American Library, 1968. 255p.
In this novel about the trip of Sigbjorn Wilderness and his wife, Primrose, to
Mexico, the author is really telling the story of his own trip with his wife to
look up his old friend, Fernando. But Fernando is already dead, and at last
Sigbjorn realizes that Fernando had really symbolized the death Sigbjorn
craved. For mature readers.

694.	McClarren, J. K. **Mexican Assignment.** New York: Funk & Wagnalls
Co., 1957. 247p.
In a Mexican village, an idealistic young American veterinarian helping to fight
hoof-and-mouth disease overcomes the reluctance of the people to use modern
ways in medicine and in agriculture.

695.	MacLeod, Ruth. **Buenos Dias, Teacher.** New York: Julian Messner,
1970. 192p.
With the help of Dave, who really understands her goals, Jennifer struggles to
be a teacher who meets the needs of deprived Mexican and white children in a
poor urban area.

696.	Madison, Winifred. **Maria Luisa.** Philadelphia: J. B. Lippincott Co.,
j	1971. 192p.
When her mother becomes ill, Maria Luisa and her younger brother are sent to
live with relatives in San Francisco where being a "Chicano" takes on new
meaning.

697.	Mantel, S. G. **The Youngest Conquistador.** Illustrated by William
j	Ferguson. New York: David McKay Company, Inc., 1963. 182p.
Cortes' conquest told from the point of view of a young boy of noble Spanish
birth whom the author fictionalizes as one of the party sent out by Cortes.

698. Means, Florence Crandell. **Alicia.** Boston: Houghton Mifflin Co.,
j   1953. 266p. o.p.
A Denver girl of Spanish background learns to appreciate her Mexican heritage
when she spends a year at the University of Mexico.

699. Means, Florence Crandell. **But I Am Sara.** Boston: Houghton Mifflin
j   Company, 1961. 231p.
An American girl in Mexico learns significant aspects of Mexican life and values.

700. Means, Florence Crandell. **Emmy and the Blue Door.** Boston: Houghton
j   Mifflin Company, 1959. 231p.
Emmy spends a summer as a participant in a Quaker workshop in Mexico where
she finds her ideals considerably strained by the realities she meets.

701. Means, Florence Crandell. **Knock at the Door, Emmy.** Boston:
j   Houghton Mifflin Company, 1956. 240p.
This story dramatizes the courage of a young migrant girl.

702. Means, Florence Crandell. **Teresita of the Valley.** Boston: Houghton
j   Mifflin Company, 1943. 166p. o.p.
Teresita's development is shown when she acknowledges and is proud of her
Mexican heritage. The adjustment of her family to a new culture and to a new
way of life is shown in the novel.

703. Millar, Margaret. **Beyond This Point Are Monsters.** New York: Random House, 1970. 213p.
The Mexican border setting, the characterizations, the plot, and the climax
are all superbly fashioned in this superior mystery story.

704. Niggli, Josephina. **Mexican Village.** Chapel Hill, N.C.: University of
North Carolina Press, 1945. 491p.
A series of ten stories centering in the village of Hidalgo in Northern Mexico,
in which the same characters appear and reappear.

705. O'Dell, Scott. **The Black Pearl.** Illustrated by Milton Johnson. Boston:
j   Houghton Mifflin Company, 1967. 140p.
A well-told story which captures effectively the life of a pearl fishing community
off Baja California.

706. O'Dell, Scott. **The King's Fifth.** Illustrated by Samuel Bryant. Boston:
j   Houghton Mifflin Company, 1966. 264p.
An historical novel about the search for the seven cities of Cibola, told from
the point of view of Esteban, the young cartographer who accompanied the
party of six sent out from Coronado's army camp. This excellent novel of
sixteenth century Mexico brings to life the people and events of the period.

707. Olsen, Paul. **The Virgin of San Gil: A Novel.** New York: Holt, Rinehart
& Winston, Inc., 1965. 189p. o.p.

In a remote mountain village of Mexico the statue of the Virgin is stolen from the church and all the jewels and gold decorations removed. An Indian charcoal seller, who is accused of theft and who is the lowliest person in San Gil, finds the statue. He is befriended by a young priest who suffers martyrdom as a consequence—but not before he has set in motion the forces of retribution.

708.　　Olson, Gene. **Sacramento Gold.** Philadelphia: Macrae Smith Company, 1961. 192p. o.p.

During the gold rush days Clancy Hawkins, a refugee from a hard homelife, tangles with Mexican desperados on his way to San Francisco.

709.　　Oppenheimer, Joan L. **Run for Your Luck.** New York: Hawthorn Books, Inc., 1971. 152p.

Eighteen-year-old Toni Weston hitchhikes to California to get a summer job and a college education. She stays with relatives and soon is involved with her new life, her cousin's "speed trips" and infatuation with a dope smuggler, her aunt's and uncle's concerns and fears, and her growing respect and understanding for a proud young Chicano.

710.　　Parish, Helen Rand. **Our Lady of Guadalupe.** Illustrated by Jean
  j　　Charlot. New York: Viking Press, Inc., 1955. 48p.

The retelling of the miraculous appearance of the Virgin Mary to the peasant, Juan Diego, near Mexico City on December 9, 1531.

711.　　Peters, Elizabeth. **The Night of Four Hundred Rabbits.** New York: Dodd, Mead & Company, 1971. 288p.

Carol Farley, a college student, and her boy friend go to Mexico seeking her long-lost father. The plot is complicated by drug traffic involving the U.S. narcotic agents. The combination of an exotic Mexican setting and a somewhat contemporary theme makes interesting reading. The title is an adaptation of the Aztec term for drunkenness. On a dark night at the Pyramid of the Sun in Teotihuacan, Carol learns about the four hundred rabbits.

712.　　Rulfo, Juan. **The Burning Plain and Other Stories.** Translated by George D. Schade. Austin, Texas: University of Texas Press, 1967. 175p.

A group of starkly powerful stories by a major figure in the history of post-revolutionary literature in Mexico, capturing single moments in the lives of the inhabitants of a harsh and isolated rural Mexico.

713.　　Rydberg, Ernie. **Bright Summer.** New York: Longmans, Green &
  j　　Company, Inc., 1953. 131p. o.p.

A Mexican-American family of fruit pickers spends the summer working near a southern California town. Presents a good picture of migrant life.

714.　　Schaefer, Jack. **Old Ramon.** Boston: Houghton Mifflin Company,
  j　　1960. 112p.

The patron's young son, who goes with Old Ramon, the shepherd, to take the sheep to graze, learns much. A simple story of a shepherd's life, sympathetically and realistically narrated.

715. Seifert, Shirley. **By the King's Command.** Philadelphia: J. B. Lippincott Company, 1962. 352p.

A novel based on the command to destroy the settlement of East Texas in 1773 and the consequences of this act.

716. Shellabarger, Samuel. **Captain from Castile.** Boston: Little, Brown & Company, 1945. 632p.

Adventures of Pedro de Bargos, who joined Hernan Cortez in the conquest of Mexico about 1518. An excellent historical novel.

717. Smith, George Harmon. **Wanderers of the Field.** New York: John
j   Day Company, 1966. 218p.

The trials and tribulations of the O'Neal family during one harvest season point out the difficulties migrant workers must face. Mexican Americans and blacks are included in the story.

718. Somerlott, Robert. **The Inquisitor's House.** New York: Viking Press, 1968. 377p.

When five people were all found dead after a fire destroyed a house in Mexico on the Day of the Dead, the officials wanted to quiet fears that the people had brought the devil's wrath upon themselves. The novel traces the lives of all five and of two who escaped death. A masterly portrayal of characters.

719. Sommerfelt, Aimee. **My Name Is Pablo.** Translated by Patricia
j   Crampton. Illustrated by Hans Norman Dahl. New York: Criterion Books, 1965. 143p.

The problems of the poor are realistically explored in this story of friendship.

720. Steinbeck, John. **The Pearl.** New York: Viking Press, Inc., 1947. 122p.

Based on an old Mexican folk tale, this is the story of the great pearl—how it was found by a Mexican family and lost again.

721. Steinbeck, John. **Tortilla Flat.** Illustrated by Ruth Gannett. New York: Modern Library, 1937. 316p.

A colorful tale of a group of carefree paisanos (those who have a mixture of Spanish, Indian, Mexican, and Caucasian blood) and their adventures in Tortilla Flat. This story gives insight into a happy, carefree life which few people ever know.

722. Stinetorf, Louise A. **A Charm for Paco's Mother.** New York: John
j   Day Company, 1965. 127p.

An easy-to-read story of a young Mexican boy's dream to pay for his mother's eye operation.

723. Summers, James L. **Don't Come Back a Stranger.** Philadelphia: Westminster Press, 1970. 192p.
This novel for young people and their parents takes a hard-hitting, potent look at today's campus, with its concerned students. Relationship of a Mexican-American and an Anglo student is portrayed.

724. Summers, James L. **Sons of Montezuma.** Philadelphia: Westminster Press, 1958. 208p. o.p.
The story of Private Jack Ransome and his march from Vera Cruz to Mexico City during the Mexican War.

725. Summers, James L. **You Can't Make It by Bus.** Philadelphia: Westminster Press, 1969. 171p.
A powerful story of a Chicano youth confused about his heritage. It is a book a Mexican American can identify with, since it gives insight into what it is like to belong to a minority group in this country.

726. Swarthout, Glendon. **They Came to Cordura.** New York: Random House, 1958. 213p.
On April 16, 1916, at Ojos Azules in Northern Mexico a provisional squadron made the last mounted charge against an enemy in the history of the United States Cavalry. The enemy was one of General Villa's bands, the provisional squadron was a unit of General Pershing's "Punitive Expedition." A book about certain fictitious events before and after the lost, last charge.

727. Taylor, Robert Louis. **Two Roads to Guadalupe.** Garden City, N.Y.: Doubleday & Company, 1964. 428p.
A picaresque novel of the Mexican War. An adventure story with almost everything—a colorful setting, enough remoteness in time to be exotic, plenty of action, suspense, violence, and even love, in the person of a beautiful girl who disguises herself as a soldier in order to follow her sweetheart.

728. Traven, B. **The Bridge in the Jungle.** New York: Hill & Wang, 1967. 216p.
A little boy disappears from a small village into the jungle. The entire settlement unites in a dramatically moving search. The psychological insights into the people's thoughts, motivations, sorrows, and joys are excellent.

729. Traven, B. **The Carreta: A Novel.** New York: Hill & Wang, 1970. 264p.
A detailed look at one of the most fascinating and least known primitive areas of the continent, the southernmost Mexican state of Chiapas.

730. Traven, B. **The Cotton-Pickers.** Rev. ed. New York: Hill & Wang, 1969. 200p.
This novel follows the career of Gerard Gales, an itinerant worker in post-World War I in Mexico.

731.   Traven, B. **Government: A Novel.** New York: Hill & Wang, 1971. 320p.
The action centers on two villages. The simple dignity of illiterate Indians is contrasted to the cynicism and corruption of ladino politicians and petty bureaucrats who live on money extorted from the Indian peons.

732.   Traven, B. **The Night Visitor and Other Stories.** New York: Hill &
            Wang, 1966. 238p.
Ten unrelated short stories of Mexico, including fantasy, adventure, philosophy, realism, and humor.

733.   Traven, B. **The Treasure of the Sierra Madre.** New York: Hill &
            Wang, 1967. 259p.
Three American derelicts search for a lost gold mine in the Mexican wilderness.

734.   Trevino, Elizabeth Borton de. **Nacar, the White Deer.** New York:
   j   Farrar, Straus & Giroux, Inc., 1963. 149p.
The legend of a deer which crossed on a Spanish galleon from the Orient to
Spain by way of Mexico, where it is befriended by a young mute herder.

735.   Trevino, Elizabeth Borton de. **The Fourth Gift.** Garden City, N.Y.:
            Doubleday & Company, Inc., 1966. 246p. o.p. Paper reprint 1971.
Tells, through the lives of seven imaginary individuals, the story of the rebellion
of the Cristeros in Mexico against the presidential decree of 1926 (banning
church and priests). The fourth gift is fortitude.

736.   Vasquez, Richard. **Chicano.** Garden City, N.Y.: Doubleday &
            Company, Inc., 1970. 376p.
An absorbing family saga presenting the problems of the Chicano by tracing
the Sandoval family through four generations, from its roots in a village in
northern Mexico during the revolution of 1910 to the present-day barrio of
East Los Angeles.

737.   Villarreal, Jose Antonio. **Pocho.** Garden City, N.Y.: Doubleday &
            Company, 1970. 157p. Reprint of 1959 ed.
A realistic novel of a young man's inner turmoil in his search for identity.
Barrio living in the United States is vividly presented.

738.   Warren, Mary Phraner. **Shadow on the Valley.** Philadelphia: West-
   j   minster Press, 1967. 192p.
Dena finds her future career and romance while working with Mexican migrants
as an after-school VISTA volunteer.

739.   Whitman, Edmund S. **Revolt Against the Rain God.** New York:
   j   McGraw-Hill Book Company, 1965. 143p. o.p.
A story about life among the ancient Mayan people. The revolt of the fictional
city of Paxil against the dictatorial policies of the High Priest.

740. Whitney, Phyllis. **A Long Time Coming**. New York: David McKay Company, 1954. 256p. o.p.
Incident after incident shows Christi Allard that good intentions alone will never change her town's prejudice against migrant Mexican-American workers in the local canning factory.

741. Wibberley, Leonard. **The Island of the Angels**. Illustrated by Leo Summers. New York: William Morrow & Co., 1965. 112p.
During a storm, a sick boy is washed ashore to the hut of a fisherman living alone on an island. After great effort he gets help from the mainland. The story offers insight into the problems of the Mexican villages. It reveals something about Mexican culture but far more about the universal need for acceptance by one's fellow man.

742. Wier, Ester. **Gift of the Mountains**. Illustrated by Richard Lewis.
j   New York: David McKay Company, Inc., 1963. 116p.
Skillful use of imagery and description evoke the Mexican atmosphere and character.

743. Wilder, Robert. **Fruit of the Poppy**: A Novel. New York: G. P. Putnam's Sons, 1965. 317p. o.p.
The men of the U.S. Federal Bureau of Narcotics and their counterparts in Mexico wage war against the forces of the underworld who constantly seek new ways to smuggle narcotics into the United States.

744. Williams, J. R. **Mission in Mexico**. Englewood Cliffs, N.J.: Prentice-Hall, 1959. 186p. o.p.
The story of an American boy living in Mexico during the struggle of Nationalist forces against the Emperor Maximilian.

745. Wilson, Carter. **Crazy February**. Philadelphia: J. B. Lippincott, 1966. 250p. o.p.
The people of Chomtick, a remote mountain village of southern Mexico, struggle to find their place in a world that seemingly has no place for them.

746. Witton, Dorothy. **Treasure of Acapulco**. New York: Julian Messner,
j   Inc., 1963. 191p.
Tony must prove his ability to earn a living from the sea before his uncle will permit him to stay in his beloved Acapulco. Vivid portrayal of a boy's love of home and of the sea.

747. Yanez, Agustin. **The Edge of the Storm**. Translated by Ethel Brinton. Illustrated by Julio Prieto. Austin, Texas: University of Texas Press, 1963. 332p.
Don Limon cannot free himself of the guilt resulting from killing a man in self-defense.

748.   Yanez, Agustin. **The Lean Lands**. Translated by Ethel Brinton. Austin,
        Texas: University of Texas Press, 1968. 328p.
The powerful story of tradition-bound farmers in an isolated region of Jalisco,
Mexico, during the early 1920s, when they are confronted with the likelihood
of the change and progress of the country.

749.   Young, Bob, and Jan Young. **Across the Tracks**. New York: Julian
        Messner, Inc., 1958. 192p.
Betty Ochoa, an Americanized Mexican in a mixed school, is haunted by the
desolation of being an "in-between." Although she meets the problem, she
finds a new understanding of her individual role in society and new pride in
her Mexican heritage.

750.   Young, Bob, and Jan Young. **Amigos**. New York: Julian Messner, Inc.,
  j   1963. 191p.
Sympathy for striking migrant workers brings conflict for an adolescent.

751.   Young, Bob, and Jan Young. **The Last Emperor: The Story of
  j   Mexico's Fight for Freedom**. New York: Julian Messner, Inc., 1969.
        192p.
History of Mexico from the Spanish conquest to the present day, with emphasis
on the 1860s and the ill-fated reign of the last foreign ruler, Maximilian.

PART II

AUDIOVISUAL MATERIALS

7. 16mm FILMS

752. **The Ancient New World.** 16mm film, 16 min., color, sound. Produced and distributed by Churchill Films, Los Angeles, Calif., 1965.
The unique use of animated figurines of the Pre-Columbian Art Collection of the Mexican Government gives the viewer a real sense of movement. The film traces the history and life of the Mayas.

753. **. . . And Now Miguel.** Rev. 16mm, 70 min., optical sound, b & w or color. Parts I and II, 35 min. each. Produced and distributed by Norwood Films, Tuxedo, Maryland.
Film version of Krumgold's book by the same title. The story of a family in the Southwest to whom the traditions of sheep-raising have come down through generations from Spanish ancestors. Portrays their family life and the fulfillment of young Miguel's dream of being accepted on equal footing by his father and older brothers.

754. **Appeals to Santiago.** 16mm film, optical sound, 27 min., color. Produced by Duane Metzger and Carter Wilson for the University of California. Distributed by McGraw-Hill Contemporary Films, New York, 1966.
A beautiful film which documents an eight-day Mayan Indian fiesta in southern Mexico. In the mountain town of Tenejapa, the burden of giving celebrations for the town's patron saints falls on private individuals. These expensive and exhausting jobs are called "cargoes." The film follows two men through their duties, which include ritual prayer and drinking sessions, offerings of candles and prayers, and large public processions of the saint's images.

755. **Architecture Mexico.** 16mm film, 20 min., sound, b & w or color. Produced and distributed by AV-ED Films, Hollywood, Calif., 1955.
History of the modern architecture of Mexico, citing new social advances and developments.

756. **Arts and Crafts of Mexico. Part I. Pottery and Weaving.** 16mm film, optical sound, 14 min., b & w or color. Produced and distributed by Encyclopaedia Britannica Educational Corporation, Chicago, 1961.
Points out the Mexicans' pride in their ability to make classically beautiful as well as useful objects by emphasizing the ancient crafts of pottery making and weaving.

757. **Arts and Crafts of Mexico. Part II. Basketry, Stone, Wood, and Metals.** 16mm film, 11 min., sound, b & w or color. Produced and distributed by Encyclopaedia Britannica Educational Corporation, Chicago, 1961.
Describes the skills and traditions which are components of Mexican craftsmanship. Shows such crafts as embroidery, basketry, onyx carving, wood carving, and metal works.

758.   **Brooms of Mexico.** 16mm film, 26 min., color, sound. Distributed
        by International Film Bureau, Inc., Chicago, 1971.
A poetic portrayal of the dreams and hopes of the Mexican people. Based on
Brooms of Mexico, by Alvin Gordon, with drawings by Ted De Grazia, including
the *Young Girl's Song* and the *Guitar Maker's Song.*

759.   **Cajititlan.** 16mm film, optical sound, 41 min., color. Produced by
        Harry Atwood, R. M. Guinn, and others. Distributed by McGraw-
        Hill Contemporary Films, New York, 1966.
Cajititlan, a highland mestizo village 20 miles from Guadalajara, in West Central
Mexico, was an Indian village a thousand years before the great city was founded.
In this ancient spot, Mr. Atwood made a poetic documentary which is evoca-
tive of the majestic beauty of the land and its people. It centers about a boy,
Cornelio, and his family and neighbors during the course of two days. From
the fishermen at dawn on Saturday until Mass and fiesta on Sunday afternoon,
the film provides an intimate view of an old, but now changing, way of life.

760.   **Californians of Mexican Descent.** 16mm film, 5 tapes (two-track),
        30 min. each. Pacifica Foundation (KPFA), Berkeley, Calif. n.d.
Pictures art, music, drama, and family life of the Californians of Mexican
descent, from a sociological approach.

761.   **California's Dawn. Part I. Part II.** 16mm film, optical sound, 28 min.,
        color. Produced and distributed by Kleinberg Films, Pasadena, Calif.,
        1963.
California history of the Spanish and Mexican periods told with art and artifacts from those periods.

761a.   **Part I. The Spanish Explorers.** Explains the origin and meaning of
        "California." Illustrates and discusses the explorations by Spain. 13 min.

761b.   **Part II. Missions, Ranchos and Americans.** Depicts the founding and
        purpose of the Spanish missions, the Rancho period, the Mexican
        Land-Grant Period, the story of the American take-over, and the
        signing of the California constitution. 15 min.

762.   **Change: Education and the Mexican American.** 16mm film, 57 min.,
        sound, b & w. Produced and distributed by Extension Media Center,
        Film Distribution, University of California, Berkeley. n.d.
Coverage of the 1968 East Los Angeles high school walkouts, including discussion by Dr. Julian Nava and other educators.

763.   **Chicano.** 16mm film, 22¾ min., sound, color. A film by J. Gary
        Mitchell. Distributed by BFA Educational Media, Santa Monica,
        Calif., 1971.
Commentaries from different points of view are offered against the background
of the Chicano Moratorium, August 1970.

764. **Chicano.** 16mm film, 27 min., sound, color. Directed by Richard Moore. Distributed by McGraw-Hill Contemporary Films, New York, 1971.
Portrays the roles of various Mexican Americans with differing occupations in American society. The new Chicano is presented in this film through the voices and thoughts of real people, accentuated with background of traditional music.

765. **Chicano from the Southwest.** 16mm film, 15 min., sound, b & w/ color. Produced and distributed by Encyclopaedia Britannica Educational Corporation, Chicago, 1970.
The story of a Mexican-American family who move from Texas to Los Angeles and their conflicts and problems of adjustment to city life and Anglo culture.

766. **Corn and the Origins of Settled Life in Meso-America, Parts I and II.** 16mm film, 41 min., sound, color. Educational Services, Inc., Newton, Mass., 1964.
A presentation of one fragment of evidence used by the archaeologist in his search for the earliest settled life in Meso-America. Dr. Paul C. Magelsdorf describes his efforts to discover the native wild corn plant from which the modern strains of corn have been cultivated. Dr. Richard MacNeish explains his search for the earliest traces of the domestication of corn in Meso-America. Discusses how these two scientists working together have created a synthesis of evidence which Dr. Michael D. Coe interprets as an indication that the earliest settled life in Meso-America occurred in the central highlands of southern Mexico.

767. **Cortez and the Legend, Parts I and II.** 16mm film, 52 min., sound, color. Produced by John Secondari. Distributed by McGraw-Hill Text Films, New York, 1968. Saga of Western Man Series.
An account of Cortez' adventures during his conquest of Mexico. Maps and views of artifacts and models enlivened by subjective camera work depict the population distribution of the Indians of Mexico, the physical plan of Aztec cities, and the entire fabric of their religious-warrior society. Re-enactments and reading of excerpts from the chronicles written by Bernal Diaz Del Castillo, one of Cortez' lieutenants, bring to life the battles, diplomacy, alliances, incredible treks, hardships, and daring of Cortez' band in its march from Veracruz to the city of Tenochtitlan. Hypothetical statements made by an Aztec warrior express the dilemma of the Indians, caught between a fear of their own gods and fear of the return of Quetzalcoatl in the form of Cortez, who also sought to destroy their gods and end their human sacrifices. Montezuma and Cortez are depicted as representatives of their religion and culture.

768. **Cultural Understanding Series.** Three 16mm films, 25 min. each, sound, color. Denver Public Schools, Denver, Colorado. Produced for ETV use on Channel 6 (KRMA).

768a. **Hispanic Cultural Arts.** Traces Hispanic influences on our language, art, music, and dance.

768b.   **Hispanic Heritage.** Through music of guitarist Alex Chavez, the young people are introduced to the past and present Hispanic heritage.

768c.   **Hispanic Life in the City.** Shows role models of successful local Spanish-surnamed citizens in such jobs as judges, educators, and state senators. These roles provide a positive image to motivate Spanish-surnamed youth.

769.   **Decision at Delano.** 16mm film, 26 min., sound, color. Produced and distributed by Cathedral Films, Burbank, Calif., 1967.
Records in vivid color and sound the drama and controversy of the historic Delano grape workers' strike, beginning in 1965. The argument between growers and strikers is presented as a running dialogue.

770.   **Down Mexico Way.** 16mm film, 28 min., sound, color. Produced by Show Associates, distributed by Cannon Associates, New York, 1965.
Pictures the splendor and beauty of Mexico in scenes of modern, colonial, and pre-Columbian architecture of the nation.

771.   **Education and the Mexican-American.** 16mm film, 57 min., sound, b & w. Two parts. Produced by the University of California, University Extension Department of Urban Affairs. Distributed by University of California Extension Media Center, Berkeley, 1969.
The first portion presents representative views of students, teachers, attorneys, and members of the public and various groups involved in the problem of education for Mexican Americans in Los Angeles. The second portion presents a panel discussion of some of the issues raised.

772.   **El Barrio.** 16mm film, 15 min., sound, b & w. Distributed by United Nation's Children's Fund, New York, 1963.
Pictures a day in the life of a seven-year-old boy whose home is in a city dump in Mexico City. Tells how the Mexican government, with aid from UNICEF, plans to help people like this young boy.

773.   **Felipa: North of the Border.** 16mm film, 17 min., sound, color. Produced by Bert Salzman and distributed by Learning Corporation of America, New York, 1971.
A study of one of the ethnic groups in American society. Shows a young Mexican-American girl helping her uncle to learn English so that he can pass the driver's test and thus maintain his dignity as a working member of society.

774.   **Fiesta Tapatia.** 16mm film, optical sound, 21 min., color. Produced and distributed by Aeronaves de Mexico, New York, 1967.
Describes the experiences of a young girl in Mexico as she vacations in Guadalajara and Puerto Vallarta.

775.   **The First Americans.** 16mm film, 10 min., color. Produced and distributed by International Film Foundation, Los Angeles, Calif., 1969.

Depicts the Indians of North America. The Indians of Mexico are shown in their beliefs, customs, religious rituals, their myths and symbols.

776. **Footprints of the Mayan Gods.** 16mm film, 29 min., sound, color.
     Produced and distributed by Hartley Productions, New York, 1969.
Speculates, using pictures of ruins, on the reasons for the fall of the Mayans, whose civilization created, among other things, spectacular architectural splendors and one of the most complicated calendars ever designed. Views of the ruins contrast with those of present-day Mayan villagers, who celebrate their Christian religion with reverence and fervor and perform folk dances in the costumes and masks of their ancestors.

777. **Guadalajara Folk Ballet.** 16mm film, 40 min., color. Programa de
     Education Interamericana, Texas A & M University, College Station,
     Texas. n.d.
A short English introduction precedes the presentation of the University of Guadalajara Folk Concert and Ballet, directed by Rafael Zemarripa. Songs in Spanish, colorful costumes, and the beauty and tempo of the music make this an outstanding work of art.

778. **The Guaymas Story.** 16mm film, 27 min., color. National Aeronautics
     and Space Administration. Houston, Texas, 1967.
The story of Americans at a NASA tracking station located in Mexico portrays their involvement with the community and their endeavors to understand the native people.

779. **The Hands of Maria.** 16mm film, 15 min., sound, color. Produced by
     Southwestern Educational Films, Inc.; distributed by RMI Film
     Productions, Kansas City, Mo., 1968.
A valley of the Rio Grande in New Mexico is the locale of this film, which documents Maria Martinez, a potter who produces pots, plates, and bowls of such exquisite craftsmanship that she and her pueblo have received many honors and have become famous. A fascinating and instructive chronicle of a remarkable talent; her technique has great significance because of the primitive skills she employs.

780. **Harvest of Shame.** 16mm film, 58 min., sound, b & w. Produced by
     CBS News, N.Y. n.d. Distr. by McGraw-Hill/Contemporary Films, New York.
Originally shown on CBS-TV, this Edward R. Murrow report shows the degradation and exploitation of millions of migratory farm workers in the United States. A strong case is made for federal legislation to improve the living, working, and educational conditions of these people.

781. **Henry . . . Boy of the Barrio.** 16mm film, 30 min., sound, b & w.
     Atlantis Productions, Inc., Thousand Oaks, Calif., 1969.
The realistic portrayal of the anguish and frustration in the life of a 14-year-old boy of Mexican ancestry who lives in the Spanish ghetto of Los Angeles. A sociological look at two years in the life of a Mexican-American boy (whose

family is on welfare and beset with a multitude of problems), his search for identity as he grows up in conflict with his Indian mother, his Mexican heritage, and the Anglo society surrounding him.

782. **History of Southern California. Part I and Part II.** 16mm film, optical sound, 34 min., color. Atlantis Productions, Inc., Thousand Oaks, Calif., 1967.

782a. **Part I. From Pre-Historic Times to Founding of Los Angeles.** Places the history of southern California in perspective with that of northern California, the West, and the nation. Depicts Indian economy and the establishment of missions, presidios, and pueblos. 16 min.

782b. **Part II. Rise and Fall of the Spanish and Mexican Influences.** Stresses the economic and cultural life of the period. Depicts mission life, establishment of ranchos, role of mountain traders and clipper ships and the decline of Indian civilization and Spanish influence. 18 min.

783. **A House to Shelter Me.** 16mm film, 30 min. By Self-Help Enterprises, Inc., Visalia, Calif. Order from Rural Housing Administration, Washington, D.C.

The film, narrated in English, describes self-help housing efforts in seven central California counties. (Loaned for one day only.)

784. **How's School, Enrique?** 16mm film, 18 min., sound, color. Produced by Frager Production. Distributed by The Learning Garden, Los Angeles, Calif., 1970.

A documentary film which depicts some of the educational and environmental problems that are faced by Mexican-American youth. One junior high school student of Mexican-American heritage, Enrique, is followed through a typical day in which his parents' interest in his education is compared to the barrio social pressure. Cinema verite is employed in contrasting the attitudes of two teachers toward Chicano children. Chosen for the December 1970 White House Conference on Children and Youth.

785. **Huelga.** 16mm film, 52 min., sound, color. Produced by King Film Productions, Seattle, Washington. Distributed by McGraw-Hill/ Contemporary Films, New York, 1967.

This chronicle of the first year of the Delano Grape Strike shows the struggles of a handful of Mexican-American workers. The strike symbolizes the yearning of all men for equality. To bring the subject up to date, a brief conclusion surveys the major advances of the National Farm Workers' Association since the end of that first year of conflict.

786. **I Am Joaquin.** 16mm film, 22 min., sound, color. Produced by El Teatro Campesino. Distributed by the Centro Campesino Cultural, Fresno, California, 1969.

An eloquent assertion of identity portrayed through still photographs by George Ballis, set to the Chicano epic poem by Rodolfo Gonzalez. Narrated by Luis Valdez.

787.   **Jose Martinez . . . American.** 16mm film, 29 min., sound, color. Produced by Audio Visual Department, Board of National Missions, United Presbyterian Church, New York, 1964.

A view of life of the major Spanish American minority groups—Puerto Ricans, Mexicans, and Spanish descendents of New Mexico. Surveys the progress made by such groups, emphasizing their cultural heritage and their growing middle class.

788.   **Juarez.** 16mm film, 29 min., sound, b & w. Produced by Teaching Film Custodians with the cooperation of the American Historical Association. Released by Teaching Film Custodians, New York, 1970.

Dramatizes the triumphant resistance of President Benito Juarez and his followers against the attempt by Louis Napoleon to install Maximilian von Hapsburg as Emperor of Mexico. Designed to be used with a text of correlated readings in a program of individualized instruction.

789.   **Lakemont High School.** 16mm film, 18 min., sound, color. Produced by Frederick P. Venditti. Distributed by Anti-Defamation League of B'nai B'rith, 315 Lexington Avenue, New York, N.Y. 10016, 1970.

An open-ended film in which viewers assume the role of a new teacher in Lakemont High School who is confronted with some of the problem incidents which confront teachers in multi-ethnic schools.

790.   **The Magic of Mexico.** 16mm film, 28 min., sound, color. Produced by Humble Oil and Refining Co., and released by Modern Talking Picture Service, Washington, D.C. n.d.

Shows many sides of Mexico: a city of skyscrapers and a small fishing village, busy vacation spots, and isolated beaches—a primitive civilization blended with modern Mexico.

791.   **Making a Pinata.** 16mm film, 11 min., sound, color. Produced and directed by John Simons. Distributed by Atlantis Productions, Inc., Thousand Oaks, California, 1969.

Three young Mexican girls are photographed making various types of pinatas which require only easy-to-get materials, basic knowledge, and imagination. The narrator describes the tools and materials being used while the camera provides close-up views of the construction from beginning to end. Although a good deal of work is involved, the project is not beyond the capabilities of elementary level boys and girls whose creativity may produce a pinata of original design.

792.   **The Many Faces of Mexico.** 16mm film, 30 min., sound, color. Produced by Douglas Aircraft Co. Released by Douglas Aircraft Co. and Sterling Movies, U.S.A., Santa Monica, Calif., 1964.

Pictures the many attractions and diverse activities which are to be found in Mexico, ranging from ancient ruins to modern industrial facilities. Includes views of Guaymas, Mazatlan, Guadalajara, Acapulco, Taxco, and Mexico City.

793.   **Maya.** 16mm film, 10 min., sound, color. Produced and distributed by Geoffrey Bell, 1007 Sutter Street, San Francisco, Calif. 94109, 1969.

This documentary film on the Maya Indian country is primarily a visual experience, with some narration excerpted from John Lloyd Stephens' "Incidents of Travel in Central America, Chiapas, and Yucatan," published in 1841. Aerial views and ground level motion pictures show the surprisingly well-preserved ruins of Chichen-Itza and Uxmal in Yucatan, and Palenque, in Chiapas, in their jungle settings. The temples and palaces, close-ups of architectural detail, carvings, and murals create wonder at the accomplishments of the Mayan civilization.

794.   **The Maya Heritage.** 16mm film, 17½ min., sound, color. Produced and distributed by Hartley Productions, New York, 1970.

This fine photographic survey of the major Mayan ruins in Mexico, Guatemala, Yucatan, and Honduras emphasizes the classic period of architecture, the period of peace that started in approximately 292 A.D. and lasted for 600 years. The narration provides information about the building materials used, descriptions of the ornamentation, and meaning of hieroglyphics found on the stelae, which have recently been identified as rulers dressed in the attributes of deities, and records their ascension to the throne, dynastic marriages, and heirs.

795.   **Maya of Ancient and Modern Yucatan.** 2nd ed. 16mm film, 20 min., sound, color. Produced by Guy Haselton. Distributed by Bailey Films, Los Angeles, Calif., 1967.

A pictorial map defines the areas once dominated by the great Mayan civilization. Other maps show the migration route of the people of Yucatan across the Bering Straits and the location of known Mayan cities. Discusses the function of the cities as religious centers and the purposes of the huge stone buildings. Views of replicas and ruins of Mayan structures, carvings, sculptures, and various artifacts illustrate the historical section, while live-action photography depicts present-day Yucatan.

796.   **The Maya of Yucatan.** 16mm film, 13 min., sound, color. Produced and distributed by RMI Film Productions, Kansas City, Mo., 1969.

The story of the rise and fall of the great Mayan civilization.

797.   **Mexican-American Culture: Its Heritage.** 16mm film, 18 min., sound, color. Produced and distributed by Communications Group West, Hollywood, Calif., 1970.

A lighthearted and lively film that depicts the song and dance traditions of Mexico, relates them to various periods in the country's history, and illustrates the influence these cultural traditions have had on the music and art of the southwestern United States. The live-action sequences displaying colorful costumes and scenery blend in well with the original watercolor drawings, historic photographs, and close-ups of old paintings. Ricardo Montalban's mellow-toned narration adds to this professional production.

798.   **A Mexican American Family.** 16mm film, 16 min., sound, color.
Produced and distributed by Atlantis Productions, Inc., Thousand
Oaks, Calif. 91360, 1970.
A brief look at the history of Mexican Americans in the Southwest. Shows the
daily activities of several members of the proud minority group, emphasizing
their close family ties, their adherence to the traditional ways, and the problems
they face in an Anglo society.

799.   **Mexican-American: Heritage and Destiny.** 16mm film, 29 min., color,
sound. Narrated by Ricardo Montalban. Produced and distributed
by Handel Film Corporation, Los Angeles, Calif., 1971.
This film will build pride in the achievements of their people among
Chicano students. The film shows the achievements of the Mexican
American in art, architecture, law, education, entertainment, and sports;
it points out that in recent wars Mexicans have become Medal of Honor
recipients beyond their proportion of the population.

800.   **Mexican American: Heritage and History.** 16mm film, 18 min., color.
Narrated by Ricardo Montalban. Available in Spanish. Produced and
distributed by Communications Group West, Los Angeles, Calif. 90028.
The film traces the contributions of Indian, Spanish, and French elements to the
music of Mexico and the Southwest. A historical perspective along with lively
music and dances.

801.   **Mexican-Americans: An Historic Profile.** 16mm film, 29 min., b & w.
By Maclovic Barraza, Chairman of the Board of the Southwest Council
of La Raza. Anti-Defamation League of B'nai B'rith, New York.
History of the Mexican American from the Spanish Conquest to the present,
with emphasis on the last hundred years. Explores development of today's
economic and political grassroots movements. Archive drawings, still photographs and documentary film footage illustrate the lecture.

802.   **Mexican-Americans: Invisible Minority.** 16mm film, 38 min., color.
Produced by National Educational Television and Radio Center and
distributed by Indiana University Audio-Visual Center, 1969.
This film portrays the Mexican Americans' struggle for a prominent place within
the poverty protest movement. Includes views of notable Chicanos: Reies
Tijerina, "Corky" Gonzales, Ernesto Galarza, Cesar Chavez, and Sal Castro.

803.   **Mexican-Americans: Quest for Equality.** 16mm film, 28 min., b & w,
sound. Produced and distributed by the Anti-Defamation League of
B'nai B'rith, New York.
Dr. Ernesto Galarza, noted author and educator, presents a moving account of
the Mexican American and his unceasing efforts to achieve full equality. His
comments are interspersed with documentary footage. Other participants are
Jose Lopez, representing the Santa Clara Valley Skill Center; Armando Valdez
of La Causa; and Polly Baca from the Southwest Council of La Raza.

804.   **Mexican Ceramic Artists—A Series: Donna Rosa, Potter of Coyotepec.**
16mm film, optical sound, 10 min., color. Distributed by Gateway
Productions, Inc., San Francisco, Calif., 1959.
Examines the black unglazed pottery of Oaxaca, ancient craft of Zapotec
Indians. Shows Rosa's primitive manner of shaping, decorating, and firing.
The film illustrates the close relation of potter to materials.

805.   **Mexican Ceramic Artists—A Series: Talavera.** 16mm film, optical
sound, 10 min., color. Distributed by Gateway Productions, Inc.,
San Francisco, Calif., 1959.
Shows famous Spanish techniques still practiced in Puebla by family units,
their skillful use of the potter's wheel and traditional Moorish shapes and designs.

806.   **Mexican Ceramics.** 16mm film, 18 min., color, sound. Distributed by
Bailey Films, Inc., Los Angeles, Calif., 1967.
Pictures low fire pottery making in Mexico as it was done by primitive methods
before the pottery wheel, and shows the manufacture of blue and white and
polychrome high fire pottery of Puebla. Shows some of the leading craftsmen
of Tonala, Metapec, Coyotepec, and Puebla as they throw, paint, model, and
fire pottery and ceramic sculpture.

807.   **Mexican Foods—The American Way.** 16mm film, optical sound, 14
min., color. Produced by Gebhardt Mexican Foods Company. Distributed by Modern Talking Pictures Service, Washington, D.C. n.d.
Presents the history of the Americanization of Mexican foods, and presents
recipes. Features Pedro Gonzalez in scenes from the old Southwest.

808.   **Mexican Handcraft and Folk Art.** 16mm film, 11 min., color, b & w,
sound. 2nd ed. Produced and distributed by Coronet Instructional
Films, Chicago, 1969.
The film shows some of the handcrafts for which Mexico is famous, and relates
them to the resources of the land, the skills of the people, and the cultural
influences of Mexico's past and present.

809.   **Mexican Impressions.** 16mm film, 15 min., color, sound. Produced by
Audio Productions, New York, 1962, for American Airlines.
Shows the historical and cultural aspects of Mexico as well as standard tourist
attractions, set against a background of native music.

810.   **Mexican Maize.** 16mm film optical sound, 10 min., color. Produced
by American Museum of Natural History and distributed by Seymour
Hymowitz, New York, 1962.
Pictures an Indian family living in the mountain region of Guerro, in southwestern Mexico, as they prepare the soil, plant seed, and care for the corn plants.

811.   **Mexican Moods.** 16mm film, 11 min., sound, color. Distributed by
the Office of the Coordinator of Inter-American Affairs, Washington,
D.C. n.d.

Describes various aspects of Mexico, including the celebration of Mexico's admittance to the United Nations, silver making in Taxco, airports throughout the country, Aztec ruins and rituals, and Mexican comedian Cantinflas.

812. **Mexican or American.** 16mm film, 17 min., sound, color. Distributed by Atlantis Production, Inc., Thousand Oaks, Calif., 1970.
A study of the conflicting cultural pressures from the Anglo and the Latin world in the life of a Mexican-American family. Emphasizes the vocational and professional decisions faced by the father as the head of the family.

813. **Mexican Rebellion.** 16mm film, optical sound, 29 min., b & w. Distributed by San Francisco Newsreel, San Francisco, Calif., 1968.
Follows the initial stages of the Mexican student rebellion during the summer of 1968. Compiled from stills, films, and film clips made by the students.

814. **Mexican Village Life.** 16mm film, 14 min., sound, color. With teacher's study guide. Produced and distributed by Coronet Instructional Film, Chicago, 1965.
Observes village life in Mexico by following the daily experiences of a young Mexican boy. Shows his family, their dress, work, and home, and the village market. Presents the contrast in rural and urban living through scenes of a visit to Mexico City.

815. **Mexican War Diary—1846.** 16mm film, optical sound, 16 min., color, b & w. Produced by Walter P. Lewissohn, American Foundation, Inc., and distributed by Coronet Films, Chicago, 1966.
A young soldier's daily military and romantic notes describe the Mexican War. Narrative and folk songs accompany watercolors of the period.

816. **Mexican Watercolor.** 16mm film, 14 min., sound, color. Produced and distributed by Show Association Films, New York, 1965.
Uses a quick-paced tour of Mexico, from Acapulco to Taxco, to present feminine apparel of the J. C. Penney Company.

817. **Mexico, a Changing Land.** 16mm, 21 min., color. Produced and distributed by Alfred Higgins Productions, Los Angeles.
Mexico is today becoming a modern nation by transferring her resources into new products to create a better life for her people. However, change is not a new phenomenon for Mexico, which had attained a climax civilization 300 years before Columbus. The enslavement by conquistadores and eventual independence of Mexico are given cursory examination. Mexico's geography is briefly explored and the changes made in the landscape by industrialization and urbanization are shown. Although the film profits from photography which cleverly employs varied angles and lush colors in presenting artifacts, adult audiences may feel that it is handicapped by its simplistic approach.

818. **Mexico: A Lesson in Latin.** 16mm film, 53 min., b & w, sound. Produced and distributed by CBS, Inc., New York, 1966.

Examines United States foreign policy with regard to Latin America from the U.S. intervention in the Mexican Revolution of 1910 to the Dominican Revolution of 1965. Emphasizes that U.S. policy has historically opposed revolution in Latin America, pointing out that despite intervention, Mexico persisted in her revolution and, instead of going Communist, became the most stable society of Latin America.

819. **Mexico at Work.** 16mm film, 17 min., optical sound, color. Produced by Paul Hoefler Productions. Distributed by Bailey Films, Inc., Los Angeles, Calif., 1960.

The film covers fishing in the Gulf of Mexico, oil wells in Veracruz, the sugar cane industry, corn raising and harvesting, and the rice culture.

820. **Mexico City: Pattern for Progress.** 16mm film, 17 min., optical sound, color. Produced by Paul Hoefler Productions. Distributed by Bailey Films, Hollywood, Calif.

With lively Spanish music in the background and colorful photography, one visits this crowded, busy city—from the old suburbs that used to be plantations to the modern section of homes and the University of Mexico.

821. **Mexico: Giant of Latin America.** 16mm film, 22 min., sound, color. Produced and distributed by Le Mont Films, Northridge, Calif., 1971.

This survey of historic and modern Mexico is a fundamental presentation of the factors contributing to her present position as a leading Latin American nation.

822. **Mexico Harnesses the Rain.** 16mm film, 11 min., optical sound, color. Produced by Charles Hathaway, distributed by Avis Films, Burbank, Calif., 1961.

Compares the old ways of farming with the new as a result of irrigation and power dams. Also shows the resultant changes in the lives of the people.

823. **Mexico in the 70's: A City Family.** 16mm film, 18 min., sound, color. Produced by Frank Gardonyi, and distributed by BFA Educational Media, Santa Monica, Calif., 1971.

Notes that Mexico is one of the fastest growing industrial economies in the world. Portrays the daily life of a Mexican family to show how this growth is affecting the lifestyle of the people.

824. **Mexico in the 70's: Heritage and Progress.** 16mm film, 12 min., sound, color. Produced by Frank Gardonyi, distributed by BFA Educational Media, Santa Monica, Calif., 1971.

Shows the blending of old and new in Mexico today as seen through the eyes of three Mexicans—a farmer, a butcher, and an architect. Points out that Mexicans take a great pride in their Indian culture and the contributions of their past civilizations.

825. **Mexico—Land of Color and Contrast.** 16mm film, 16 min., optical sound, color. Produced and distributed by Neubacher-Vetter, Los Angeles, Calif., 1967.

Contrasts the early civilizations of Mexico with its present cultures, and ancient pyramids and old villages with modern cities, such as Mexico City and Acapulco.

826. **Mexico Lost—Mexico Found.** 16mm film, 21 min., optical sound, color. Produced and distributed by Aeronaves de Mexico, New York, 1967.
Views monuments and ruins which represent Mexico's past. Pictures tourist attractions that a young couple visit on their vacation, including the Museum of Anthropology, the cities of Yucatan, the pyramids, and the crafts area of Mexico City.

827. **Mexico, Part I: Northern and Southern Regions.** 16mm film, 17 min., sound, color. Distributed by McGraw-Hill/Contemporary Films, New York, 1964.
Illustrates the basic differences in the natural settings and ways of living in northern and southern Mexico. Shows the Indian and Spanish influences on present-day life in Mexico, examines the social and economic ties between Mexico and the United States, and discusses the economic and social changes taking place.

828. **Mexico, Part II: Central Gulf Coast Regions.** 16mm film, 18 min., sound, color. Distributed by McGraw-Hill/Contemporary Films, New York, 1964.
Explains why the central plateau is the economic, political, and social core of Mexico. Discusses the character of rural life in the central plateau and eastern lowland regions, describes the historical and cultural background of modern Mexico, and points out the economic changes that are taking place.

829. **Mexico: The Changing World of Carlos Flores.** 16mm film, 16 min., color, sound. Distributed by Universal Education and Visual Arts, New York, 1969.
The story of Carlos Flores, a Mexican farmer, and what he did to overcome the problems facing him and other small farmers who were being driven from their land by changing times.

830. **Mexico: The Land and the People.** Rev. ed. of **People of Mexico.** 16mm film, optical sound, 21 min., color, b & w. Produced and distributed by Encyclopaedia Britannica Educational Corporation, Chicago, 1961.
Illustrates the contrasts between aristocrat and farmer, city and village, and the old and new methods in industry and agriculture. Traces the cultural, religious, and economic heritage of the Mexican people.

831. **Mexico Today.** 16mm film, 28 min., sound, color. Distributed by Rothchild Film Corporation, Brooklyn, N.Y., 1967.
Presents a modern view of Mexico, its cities, churches, and inhabitants. Pictures silver manufacturing, art expressions in architecture, religious observances, favorite tourist attractions, and aspects of the diversity of Mexico's culture.

832. **Mexico, 1200 Years of History.** 16mm film, 23 min., sound, color. Distributed by Educational Systems Corporation, Washington, D.C., 1970.

Portrays the history of Mexico from the crossing of the Bering Strait by nomadic tribes and the eventual settling of some of these tribes into what is present-day Mexico. The final scenes portray modern Mexico.

833. **Mexico's Heritage.** 16mm film, optical sound, 17 min., color. Produced by Paul Hoefler and distributed by Bailey Films, Inc., Los Angeles, Calif., 1960.

Shows the ruins of Aztec and Toltec civilization and explains colonial influence on architecture and religion; includes an Aztec sacrificial dance.

834. **Mexico's History.** 16mm film, 16 min., sound, color, b & w. Produced and distributed by Coronet Films, Chicago, 1969.

An overview of Mexico's history from the early Mayan civilization to modern times.

835. **Migrant.** 16mm film, 53 min., sound, color. Produced and distributed by NBC Educational Media, Santa Monica, Calif., 1971.

Angie relates her personal feelings about being a Mexican American. She takes pride in the fact that her family, like other Mexican-American families, "surround their kids with love instead of material things."

836. **Modern Mayan.** 16mm film, 14 min., sound, color. Produced and distributed by Hartley Productions, New York, 1969.

The story of one Mayan, a school teacher, and the life he leads in the state of Chiapas. Relates how the Mexican government is attempting to improve the lot of these people.

837. **The Most Hated Man in New Mexico.** 16mm film, 29 min., color, sound. Distributed by NBC Educational Enterprises, New York, 1970.

Reies Lopez Tijerina, originally a migrant worker, has become a spokesman for his people to reclaim ancient land grants.

838. **North From Mexico.** 16mm film, 20 min., color, sound. Produced by Center for Mass Communication of Columbia University Press. Distributed by Greenwood Press, Westport, Conn., 1971.

Adapted from Carey McWilliams' book with the same title, this film does a respectable job of tracing 400 years of Mexican-American history—from Coronado's exploration into North America in 1540 to the current socioeconomic status of the modern Chicano.

839. **Not for Any Other Nation.** 16mm film, 26 min., sound, color. Produced and distributed by Ralph O. Lund, New York, 1970.

Discusses the development of religious devotion in the Mexican people from the time of the Aztecs to the present.

840.   **Pancho.** 16mm film, 25 min., sound, color. Produced by Robert K. Sharpe. Produced and distributed by the U.S. Office of Economic Opportunity, Washington, D.C., 1967.

Surveys features of the Head Start Program. Follows the development of a young boy of Mexican descent, showing his miraculous physical and mental change from cretin to normal child through the aid of the Head Start Program.

841.   **People: Bringing Life to the City** . . . 16mm film, 12½ min., sound, color. Produced by Gilbert Altschul Productions, Inc., and distributed by Journal Films, Chicago, 1971.

The customs perpetuated by Chinese, Mexican, Negro, Jewish, Canadian, Italian, and Irish families who immigrate to a city are viewed as contributions to its variety of life patterns.

842.   **Pepito and the Machine.** 16mm film, optical sound, 29 min., sound, b & w. Produced by United Nations International Zone Series and distributed by McGraw-Hill/Contemporary Films, New York, 1963.

Only a relative few of the world's homes have water piped in. Otherwise it has to be carried—sometimes for miles—from well, lake, or stream. This drudgery ties up manpower needed for more rewarding work. In the Mexican village of San Pedro, water was carried three miles. Pepito went to another village and saw the machine that meant clean water and a better way to get it.

843.   **Pilgrimage (Delano to Sacramento).** 16mm film, 1 record, 10 min., color. Distributed by Multi-Media Productions, Palo Alto, Calif.

An account of the Huelga march to Sacramento, which dramatized the goals of the Grape Strike.

844.   **Real Self.** 16mm film, 14 min., sound, b & w. Produced by Guggenheim Productions, distributed by National Education Association, Washington, D.C., 1970.

A look at the cultural differences of minority groups—the people of the black ghetto and those of the Chicano barrio. Describes the feelings of parents and children about the present educational system.

845.   **Salazar Family: A Look at Poverty.** 16mm film, optical sound, 14 min., b & w. Produced and distributed by the University of California, Media Extension Center, Berkeley, Calif., 1970.

An introduction to each member of the Salazar household, in a small community in Utah, and their collective poverty-produced problems. This is a graphic illustration of the inability of existing social institutions to relate to and cope with the needs of the poverty stricken.

846.   **Sentinels of Silence.** 16mm film, 18 min., sound, color. Produced and distributed by Pyramid Films, Santa Monica, Calif., 1971.

Panorama of Mexico's pre-Columbian ruins. Narrated by Orson Welles.

847.   **The Siege of the Alamo**. 16mm film, 21 min., sound, color. Produced by Columbia Broadcasting System. Distributed by BFA Educational Films, Los Angeles, Calif.

Complete coverage of the siege of the Alamo and the later capture of Santa Anna.

848.   **Siqueiros—"El Maestro"—March of Humanity in Latin America**. 16mm film, 14 min., sound, color. Produced and distributed by Encyclopaedia Britannica Educational Corporation, Chicago, 1969.

Siqueiros, Rivera, and Orozco were leaders of the renaissance in mural painting in Mexico. Now only Siqueiros remains to carry on the work of that trio of giants in Mexican art. The artist speaks of his political and artistic philosophy while the camera shows his assistants working on sculpture, flat paintings, and bas-relief, to be combined in a vast work that will be housed in a specially designed and constructed building in Mexico City. A splendid film record of a mural which is sure to become one of the major art works of contemporary Mexico—where the history of art is counted in milleniums.

849.   **Sun Break Fantasy**. 16mm film, 29 min., sound, color. Distributed by Western Air Lines, Los Angeles, Calif., 1966.

An overview of the tourist attractions of seven southern cities—Phoenix, Las Vegas, Palm Springs, Los Angeles, San Diego, Mexico City, and Acapulco.

850.   **Taxco de Mis Amores**. 16mm film, 11 min., color, sound. Distributed by Instructional Media Center, University of Texas, Austin, Texas, 1966.

The song *Taxco de Mis Amores* is heard in Spanish, as scenes of the city and its people are shown.

851.   **This Is Mexico**. 16mm film, 27 min., sound, color. Produced by Sim Productions. Released by Western Woods Studios, Weston, Conn., 1963.

Discusses the history, culture, customs, art, architecture, cities, religion, education, industry, and tourist attractions of Mexico. Includes views of Mexico City, Acapulco, and Yucatan.

852.   **Tijerina**. 16mm film, 30 min., b & w, bilingual. Distributed by University of California, Extension Media Center, Berkeley, Calif.

A film of a speech by Reies Tijerina on the grievances and injustices committed against the Spanish-speaking people.

853.   **Unfinished Revolution**. 16mm film, 54 min., sound, b & w. Produced and distributed by National Educational Television and Radio Center, and Westinghouse Broadcasting Company, New York, 1962.

Relates the rapid economic and political development which Mexico has experienced in the past 20 years. Mexican intellectuals, artists, and businessmen discuss the country's achievements and objectives.

854.   **U.S. Chases Villa**. 16mm film, 3 min., sound, b & w. Distributed by Official Films, Ridgefield, N. J., 1960.

Describes the border troubles with Mexico in 1916 that culminated in Villa's raid on Columbus, New Mexico, on March 9 and President Wilson's selection of General Pershing to head an expeditionary force in pursuit of the bandit.

855. **United States Expansion: California.** 16mm film, 16 min., sound, color. Produced and distributed by Coronet Films, Chicago, 1969.
The history of California is told through graphic materials, historical quotations, present-day scenes, and early photographs. The film begins with the concept that the state was initially an island and continues to sequences that show the state as it is today.

856. **Vacation Land de Amigos.** 16mm film, 25 min., sound, color. Distributed by Joe Kelley Film Productions, Corpus Christi, Texas, 1967.
A tour of Mexico beginning at Laredo, Texas, and at the Mexican border town of Nuevo Laredo. Includes views of Monterrey, Mexico City, Taxco, Acapulco, the Yucatan, and the Mayan and Aztec ruins. Returns to the United States through the Reynosa-McAllen Gateway of Texas.

857. **Viva La Causa—The Migrant Labor Movement.** 16mm film, 40 min., sound, color. Produced and distributed by Denoyer Geppert Company, Chicago, 1971.
Traces the rise of Cesar Chavez's farm workers' union through a series of interviews with migrant workers and union organizers. Shows how non-violence can be used to achieve social and economic reforms.

858. **Viva Mexico.** 16mm film, 30 min., sound, color. Distributed by Sterling Films, Los Angeles, Calif., 1970.
Describes the blend of modern Indian and Spanish cultures in Mexico. Shows views of Acapulco, Mexico City, and various off-beat retreats during fiesta time. Includes archaeological sequences of a visit to the new National Museum of Anthropology.

859. **Viva Mexico.** 16mm film, 17 min., sound, b & w. Distributed by the RKO Radio Pictures Film Company, New York.
Presents the geography and history of Mexico, emphasizing the country's participation in the war effort.

860. **Voice of La Raza.** 16mm film, 60 min., sound, color. Distributed by William Graves Productions, New York.
Narrated by Anthony Quinn, the film gives an overview of the Mexican Americans today.

861. **The Westward Movement: Texas and the Mexican War.** 16mm film, 18 min., sound, color. Distributed by Encyclopaedia Britannica Educational Corporation, Chicago, 1966.
Reviews the causes of the Texas settlers' revolt which led to independence for Texas. Ties the annexation of Texas to issues of slavery and territorial expansion. Points out that the U.S. paid the price of ill will in Latin America and political crisis at home by winning the war with Mexico.

862. **Who Needs You?** 16mm film, 11 min., sound, color. Distributed by AIMS Instructional Media Services, Hollywood, Calif., 1971.
Features a Spanish American boy who discovers that he can derive self-esteem through his relationships with his friends and through pride in his heritage.

863. **Why? La Basta: Chicano Moratorium at Laguna Park.** 16mm film, 12 min., color, sound. Produced and distributed by Cintech Productions, Long Beach, Calif.
Portrays the events that took place August 29, 1970, when Ruben Salazar was killed and a riot occurred in East Los Angeles. The reasons for the events are examined and questioned.

864. **Wings to the Land of the Maya.** 16mm film, 29 min., sound, color. Distributed by Pan American World Airways, Inc., New York, 1963.
Presents the countries of Mexico, Yucatan, and Guatemala, and the island of Cozumel, explaining that these countries are growing in popularity yet are among the least exploited areas of Latin America. Shows scenes of typical tourist attractions, including the Maya ruins of Chichen Itza and Uxmal, and an Indian dance ceremony at Uxmal.

8: 35mm FILMSTRIPS

865.   **The Agricultural Revolution in Mexico.** 35mm filmstrip, 59 frames, color. Encyclopaedia Britannica Educational Corporation, Chicago, 1968. Mexico in Transition Series.
Portrays Mexico as a totally agricultural country struggling to become industrialized and discusses the continuing revolution in agriculture.

866.   **The Artistic Revolution in Mexico.** 35mm filmstrip, 55 frames, color. Encyclopaedia Britannica Films, Chicago, 1968. Mexico in Transition Series.
Presents reproductions of murals by leading Mexican artists to show the art and history of the country and the way of life of the Mexican people.

867.   **Arts and Crafts of Mexico.** 35mm filmstrip, 49 frames, color. Encyclopaedia Britannica Films, Chicago, 1968. Mexico in Transition Series.
Pictures various types of Mexican arts and crafts and discusses how the social and economic revolutions in the country have affected them.

868.   **Assignment Mexico.** 35mm, 9 min., sound, color. 20th Century Fox Film Corporation, Los Angeles, Calif., 1961.
A tour of Mexico pointing out the importance of both the Indian and the Spanish heritage in the nation today. Points out how conditions have changed in the twentieth century.

869.   **Audio-Visual English.** Ten 35mm filmstrips, color, records, and teacher guide. Prepared by Patricia H. Cabrera. Collier-Macmillan International, New York, 1971.
A new series of filmstrip sets designed to complement basic courses in English as a second language. Sets 1 and 2 are designed for the beginning student. Contact Collier-Macmillan International, 866 Third Avenue, New York, N.Y. 10022, for sample kit.

870.   **The Aztecs and Cortes (Los Aztecas y Cortez).** 35mm filmstrip, 51 frames, color, and disc. 1 side, 12 inches, 33 1/3 rpm, 20 min., microgroove (Mex.) International Communications Foundation, Monterey Park, Calif., 1962. Mexico Series.
Describes the migrations of the Aztec people and explains how they chose the site for their first capital city. Gives a brief history of the first Spanish encroachments in Latin America, including the landing of Cortes and the conquest of the Aztec nation.

871.   **The Aztecs, the Maya, the Incas—A Comparison.** 35mm filmstrip, 49 frames, color. Encyclopaedia Britannica Educational Corporation, Chicago, 1966. Ancient Indian Civilizations Series.
A study of the three ancient civilizations up to the Spanish conquest.

872. **Brooklyn Goes to Mexico.** 35mm filmstrip, 9 min., sound, color. Produced by Thomas Mead. Distributed by Universal Pictures Company, New York, 1961.

A tour of Mexico as seen through the eyes of a native of Brooklyn, N.Y. Includes views of Mexico City and its traffic, of Chapultepec Park, of the ruins of the Aztecs, and of Acapulco.

873. **Changing Mexico.** 35mm filmstrip, 43 frames, color. Popular Science Publishing Company, Inc., Audio-Visual Division, New York, 1967.

Describes changes that are taking place in the economic and social life of Mexico today with emphasis on the fields of agriculture, industry, commerce, education, and social welfare. Points out the progress that has been achieved and the major problems that the nation is striving to resolve. With captions.

874. **The Cities of Mexico.** 35mm filmstrip, 72 frames, color, and disc: 1 side, 12 inches, 33 1/3 rpm, 19 min., microgroove. International Communications Foundation, Monterey Park, Calif., 1962. Mexico Series.

Presents some of the important cities of Mexico, including Juarez, Monterey, Chihuahua, Puebla, Veracruz, Acapulco, and Mexico City, and outlines reasons for their economic development.

875. **Civilizations of Early America.** A Series. Six 35mm filmstrips with 3 discs or 6 cassettes, 51 frames each, color, 13 min. each. Automatic. Coronet Instructional Films, Chicago, 1971.

The Olmecs.	**The Aztecs.**
Teotihuacan to Toltec.	**Chavin to Inca.**
The Mayas.	**The Incas.**

Depicts their history, life, and achievements. Available with teacher's guide. Preview available.

876. **Exploring Ancient Mexico: The Maya.** 35mm filmstrip, 41 frames, color. Imperial Film Company, Inc., Lakeland, Florida, 1965.

A study of the ancient cities of the Yucatan Peninsula. Traces the historical background of these ruins, especially that of Chichen Itza, with the aid of maps.

877. **Exploring Ancient Mexico: Pre-Aztec.** 35mm filmstrip, 38 frames, color. Imperial Film Company, Inc., Lakeland, Florida, 1965.

A study of the pre-Aztec civilization in ancient Mexico. Sketches a simple time sequence for the Tolnac, Toltec, and Zapotec Indian cultures. Explores the ruins of four ancient cities: Tajan (Totonac), Tula (Toltec), Mitla, and Monte Alban (both Zapotec).

878. **Exploring the Sacred Mayan Well.** Two 35mm filmstrips and 2 cassettes, 38 frames each, color. Imperial Film Company, Lakeland, Florida, 1970.

A fascinating account of the recent exploration of an ancient Mayan sacrificial well in the Yucatan region of Mexico. Excellent photographs, some taken under water, and narration, accompanied by effective orchestral music, record the expedition from its inception to completion, conveying the difficult working conditions, the long and dedicated hours of work by archaeologists, and the excitement of their discoveries as they first lowered the water level, excavated the banks of the well, and eventually sent divers to the bottom of the lake. The bones of victims, predominantly children, religious pottery and sculpture, and magnificent ceremonial gold jewelry were recovered.

879. **Fiesta Time—Mexico.** 35mm filmstrip, 58 frames, 33 1/3 rpm disc recording, 20 min. International Communications Foundation, Monterey Park, Calif., 1962. Mexico Series.

The Cinco de Mayo, famous Mexican fiesta, is featured in this film. The parades, rodeos, Indian gymnasts, and cultural and handicraft exhibits reveal the gaiety and bright color of a typical fiesta in Mexico.

880. **Folksongs and Cowboys.** Two 35mm filmstrips and two 33 1/3 rpm disc recordings, average 69 frames, color. Warren Schloat Productions, Pleasantville, N.Y., 1970.

Illustrates the cowboy's life before 1836, showing the Mexican influence on the American ranching culture.

881. **A History of Mexican Art. Set 2: Mayan Art.** 35mm filmstrip, 40 frames, color. Herbert E. Budek Films and Slides, Santa Barbara, Calif., 1964.

Describes the Mayan civilization at Dzibilichaltun, Edzna, Kahah, and Uxmal, showing the relationship between religion and architecture.

882. **A History of Mexican Art. Set 3: Ciucuilo, Tula, and a Selection of Indian Sculpture.** 35mm filmstrip, 40 frames, color. Herbert E. Budek Films and Slides, Santa Barbara, Calif., 1966.

A study of the monuments at Ciucuilo and the civilizations of the Toltecs at Tula. Includes some examples of Indian sculpture.

883. **A History of Mexican Art. Set 4: Zapatec and Mixtec Art in the Valley of Oaxaca: Monte Alban and Mitla.** 35mm filmstrip, 40 frames, color. Herbert E. Budek Films and Slides, Santa Barbara, Calif., 1966.

Traces the history of the Valley of Oaxaca, and pictures the Zapotec and Mixtec civilization at Monte Ablan and Mitla.

884. **A History of Mexican Art. Set 5: Aztec and Pre-Aztec Art.** 35mm filmstrip, 40 frames, color. Herbert E. Budek Films and Slides, Santa Barbara, Calif., 1964.

Describes the last two Aztec cultures before the arrival of the Spaniards in Mexico.

885. **A History of Mexican Civilization. Set 1: Mayan Art in Chichen Itza.** 35mm filmstrip, 51 frames, color. Herbert E. Budek Films and Slides, Santa Barbara, Calif., 1967.

Explores the important centers of the ruins at Chichen Itza, explaining the religious significance of the intricate motifs used in the buildings. With captions.

886. **A History of Mexican Civilization. Set 5: Aztec and Pre-Aztec Art.** 35mm filmstrip, 51 frames, color. Herbert E. Budek Films and Slides, Santa Barbara, Calif., 1967.
Describes the Aztec history and culture before the arrival of the Spaniards. With captions.

887. **A History of Mexican Civilization. Set 6: Colonial Art of the 16th Century.** 35mm filmstrip, 42 frames, color. Herbert E. Budek Films and Slides, Santa Barbara, Calif., 1967.
Gives special attention to the cultural fusion which developed in Mexico during the sixteenth century. With captions.

888. **How People Live in Mexico.** 35mm filmstrip, 36 frames, color. Benefic Press, Westchester, Illinois, 1970.
Less concerned with how its people live than with what kind of country they live in, this filmstrip highlights Mexico's discovery, contrasting landscape, early Aztec culture, rule by Spain, and eventual revolution in 1821. The rest of the strip briefly points to current trends in Mexico, including its agriculture, education, sports, industry, government, and international affairs. A scattered treatment in bright photographs and watercolor drawings for quickly introducing Mexico in social studies, history, and geography classes.

889. **Indian Mexico: A Glimpse of Daily Life.** 35mm filmstrip, 45 frames, color. Educational Filmstrip, Huntsville, Texas, 1964.
Oaxaca, living and dressing much as it did before the Spanish invasion, is illustrated with colorful pictures of scenery, special costumes, and dances.

890. **Indian Mexico: Crafts and Customs.** 35mm filmstrip, 42 frames, color. Educational Filmstrip, Huntsville, Texas, 1964.
This filmstrip takes a look at various Mexican villages and the crafts they specialize in, such as Teotitlan, the serape center, and Coyotepec, the black pottery center.

891. **Indian Mexico: Heritage of the Past.** 35mm filmstrip, 58 frames, color. Educational Filmstrip, Huntsville, Texas, 1964.
The historical background of Mexico's culture, people, traditions, ancient dances, and ruins are shown with pictures.

892. **The Industrial Revolution in Mexico.** 35mm filmstrip, 57 frames, color. Encyclopaedia Britannica Films, Chicago, 1968. Mexico in Transition Series.
Portrays Mexico as a totally agricultural country struggling to become industrialized, and describes the continuing revolution in industry.

893. **Into the Silent Land.** 35mm filmstrip, sound, color. 20th Century
Fox Film Corporation, 1964.
A tour of southern Mexico. Pictures the historic sites and ancient monuments
that once were part of the great Mayan empire, including Uxmal, Chichen Itza,
and the island of Cozumel.

894. **Introduction to Mexico.** 35mm filmstrip, 25 frames, color. Produced
by F. W. Hayman Chaffery. Distributed by Carman Educational Association, Ontario, 1966.
Pictures the varied landscape of Mexico, showing the colorful pageantry and
the influence of the great Indian civilizations.

895. **The Land of Mexico.** 35mm filmstrip, 59 frames, color. Encyclopaedia
Britannica Films, Chicago, 1968. Mexico in Transition Series.
Describes the topography of Mexico, pointing out reasons why the country is a
totally agricultural one.

896. **Let's Visit Mexico.** 35mm filmstrip, 42 frames, color, sound with audio
tape, 15 min. 3¾ ips. Educational Audio Visual, Inc., New York, 1967.
The history of Mexico as illustrated by Orozco, Rivera, O'Gorman, and other
muralists adds authenticity to this film.

897. **Life in Ancient America.** 35mm filmstrip, 30 frames, color. Produced
by Isatype Institute. Distributed by Carman Educational Associates,
1966.
Uses authentic photographs in combination with time and flow charts and
diagrams to examine the social life, advanced agricultural methods, arts and
crafts, and religions of the most flourishing early American civilizations: Mayan,
Toltec, and Aztec in Mexico, and the Inca in Peru.

898. **Life of Benito Juarez.** 35mm filmstrip, 34 frames, color, 33 1/3
rpm disc, 12 min. International Communications Foundation, Monterey Park, Calif., 1962. Mexico Series.
Photographed in the actual locales in Mexico, this filmstrip traces the story of a
pureblooded Indian boy who became one of the great presidents of Mexico.

899. **Living in Mexico—City and Town.** A Series. Four 35mm filmstrips,
two 12" records, 45 frames each, color. Bailey Film Association, Los
Angeles, Calif., 1967.
Modern Mexico City.   **Cuetzalan: A Small Town in Puebla.**
Four Poor Families in   **Sunday Market in Cuetzalan.**
    Mexico City.
Mexico City and a small agricultural town in the mountains provide two diverse
views of life in Mexico today. Modern Mexico City has theatres, parks, supermarkets, housing projects, modern buildings, wide boulevards. It also has its
poor, as seen in the strip focusing on four families on the city's outskirts. The
other two strips show the rural side of Mexican life for a closer understanding
of Mexico's heritage and expectations for the future.

900. **Living in Mexico Today.** Seven 35mm filmstrips, 35 frames each, color, 7 phonodiscs, 2 sides each: 1 side English, 1 side Spanish, 12 in., 33 1/3 rpm, 30 min. each, microgroove. Spanish text issued also on phonotape: plastic, dualtrack, 1 reel (7 in.), 3 ¾ ips, 84 min. Study-scopes Productions, Los Angeles, 1960.

Transportation.	**Education.**
Recreation.	**Housing.**
Working.	**Markets and Shopping.**
Places of Interest.	

A socio-economic study of Mexico, noting the effects of the expanding middle class society on the country.

901. **Masterworks of Mexican Art—A Series.** Sic 35mm filmstrips, 52 frames each, color, six 12-in. records, 2 sides each, 33 1/3 rpm, 10 min. each. Bailey Films, Los Angeles, Calif., 1966.

Pre-Classic Art .	**Toltec Civilization.**
Cultures of the Pacific Coast.	**Maya Civilization.**
Teotihuacan Civilization.	**New Spain to Mexico.**

Thirty-five centuries of art reveal superstitions, religions, agriculture, dances, family life, and sports, and give other insights into life as it existed in our continent's earliest civilizations. The series begins with the pre-classic art of 1500 B.C. and includes sculpture, jewelry, ceramics, painting, and weaving through the time of the conquistadores to the recent works of Orozco and Rivera in the folk arts of today. Maps establish locations and dates of the several cultures represented. The remarkable civilizations of Mexico are given reality in this unusually comprehensive exhibition of Mexican art which toured the United States under the sponsorship of the Mexican government.

902. **Mexican-Americans.** 35mm filmstrip, 68 frams, color, and phonodisc: 1 side, 12 in., 33 1/3 rpm, 15 min., microgroove. Warren Schloat Productions, Pleasantville, N.Y., 1968.

Describes the settling of the Mexicans in the United States. Includes information on the struggle of the grape pickers in La Huelga.

903. **Mexican Art, Architecture, and Education.** 35mm filmstrip, 58 frames, color, phonodisc: 1 side, 12 in., 33 1/3 rpm, microgroove. Anne Marie Rambo. Distributed by BFA Educational Media, 1970. Mexico in the 20th Century Series.

A summary of the art, architecture, and education of Mexico. Discusses the influence of Indian art, history, and social conditions on many of the modern artists. Points out the problems in education that Mexico still faces in the rural areas. Includes scenes of statues and monuments which show the Spanish influence and the bold, modern style of architecture.

904. **Mexican Cecession and the Gadsden Purchase.** 35mm filmstrip, 43 frames, color. Produced by Curriculum Materials Corporation. Distributed by Herbert M. Elkins Co., Tujunga, Calif., 1968.

Describes the acquisition of the far Western territory through the Gadsden Purchase. Traces the development of states and the migration of Americans into the Spanish region. From the Western Expansion of the United States Series.

905. **Mexican Epic—Before the Conquest.** Five 35mm filmstrips, average 57 frames, color. Educational Filmstrips, Huntsville, Texas, 1968.

Beginnings.   **Toltecs.**
Classic Maya.   **Aztecs.**
Classic Mexicans.

906. **The Mexican Epic—From Conquest to Nation.** Three 35mm filmstrips, average 56 frames, color. Educational Filmstrips, Huntsville, Texas, 1968.

Conquest.   **Mexico Since Independence.**
Colonial Heritage.

907. **Mexican Kaleidoscope.** 35mm filmstrip, 70 frames, color phonodisc: 1 side, 12 in., 33 1/3 rpm, 15 min., microgroove (Mex.). International Communications Foundation, Monterey Park, Calif., 1962. Mexico Series.

Pictures different types of Mexican people. Shows scenes of present-day urban and rural environments, recreational activity, old and new world schools, and agricultural and social progress. Discusses a bracero farm program.

908. **Mexican People of Today.** 35mm filmstrip, 31 frames, color. Imperial Film Company, Lakeland, Florida, 1965.

A study of the way of life of the people in rural Mexico, including the Mayas of Chiapas, Oaxacan farmers, and Taxco workers. Shows the native and modern dress of the rural people and describes the recreational life of people in and around Mexico City. With captions.

909. **The Mexican Revolution of 1910.** Two 35mm filmstrips, color, one lp record, one cassette. Multi-Media Productions, Palo Alto, Calif., n.d.

Using the Mexican Revolution of 1910 as a basis, and the protest against authoritarian one-man rule as a start, the program traces the change from mob rule to revolution to civil war to revolution again. The use of simplistic slogans is contrasted with the basic problems of Mexico; the approaches used by the revolution and the post-revolutionary period in attacking these problems. A panorama of contemporary photographs, mural paintings, and political cartoons is presented.

910. **Mexican Town, Population 14,000: At School.** 35mm filmstrip, 35 frames, color. Warren Schloat Productions, Pleasantville, N.Y., 1964.

Accompanies 11-year-old Conchita and 13-year-old Juan during their school activities.

911. **Mexicans at Play.** 35mm filmstrip, 40 frames, color, phonodisc: 1 side, 12 in., 33 1/3 rpm, microgroove (Mex.). Anne Marie Rambo. Distributed by BFA Educational Media, Santa Monica, Calif., 1970.
Shows scenes of various forms of recreation in which Mexicans engage. Includes views of fiestas, golf and soccer games, swimming, bullfighting, mineral spas, parks, and plazas.

912. **Mexicans at Work.** 35mm filmstrip, 56 frames, color, phonodisc: 1 side, 12 in., 33 1/3 rpm, microgroove. Anne Marie Rambo. Distributed by BFA Educational Media, Santa Monica, Calif., 1970. Mexico in the 20th Century Series.
Discusses some of the occupations of Mexicans—including farming, mining, and tourism as well as industries concerned with petroleum, textiles, handicrafts. Points out that the country is an agricultural nation with a growing industrial segment.

913. **Mexicans on the Move.** 35mm filmstrip, 48 frames, color, phonodisc: 1 side, 12 in., 33 1/3 rpm, microgroove. Anne Marie Rambo. Distributed by BFA Educational Media, Santa Monica, Calif., 1970. Mexico in the 20th Century Series.
Shows scenes of old and new methods of transportation, including people carrying parcels and loads on their heads and backs, rural families using burros and mule trains supplying isolated villages and farms. Includes scenes of buses, bicycles and airplanes.

914. **Mexico—A Study in Peaceful Evolution.** 35mm filmstrip, 41 frames, b & w. Current Affairs Films, New York, 1967.
Traces the history of political unrest in Mexico from 1810 to the 1900s and describes the effect of recent political stability on economic, agricultural, and industrial development in Mexico. Discusses the role of Mexico as a key link between North America and the developing nations to the south. Emphasizes the efforts of the Mexican government to raise living standards and to eradicate illiteracy.

915. **Mexico City (La Ciudad de Mexico).** 35mm filmstrip, 73 frames, color, phonodisc: 1 side, 12 in., 33 1/3 rpm, 21 min., microgroove (Mex.). International Communication Foundation, Monterey Park, Calif., 1962. Mexico Series.
Pictures a visit to Mexico City showing why it is the focal point of the economic, political, and cultural life of Mexico. Discusses the industrial development of the country. Shows events in the daily life of a skilled worker and includes views of the city school that his children attend.

916. **Mexico City and Acapulco.** 35mm filmstrip, 30 frames, color. Imperial Film Company, Lakeland, Florida, 1965.
Shows scenes of ultra-modern city living as observed in Mexico City and Acapulco. With captions.

917. **Mexico City to Yucatan.** 35mm filmstrip, 70 frames, color, sound, 33 1/3 rpm disc, 17 min. International Communications Foundation, Monterey Park, Calif., 1962. Mexico Series.
This color filmstrip takes us to the capital, where we see the farmer's market, and life in and near the capital. Some of the highlights are a pineapple harvest, drying coconuts, a sulphur port, and a fishing port.

918. **Mexico History—Yucatan: The Age of the Maya.** Five 35mm filmstrips, and five 33 1/3 disc recordings, 60 frames, color. RMI Educational Films, Kansas City, Missouri, 1968.
Mayan civilization that existed from around 2000 B.C. to 1650 A.D. is shown by means of its temples and artifactual remains.

919. **Mexico in Revolution.** 35mm filmstrip, 52 frames, color. Encyclopaedia Britannica Films, Chicago, 1965. Mexico in Transition Series.
Describes Mexico as a totally agricultural country struggling to become industrialized, and shows the continuing revolutions in agriculture, industry, education, and art.

920. **Mexico in the 70's Series.** Six 35mm filmstrips, color, 3 disc or 5 cassettes. Automatic or manual, study guide. Preview available. Distributed by BFA Educational Media, Division of Columbia Broadcasting System, Santa Monica, Calif., 60404.

Foods.	**Indians and Their Heritage.**
Handicrafts.	**Housing—Village and City**
Fine Arts and Architecture.	**Recreation.**

Presents cultural changes resulting from industrialization and increased technological advances in Mexico in the 1970s.

921. **Mexico: Landform, Climate, Vegetation.** 35mm filmstrip, 35 frames, color. Budek Films and Slides, Santa Barbara, Calif., 1965.
Describes the differences in landforms, climate, vegetation, economy, and cultural activities of the eastern lowlands, the central plateau, and the southern lowlands of Mexico. With captions.

922. **Mexico Lost—Mexico Found.** 16mm film, 21 min., sound, color. Made by Shaw Associates, distributed by Aeronaves de Mexico, S.A., 1967.
Presents views of some of the monuments and ruins which represent Mexico's past. Pictures various tourist attractions that a young couple visits on their vacation, including the Museum of Anthropology, the city of Yucatan, the pyramids, and the craft areas of Mexico City.

923. **Mexico, Our Next Door Neighbor. Parts I and II.** Two 35mm filmstrips, 45 frames each, color. Produced by Psfom Productions. Distributed by McGraw-Hill/Contemporary Films, New York. n.d.
Provides an introduction to and an overview of the country. Illustrates the

scenic wonders, peoples, ancient origins, customs, climate, products, transportation, industries, and flora and fauna. With captions.

924.   **Mexico, Our Southern Neighbor.** 35mm filmstrip, 40 frames, color.
         Popular Science Publishing Company, Inglewood, Calif., 1956.
Presents pictures of various parts of Mexico from large haciendas and great
urban centers to small villages and farms. Depicts ancient Aztec glories. With
captions.

925.   **Mexico. Parts I and II.** Two 35mm filmstrips, 39 frames each, color.
         McGraw-Hill, New York, 1965.
Discusses the problems of the country growing out of natural environments,
cultural heritage, and present-day economic, social, and political activities.

925a.   **I. Northern and Southern Regions.** Describes the differences in land-
         forms, climate, and culture in Mexico and shows how life in northern
         Mexico differs from life in the southern region.

925b.   **II. Central and Gulf Coast Regions.** Shows farming methods and the
         way of life of the people who live in the Central Plateau of Mexico.
         Pictures Mexico City as a tourist attraction and as the center of the
         nation's commerce, government, and education. Includes views of a
         fiesta, of monuments, and of the seaport city of Veracruz.

926.   **Mexico, the Country and Its People, No. 1: Pre-Columbian Mexico.**
         35mm filmstrip, 37 frames, color, phonodisc: 1 side, 10 in., 33 1/3
         rpm, 10 min., microgroove. Filmstrip House, New York, 1965.
A view of the early Indians of Mexico—where they came from, how they lived,
and the civilization they developed. Discusses the geography of the country, and
the languages, folkways, art, and music of the country.

927.   **Mexico, the Country and Its People, No. 2: The Spanish Colonial
         Period.** 35mm filmstrip, 41 frames, color, phonodisc: 1 side, 10 in.,
         33 1/3 rpm, 10 min., microgroove. Filmstrip House, New York, 1965.
Dramatizes the conquest of the Aztecs by Cortes and shows the spread of
Spanish influence—religion, education, exploitation, and economic development.

928.   **Mexico, the Country and Its People, No. 3: First Century of Indepen-
         dence.** 35mm filmstrip, 33 frames, color, phonodisc: 1 side, 10 in.,
         33 1/3 rpm, 10 min., microgroove. Filmstrip House, New York, 1965.
Surveys the first hundred years of the attempts of the Mexicans to govern themselves (1821-1921). Highlights the lack of education and preparation for self-
government, foreign interference, recurring dictatorships, the 1910 revolution,
and the slow emergence of a distinctive Mexican civilization.

929.   **Mexico, the Country and Its People, No. 4: Modern Mexico.** 35mm
         filmstrip, 37 frames, color, phonodisc: 1 side, 10 min., microgroove.
         Filmstrip House, New York, 1965.
Emphasizes recent economic and cultural developments and the current

problems of agricultural poverty and limited educational opportunities which are characteristic of modern Mexico. Includes many examples of art and architecture.

930.   **Mexico, the Land and Its History (La tierra y su historia).** 35mm filmstrip, 75 frames, color, phonodisc: 1 side, 12 in., 33 1/3 rpm, 14 min., microgroove. International Communications Foundation, Monterey Park, Calif., 1962. Mexico Series.
Illustrates the geographic and historic setting in which the Mexican nation has developed, discussing the basic geographic features, vegetation, and animal life. Shows how the native materials were adapted to suit human needs and presents the struggle for independence up to the present time.

931.   **Mexico's History.** 35mm filmstrip, 42 frames, color, phonodisc: 1 side, 12 in., 33 1/3 rpm, microgroove. Anne Marie Rambo. Distributed by BFA Educational Media, Santa Monica, California, 1970.
Traces the history of Mexico, including the 300-year exploitative rule of the Spanish rebellions led by Hidalgo and Morelos, Benito Juarez's crusade for reform, and the dictatorship of Porfirio Diaz.

932.   **Mexico's History.** 35mm filmstrip, 43 frames, color, sound. Encyclopaedia Britannica Educational Corporation, Chicago, 1968. Mexico in Transition.
Briefly recounts the contributions of Mexico's ancient Indian civilizations, the invasion, conquest, and exploitation of natives by the Spanish in the nineteenth century, and the early twentieth century land reform gained by the common people of Mexico.

933.   **Mexico's Physical Heritage.** 35mm filmstrip, 50 frames, color, phonodisc, 1 side, 12 in., 33 1/3 rpm, microgroove. Anne Marie Rambo. Distributed by BFA Educational Media, Santa Monica, Calif., 1970. Mexico in the 20th Century Series.
Describes the geography of Mexico pointing out that it has climatic regions ranging from hot, tropical jungles to snowy mountain ranges. Includes scenes of the highlands and of the Yucatan Peninsula.

934.   **The Mid-Atlantic. Part 2: Later Waves of Immigration.** 35mm filmstrip, 76 frames, color, phonodisc: 2 sides, 10 in., 33 1/3 rpm, 15 min., Filmstrip House, New York, 1970.
Cites the contribution of each major national group of immigrants. Discusses migration in the mid-Atlantic States and the present-day black and white situation.

935.   **Minorities Have Made America Great. Part II, Mexican-Americans.** 35mm filmstrip, color, lp record. Warren Schloat Productions, Inc., Pleasantville, N.Y. n.d.
This film traces the story of the Mexican Americans from early in American history to the present time, relating their accomplishments, their struggles, and the obstacles they have faced.

936.　**Modern Mexico: The Dynamic Northeast.** 35mm filmstrip, color, 3 strips, 49 frames, 57 frames, 55 frames. Educational Filmstrips, Huntsville, Texas, 1966.
Contents: 1) History and development; 2) Geography and economy; 3) Family life and recreation.

937.　**Nations of Today—Mexico: The Country and Its People.** Four 35mm filmstrips and two 33 1/3 disc recordings, color. Filmstrip House, New York, 1965.
The distinctive Mexican culture, a blend of the Spanish and the Indian, is covered in these filmstrips, which show the pre-Columbian background, the conquest, the revolutions and succession of dictatorships, and modern Mexico. Strips are 37, 41, 33, and 37 frames, respectively; each takes 10 minutes.

938.　**Northern Mexico and the Central Highlands.** 35mm filmstrip, 45 frames, color, and phonodisc: 1 side, 12 in., 33 1/3 rpm, 16 min. Society for Visual Education, Chicago, 1967.
Compares the New Mexico with the old. Points out the influence of the Aztec who established a great empire in the valley of Mexico, and that of the Spaniards, who conquered Mexico in 1521. Examines the major sources of income—farming, industry, and tourism.

939.　**The People of Mexico.** 35mm filmstrip, 52 frames, color. Encyclopaedia Britannica Film Corporation, Chicago, 1965. Mexico in Transition Series.
Describes the people of Mexico and their part in the continuing revolutions in agriculture and industry, education and art.

940.　**La Raza.** 24 35mm filmstrips and 12 33 1/3 rpm disc recordings, 45 to 52 frames, color. Multi-Media Productions, Palo Alto, Calif.
An excellent series which cover material from Montezuma to Chavez. Good comparative approach in a classroom situation, and a good reference source to offer. Each lesson consists of two color filmstrips and one record. Comprehensive teacher's manual. Each of the programs is available in Spanish or English.

THE PIONEER HERITAGE

940a.　**The Far Frontier.** Northward expansion of New Spain. Motives of gold, land, religion, and protection of the frontiers. Early exploration and settlement of borderlands.

940b.　**The First Pioneers.** Settlement of the borderlands. Development of differing societies in different locations.

THE AWAKENING

940c.　**Awakening: The Great Migration.** Emigration of thousands of Mexicans to the United States. Revitalization of folk culture in the United States. The bracero program. The Mexican-American contribution to economic development in industry and agriculture.

940d.   **Awakening: The New Experiences.** Discrimination: examples, reactions, and solutions. Education, including problems and advantages of bilingual education.

940e.   **Awakening: The Political Experience.** Mexican-American social and political awakening. Individualism in politics. Efforts to unite politically: the movements and the men. The story of Reies Tijerina (New Mexico).

940f.   **Awakening: Huelga.** Early unionization and strikes. Cesar Chavez and the farm labor movement; the story of the Delano, California, strike. Spread of the movement in the Southwest.

THE MEXICAN HERITAGE

940g.   **Of Gods and Men.** Development of civilization in pre-Hispanic Middle America. Emergence of theocratic, militarist societies. Establishment of the Aztec Empire.

940h.   **Mexico of the Indians.** Daily life in pre-Hispanic Mexico. Advanced civilization of the Aztecs.

940i.   **Twilight of the Gods.** The Spanish Conquest of Mexico. Consolidation and cultural synthesis; combination of Spanish and Indian in development of Mexican folk culture.

CONFLICT OF CULTURES

940j.   **Conflict of Cultures: Invasion of the Borderlands.** Early entrance into life of the borderlands: trappers, Santa Fe Trail, pioneer settlement in Texas and formation of the Texas Republic. Effects on Mexican population.

940k.   **Conflict of Cultures: Conquest of the Borderlands.** Mexican-American war. The Treaty of Guadalupe Hidalgo and its heritage of bitterness. The California gold rush and the contribution of Mexican miners. Aftermath of war. The loss of land grants.

940l.   **Revolution.** Mexican Revolution (1910 to the present) and its effect on the society and culture of the borderlands. Political changes. The rural revolution, chaos, and immigration to the United States.

941.   **Revolution: China and Mexico.** 35mm filmstrip. Set disc or cassette, automatic and manual, color and b & w. 2 strips with 2 discs or 2 cassettes, 108 frames each, 20 min. each. Produced by World Law Fund. Distributed by Current Affairs Films, New York, 1971.
Explores two revolutions of the twentieth century, showing how major changes brought on by the revolutionary process in Mexico and China resulted in significantly different consequences. Narrated against background of authentic music and outstanding works of art. Teacher's guide available.

942.   **Seeing Mexico.** Six 35mm filmstrips and three 33 1/3 disc recordings, color. Coronet Films, Chicago. n.d.
A series of filmstrips showing modern and historic Mexico.

151

943.   **Seeing Mexico, No. 1.** 35mm filmstrip, 51 frames, phonodisc: 1 side, 12 in. 33 1/3 rpm. Coronet Instructional Films, Chicago, 1968. With user's guide.

Uses photographs and maps to illustrate the variety of land forms and climates in Mexico, including the Central Plateau, the Sierra Madres, and the coastal lowlands.

944.   **Seeing Mexico, No. 2: Agriculture.** 35mm filmstrip, 52 frames, color, phonodisc: 1 side, 12 in., 33 1/3 rpm, 11 min. Coronet Instructional Films, Chicago, 1968. With user's guide.

Describes how and where the principal agricultural products of Mexico are arised, points out some of the factors that limit agricultural production, and shows some of the methods being used to overcome some of the farming problems.

945.   **Seeing Mexico, No. 3: Industry and Commerce.** 35mm filmstrip, 52 frames, color, phonodisc: 1 side, 12 in., 33 1/3 rpm, 12 min. Coronet Instructional Films, Chicago, 1968. With user's guide.

Discusses such industries as textiles, steels, and chemicals. Notes that important exports such as agricultural products and raw materials are traded for machinery and transportation equipment.

946.   **Seeing Mexico, No. 4: Its People.** 35mm filmstrip, 54 frames, color, phonodisc: 1 side, 12 in., 33 1/3 rpm, 13 min. Coronet Instructional Films, Chicago, 1968. With user's guide.

Describes the differences in ways of life in the small towns and in the cities of Mexico.

947.   **Seeing Mexico, No. 5: Its History.** 35mm filmstrip, 54 frames, color, phonodisc: 1 side, 12 in., 33 1/3 rpm, 15 min. Coronet Instructional Films, Chicago, 1968. With user's guide.

Traces the history of Mexico from the ancient Mayans through the conquests and the revolutions to the establishment of a constitutional government similar to that of the United States.

948.   **Seeing Mexico, No. 6: Its Culture.** 35mm filmstrip, 45 frames, color, phonodisc: 1 side, 12 in., 33 1/3 rpm, 11 min. Coronet Instructional Films, Chicago, 1968. With user's guide.

Describes the Indian, Spanish, and Mestizo cultures in Mexico, and shows some of the murals, mosaics, handicrafts, and architecture produced by the different cultures.

949.   **Spain in the New World.** 35mm filmstrip, 78 frames, color. Produced by Producers' Color Service, Detroit. Distributed by Encyclopaedia Britannica Educational Corporation, Chicago, 1968.

Examines a Mexican colony as a prototype of the kind of colony that the Spanish established in the New World.

950. **Spanish Mexico—A Series.** Three 35mm filmstrips, average 57 frames, color. Educational Filmstrips, Huntsville, Texas, 1968.
This filmstrip gives an understanding of the blend of Spanish and Indian influences in the development of the Mexican culture.

951. **Spanish Mexico: The Heartlands.** 35mm filmstrip, 58 frames, color. Educational Filmstrips, Huntsville, Texas, 1968. With manual.
Describes the heartlands of Mexico and their surrounding areas. With captions.

952. **Spanish Mexico: The Spanish Heritage.** 35mm filmstrip, 57 frames, color. Educational Filmstrips, Huntsville, Tex., 1968. With manual.
Traces the Spanish heritage of Mexico through her art, architecture, and customs. With captions.

953. **Spanish-American Leaders of the 20th Century.** Eight 35mm filmstrips and four 33 1/3 disc recordings, color. International Book Corporation, Miami, Florida, 1971.
Biographical filmstrips presenting the personal achievements and contributions to American life of various Spanish-American leaders, including Cesar Chavez, Henry Gonzales, Leopold Sanchez, and Jose Feliciano.

954. **The Story of the Spanish-Speaking American.** 35mm filmstrip, 41 frames, color. Eye Gate House, Jamaica, N.Y., 1966. With teacher's manual. The Story of America's People, Series 1, No. 4.
Discusses such famous Spanish explorers as Columbus, Pizarro, Cortez, and Ponce De Leon. Describes the struggle for Mexican Independence, the war, and purchase of Mexican lands. Discusses the contributions of Spanish-speaking Americans to the United States.

955. **A Trip Through Southern Mexico.** 35mm filmstrip, 62 frames, color, discs: 1 side, 12 in., 33 1/3 rpm, 19 min., microgroove. Communications Foundation, Monterey Park, Calif., 1962. With teacher's study guide. Mexico Series.
Presents the geography, history, and living conditions of the area south of Mexico City, pointing out the various Indian cultures, and showing the ruins of Alban and Mitla. Uses a visit to rural markets to explore the economy of the area.

956. **A Trip to Mexico City, Part 1.** 35mm filmstrip, 64 frames, color, disc: 1 side, 12 in., 33 1/3 rpm, 12 min., microgroove. International Communications Foundation, Monterey Park, Calif., 1962. With teacher's guide. Mexico Series.
Recreates the geographic and historic setting in which the present Mexican nation has developed, using photographs of ancient times to present the cultural background. Surveys the struggle for independence to the present time.

957. **A Trip to Mexico City, Part 2.** 35mm filmstrip, 71 frames, color, disc: 1 side, 12 in., 33 1/3 rpm, 15 min., microgroove. International

Communications Foundation, Monterey Park, Calif., 1962. With
teacher's guide. Mexico Series.
Illustrates the various degrees of development in transportation and communication facilities in Mexico City. Pictures the tropical vegetation, birds, animals,
and crops, and shows how the Mexican people use the vegetation and animal
life which grow in the area.

958.   **We Are All Brothers**. 35mm filmstrip, 53 frames, color. Teacher's
        guide and pamphlet written by anthropologists Ruth Benedict and
        Gene Weltfish. Public Affairs Committee. Distributed by Social
        Studies School Service, 10000 Culver Blvd., Culver City, Calif. 90230.
A basic introduction to the problems of racial prejudice. The filmstrip, guide,
and accompanying pamphlet bring to light the facts that race, religion, and
nationality do not make one man superior or inferior to another. It explains
differences in skin color, intelligence, race, language, and customs; and it shows
how fear and ignorance bring about prejudice.

959.   **Yucatan—Land of the Mayas**. 35mm filmstrip, 70 frames, color,
        33 1/3 rpm, disc, 17 min. International Communications Foundation,
        Monterey Park, Calif., 1962. Mexico Series.
This filmstrip presents a contrast between the modes of life of a Spanish, a
Mayan, and a Mestizo family. Aspects which are included in the film are: the
processing of henequen, the major crop of the Yucatan; the weaving of the
hammock; the marketplace; and the manufacturing of gold jewelry.

9: 8mm FILM LOOPS

960.   **America, the Melting Pot: Myth or Reality?** Super 8mm filmstrip,
        1 lp record, disc or cassette, automatic and manual, color, 64 frames,
        18 min. Current Affairs Films, New York, 1971.
Shows why some ethnic groups have found it more difficult than others to
become assimilated into America's national life. Explores validity of "melting
pot" concept. Previews available. A detailed discussion guide accompanies the
set.

961.   **The Americana Series.** Includes **The Mexican-American.** 2 super 8mm
        filmstrips, sound, color, 15 min. Handel Film Corporation, West
        Hollywood, Calif., 1971.
Shows the Mexican-American background and his present status in the United
States. Includes teacher's guide. Preview available.

962.   **The Bounteous Earth.** Super 8mm film cartridge, optical sound, color,
        9 min. Produced by U.S. Office of Inter-American Affairs. Distributed
        by U.S. National Audiovisual Center, Washington, D.C., 1949.
        Mexican Fiestas Series.
Pictures two fiestas closely related to the agricultural life of the Mexicans:
Candlemas Day blessing of the animals, and the harvest festival.

963.   **City Life in Middle America.** 8mm filmstrip, silent, color, 3 min.
        Middle America Series with teacher's study guide. Released by Inter-
        national Communications Foundation, Monterey Park, Calif., 1965.
A pictorial study of the ultra-modern and distinctly colonial aspects of the
urban centers of Middle America.

964.   **Cuernavaca.** Super 8mm cartridge, optical sound, color, 11 min. Pro-
        duced by U.S. Office of Inter-American Affairs. Distributed by U.S.
        National Audiovisual Center, Washington, D.C., 1943.
Beautiful views of the resort towns of Acapulco and Cuernavaca and the silver-
mining town of Taxco.

965.   **The Day Is New.** Super 8mm cartridge, optical sound, b & w, 10 min.
        Produced by U.S. Office of Inter-American Affairs. Distributed by
        U.S. National Audiovisual Center, Washington, D.C., 1949.
Depicts the life and daily pursuits of the residents of Mexico City.

966.   **Fiestas of the Hills.** Super 8mm film cartridge, optical sound, color,
        10 min. Produced by U.S. Office of Inter-American Affairs. Distri-
        buted by U.S. National Audiovisual Center, Washington, D.C., 1949.
        Mexican Fiestas Series.
Ceremonies at Amecameca where dancers climb the trail to Sacramento, re-
enacting that part of the passion called Via Crucia. Pictures Lenten pilgrims
visiting the once sacred grotto of Oztocteatt.

967.   **Geography of the Americas.** Super 8mm cartridge, optical sound, 11
         min., color, b & w. Produced and distributed by Coronet Films,
         Chicago, 1955.
Describes the occupations and crops of the three main geographic regions of
Mexico. Includes scenes of farmers, miners, cattle ranchers, factory workers,
and city dwellers. Touches on history and current events.

968.   **Guadalajara.** Super 8mm cartridge, optical sound, 17 min., color.
         Produced by U.S. Office of Inter-American Affairs. Distributed by
         U.S. National Audiovisual Center, Washington, D.C., 1943.
Provides a view of the Mexican city of Guadalajara.

969.   **Guadalajara Family.** Super 8mm cartridge, optical sound, 20 min.,
         b & w. Produced by Paul Hoeffler Productions, LaJolla, Calif. Dis-
         tributed by Bailey Film Association, Los Angeles, Calif., 1958.
Shows the life and culture of a family in modern, industrialized Mexico.

970.   **Market Day in a Mexican Town.** Super 8mm cartridge, silent, 4 min.,
         color. Produced and distributed by Ealing Corporation, Cambridge,
         Mass., 1968. How Man Lives Series.
Presents scenes of a country town in the state of Chiapas in south Mexico where
a family of mixed Spanish-Indian ancestry prepares articles for sale on market
day. Shows the exchange system between town and country on market day.

971.   **Maya of Ancient and Modern Yucatan.** 2nd ed. Super 8mm car-
         tridge, optical sound, 20 min., color. Produced by Guy D.
         Haselton. Distributed by Coronet Films, Chicago, 1967.
This cartridge illustrates the fact that Mayan civilization paralleled those
of other continents, even though it did not reach the same height.

972.   **Mexican-Americans.** Super 8mm film loop, color, silent. Valiant
         IMC, Hackensack, N.J., 1970.
Biographies of well-known Mexican Americans.

973.   **Mexican Ceramics.** Super 8mm film loop, cartridge, optical sound,
         18 min., color. Produced by Randall and Townsend. Distributed by
         Bailey Film Association, Los Angeles, Calif., 1966.
Shows how low-fire pottery was made before the pottery wheel, and the manu-
facture of the beautiful blue and white and polychrome high-fire pottery of
Puebla.

974.   **Mexican Fishing Village.** Super 8mm film, cartridge, optical sound,
         8 min., color. Produced by Stuart Roe, Sunnyvale, Calif. Distributed
         by Bailey Films, Inc., Los Angeles, Calif., 1957.
Shows spinning, weaving, and mending of the huge cotton fishing nets at Lake
Patzcuaro, where fishing is the principal occupation.

975. **Mexican Potters—Clay Art in Old Mexico.** Super 8mm film, cartridge, optical sound, 11 min., color. Produced by Paul Hoeffler Productions. Distributed by Bailey Film Association, Los Angeles, Calif., 1959.
Shows how regional traditions of design and available materials have led to distinctive types of pottery in various sections of Mexico.

976. **Mexican Village Coppermakers.** Super 8mm film, cartridge, optical sound, 10 min., color. Produced by Stuart Roe. Distributed by Bailey Film Association, BFA Educational Media, Los Angeles, Calif., 1957.
Life in a mountain village of Mexico where copper is mined, melted, and beaten into plates and bowls as it has been for generations.

977. **Mexican Village Life.** Super 8mm cartridge, optical sound, 17 min., color. Produced by Paul Hoeffler Productions. Distributed by Bailey Film Association, Los Angeles, Calif., 1958.
Depicts the daily lives of the people in a small village in the great valley of Mexico, showing how the people depend on each other for such simple needs as water, fuel, and food.

978. **Mexico.** Super 8mm film loops, 4 loops, each approximately 4 min., silent, with manual. Bailey Film Associates, Los Angeles, Calif., 1968. Released in 1969.
Each loop documents a specific native industry in an attempt to show that primitive arts are based on utilitarian needs.

979. **Mexico at Work.** Super 8mm cartridge, optical sound, color, 17 min. Produced by Paul Hoeffler Productions. Distributed by Bailey Film Associates, Los Angeles, Calif., 1960.
Fishing in the Gulf of Mexico, oil wells in Veracruz, sugar cane industry, corn harvesting, and rice culture.

980. **Mexico Builds a Democracy.** Super 8mm cartridge, optical sound, color, 20 min. Produced by U.S. Office of Inter-American Affairs. Distributed by U.S. National Audiovisual Center, Washington, D.C., 1949.
Pictures rural education in Mexico, including the government's efforts to bring modern education to a Tarascan Indian group. Included are a government boarding school program for teachers and the work of an itinerant instructor.

981. **Mexico City—Pattern for Progress.** Super 8mm cartridge, optical sound, color, 17 min. Produced by Paul Hoeffler Productions. Distributed by Bailey Film Associates, Los Angeles, Calif., 1959.
The various aspects of Mexico City as seen through the eyes of a middle class family, a university student, and a civil engineer.

982. **Mexico Harnesses the Rains.** Super 8mm film, optical sound, color, 11 min. Produced by Charles Hathaway. Distributed by Avis Films, Burbank, Calif., 1961.

Explains how irrigation and power dams are changing the lives of people in Sonora and Senalsa, Mexico. Compares the old and the new ways of farming and also indicates some changes in city living patterns.

983. **Mexico—Making Copper.** Super 8mm cartridge, silent, color, 3 min. Produced by Stuart Roe. Distributed by Bailey Film Associates, Los Angeles, Calif., 1968. Mexico Series.

Each step in copper work is clearly illustrated from the beginning to the finished piece.

984. **Mexico—Making Ollas.** Super 8mm cartridge, silent, 9 min., color. Produced by Charles Hathaway. Distributed by Bailey Film Associates, Los Angeles, Calif., 1959. Mexico Series.

Shows the Mexican Indians making ollas, large earthenware jars, and how they trade this product for the necessities of life. Stresses the importance of this primitive industry and culture.

985. **Mexico—Net Fishing.** Super 8mm cartridge, silent, color, 3 min. Produced by Stuart Roe. Distributed by Bailey Film Associates, Los Angeles, Calif., 1968. Mexico Series.

Shows native fishermen going out each day net fishing to supply the necessities of life.

986. **Mexico—Net Makers.** Super 8mm cartridge, silent, color, 3 min. Produced by Stuart Roe. Distributed by Bailey Film Associates, Los Angeles, Calif., 1968. Mexico Series.

Shows the handicraft of spinning and weaving the nets used in the occupation of fishing.

987. **Mexico's Heritage.** Super 8mm film, cartridge, optical sound, 17 min., color. Produced by Paul Hoeffler Productions. Distributed by Bailey Film Associates, Los Angeles, Calif., 1960.

Shows ruins of Aztec and Toltec civilizations and explains colonial influence on architecture and religion, and includes Aztec sacrificial dance.

988. **Patzcuaro.** Super 8mm cartridge, optical sound, 11 min., color. Produced by U.S. Office of Inter-American Affairs. Distributed by U.S. National Audiovisual Center, Washington, D.C., 1944.

Portrays a day in the life of the Tarascan Indians on the shores of Lake Patzcuaro west of Mexico City.

989. **People of Middle America.** 8mm Specialists, 4 min., color. With teacher's study guide. Released by International Communications Foundation, Monterey Park, Calif., 1965. Middle America Series.

Presents a fast-moving mosaic of the greatly varied types of people who compose the population of Middle America, as revealed in a study of clothes, living quarters, and customs of the area.

990. **Progress in Middle America.** 8mm Specialists, 4 min., silent, color. With teacher's study guide. Released by International Communications Foundations, Monterey Park, Calif., 1965. Cinematographer and author of study guide, L. Van Mourick, Jr. Middle America Series.
Presents a mosaic of scenes which symbolize significant progress now taking place in Middle America.

991. **Rural Life in Middle America.** 8mm Specialists, 4 min., silent, color. With teacher's guide. Released by International Communications Foundation, Monterey Park, Calif., 1965. Middle America Series.
An overview of the conditions of life in rural areas of Mexico and Central America.

992. **Volcanoes of Mexico.** Super 8mm cartridge, optical sound, 8 min., color. Produced by G. B. Instructional, London, England. Distributed by Universal Education and Visual Arts, New York, 1965.
Presents physical and geological factors which cause volcanic eruptions. Traces the complete cycle of the volcanic Paricutin in Mexico and explains why people continually return to farm volcanic regions despite the ever-present danger of eruptions.

993. **Yucatan—Land of the Maya.** Super 8mm cartridge, optical sound, 17 min., color. Produced by Paul Hoeffler Productions, La Jolla, Calif. Distributed by Bailey Film Associates, Los Angeles, Calif., 1962.
Portrays the ancient cities of Chichen Itza and Uxmal. Shows examples of handicrafts made by descendants of the Mayas and the conquistadores living in Yucatan today. Includes views of the modern city of Merida and the country villages.

10: RECORDINGS

TAPES

994. **Acculturation of the Hispanic American.** Audio tape. Southern Colorado State College, Pueblo, Colo. 81005.
This tape, prepared by Dr. Louis Medina, is accompanied by "ditto" charts for use with the tape.

995. **Ballet Folklorico de Ballas Danza Azteca.** Audio tape. 60 min., Texas Educational Agency.
Various types of dance rhythms are played and sung.

996. **Californians of Mexican Descent.** Audio tape. Pacifica Tape Library, Berkeley, Calif. KPFA Division of Documentaries. Programs prepared by Colin Edwards.
The program contents are: How, when and why they came; The culture they brought; Culture and the question of language; Drama in the Mexican community; Their taste and talent in music; Their dancers and artists; The matter of taste; The question of faith; Their values and psychology.

997. **Distortion of Mexican American History.** Audio tape. Pacifica Tape Library, Berkeley, Calif. Narrated by Dr. Octavio Romano.
A discussion of the "twisting" of facts in Mexican-American history.

998. **Educational Needs of Chicanos.** Audio tape. Pacifica Tape Library, Berkeley, Calif. Narrated by Y. Arturo Cabrero.
Bilingualism, discrimination, and educational programs and needs of the Mexican American are brought forth in the talk.

999. **The High School Student in Mexico.** 6 cassette tapes, 15 min. each. Educational Sensory Programming, Jonesboro, Arkansas, 1970.
Mexico's amusements and cultural development.

1000. **History and Contributions of the Spanish and Why We Should Recognize These Contributions.** Video tape. 60 min. Prepared by Horacio Ulibarri. Colorado Department of Education, Denver, Colo.
This video tape was made on a Sony ½-inch recorder. It is also available in audio tape at 3¾ inches per second, with accompanying color slides taken during the presentation of the program.

1001. **The Interesting and Unusual in Mexico.** 1 reel-to-reel tape, 30 min. Educational Reading Service, Paramus, N.J., 1970.
Touring ancient and modern Mexico.

1002. **Interview with Reies Tijerina.** Audio tape. Pacifica Tape Library, Berkeley, Calif.

160

Tijerina is a leader of the Mexican-American group attempting to reclaim confiscated land grants in New Mexico.

1003. **Mexican-American: An Examination of Stereotypes.** Tape, 8 cassettes with teacher's guide. Produced by Henry Olguin and distributed by BFA Educational Media, Division of Columbia Broadcasting System, Santa Monica, Calif. 60404.
The tape analyzes the sources, development, and effects of stereotyping on both the Mexican-American and the Anglo.

1004. **Mexican-American Series.** Audio tape. Center for Study of Democratic Institutions, Santa Barbara, Calif.
A history and survey tape series.

1005. **Mexican Folk Songs.** Tape. Open 7 in. reel or cassette. 30 min., 1965. Produced by Pennsylvania Department of Public Instruction. Distributed by the National Center for Audio Tapes, Bureau of Audiovisual Instruction, University of Colorado, Boulder, Colorado.
Singing and native instruments are used to illustrate the idea that a people can be understood through its music.

1006. **Teaching English Through Television to a Spanish Speaking Population.** University of Arizona Radio-TV Bureau, 1968.
A series of videotapes designed to teach English to Spanish-speaking adults by using an innovative television format. This approach to learning English takes advantage of television in remote communities where a television set is the day-to-day link with the outside world. It teaches English in a short time to enable the target viewer to negotiate "need situations."

DISCS

1007. **Folk Music of Mexico.** Recorded and edited by Henrietta Yurchenco. LP 33 1/3 rpm. Record No. AAFS L19 available from the Music Division, Recording Laboratory, Reference Department, Library of Congress, Washington, D.C.
A recording of various folk songs of Mexico.

1008. **Loyalties—Whose Side Are You On?** A Scope Literature Contact Record. Produced by Sheila Turner and Robert Mack. Scholastic Records, Englewood Cliffs, N.J.
Actual recordings of a street gang, an antiwar demonstration, Viet Nam veterans, and two Mexican Americans who achieved success in different ways.

1009. **Mexican Folk Dances.** 33 1/3 disc. Bowmar, Glendale, Calif.
This record includes eight popular Mexican dances.

1010.   **Mexican Folk Songs.** 33 1/3 disc. Folkways/Scholastic Records, Englewood Cliffs, N.J.
Alfonso Cruz Jimenez is a blind singer from Oaxaca who accompanies himself on a guitar.

1011.   **Selections from Spanish Poetry.** Read in English and Spanish by Seymour Resnick. CMS Records, New York.
The record includes 28 selections representing the popular favorites among native speakers of Spanish as well as among teachers and students of the Spanish language.

1012.   **Spanish Folk Songs of New Mexico.** 33 1/3 disc. Educational Reading Service, Paramus, N.J.
A group of Spanish folk songs.

1013.   **Tarascan and Other Music of Mexico.** 33 1/3 disc. Folkways/Scholastic Records, Englewood Cliffs, N.J.
Native instruments illustrate the music of different regions of Mexico.

1014.   **Traditional Songs of Mexico.** 33 1/3 disc. Folkways/Scholastic Records, Englewood Cliffs, N.J.
An excellent rendition of the traditional songs of Mexico.

11: MAPS, TRANSPARENCIES AND OTHER MEDIA

MAPS

1015.   **Indian Tribes and Settlements in the New World, 1500-1750.** One 50 x 38 map on spring roller. Educational Enterprises, Inc., Tyler, Texas. n.d.

1016.   **Mexico, Central America.** One 62 x 50 map. Educational Enterprises, Inc., Tyler, Texas, 1970.

TRANSPARENCIES

1017.   **Mexico.** 10 x 10 prepared transparency, color. American Map Company, Inc., New York, 1968.
Outlines, boundaries, rivers, and mountains are shown.

1018.   **Mexico.** 6 multiple-overlay colored transparencies. AEVAC. Social Studies School Service, Culver City, Calif.
Individual transparencies explore Mexico's culture from six vantage points of history, geography, anthropology, sociology, economics, and political science. The 22 overlays emphasize the wholeness of the approach.

1019.   **Mexican War.** 3 vol., color, 10 x 10 transparencies. From the American History and Government Projects-Aid Series. Western Publishing Educational Series, Racine, Wisconsin.

SLIDE SETS

1020.   **Mexican Art.** Color slide sets, 72 slides per set. Sets prepared by Professor James Reuter, University of Mexico. Demco Educational Corporation, Madison, Wisconsin.
An in-depth study of Mexican art.

1021.   **Mexico, the Land and Its People.** 2 x 2 color slide set, framed. SVE (Society for Visual Education), Chicago.
The set provides the cultural background of Mexico. Full-color photographs depict the people, places and activities of interest in the country.

1022.   **Slide Presentation: Mexican Family Life.** Prepared by Jearl B. Nunnelee. Arkansas Valley Board of Cooperative Educational Services, 1968.
Approximately one hour in length, this program provides an in-depth look at Mexican family life in the Arkansas Valley Area of Colorado.

STUDY PRINTS

1023.   **Mexico, Central America and the West Indies Today**. 3 sets, 8 pictures per set, full color photographs with text material on back of pictures. Each set $8.00. SVE (Society for Visual Education, Inc.), Chicago.

   Mexico, The Cities
   Mexico, The Countryside
   Mexico, Crafts and Industries

The photos present the peoples, their activities, large cities and small rural areas, agriculture and other industries, ancient and modern ways of life.

MULTIMEDIA KITS

1024.   **Mexico**. Multimedia kit in full color including 6 sound filmstrips/records, 24 picture-story study prints, 4 games. Society for Visual Education, Chicago. $87.00.

1024a.   **Living in Mexico Today**. 4 filmstrips, 2 records, 4 word games.
1024b.   **Christmas Songs in Spanish**. 1 filmstrip, 1 record.
1024c.   **Christmas in Mexico**. 1 filmstrip, 1 record.
1024d.   **Mexico—The Cities**. 8 study prints.
1024e.   **Mexico—The Countryside**. 8 study prints.
1024f.   **Mexico—Crafts and Industries**. 8 study prints.

1025.   **Multimedia Mexico**. 6 tapes, 30 pupil materials kits, teacher's manual (cassettes or tapes available), 15-22 min. Imperial International Learning, Kankakee, Illinois. Distributed by Miller's Visual Aids, Fort Worth, Texas.

All the excitement, the color, and the vivid tradition of Mexico are captured in this series of six tapes. The tapes, consisting of interviews and reports recorded on location in Mexico by George Volger, give students a unique insight into life "south of the border." A narrator bridges the interviews and fills in background information as students hear interviews with Mexican citizens, join the crowd for a bullfight and step into an ancient monastery kitchen to learn about favorite Mexican foods.

1025a.   Tape 1. The land of Mexico is introduced on this tape, with emphasis on the geography of the country.
1025b.   Tape 2. The turbulence of Mexico's history, from Aztec times to the present, is brought to life through the study of Mexican art forms. A trip to the Aztec Pyramid of the Sun, and a report from the historic Zocalo Square in the heart of Mexico City add to the historical background provided on this tape.
1025c.   Tape 3. This tape examines the influence of religion on Mexico's history and present-day life.
1025d.   Tape 4. Problems and progress in Mexican agriculture are examined through interviews and reports on this tape.
1025e.   Tape 5. Education is a field of many problems in a country such as Mexico, and this tape deals with efforts to cope with the varied needs of students across the country.

1025f.   Tape 6. The fields of sport and the arts—which sometimes blend
          together in Mexico—are discussed. The intense excitement of a bull-
          fight and the smacking fury of a jai alai meet are brought to life in
          on-the-scene descriptions and interviews.

PORTFOLIOS

1026.   **Portfolio of Outstanding Americans of Mexican Descent.** 37 11 x 14
          portrait-prints. Order from Social Studies School Service, Culver
          City, Calif., 1970. $7.50.
37 black and white portraits and biographical sketches in both English and
Spanish of important and famous Mexican-Americans. Among individuals portrayed: Cesar Chavez, Ernesto Galarza, Congressman Henry Gonzalez, Congressional Medal of Honor recipient Rodolfo R. Hernandez, Julian Navo, Congressman Edward Roybal, Ambassador Raymond L. Telles, and Judge Carlos
M. Teran.

1027.   Rodriguez, David, and Benjamin Lelevier. **A Portfolio of Outstanding
          Americans of Mexican Descent.** Menlo Park, Calif., Educational
          Consulting Associates, 1971.
Portraits (11 x 14) of distinguished Mexican Americans.

HISTORICAL CALENDAR

1028.   **Schlitz Mexican-American Historical Calendar.** $1.00. (Schools and
          non-profit organizations may receive free of charge.) The Joseph
          Schlitz Brewing Company, Libraries 10, P.O. Box 1766, FDR Station,
          New York, N.Y. 10022.
The Mexican American Historical Calendar carries portraits of great men of
Spanish, Mexican, and Indian heritage and their significant contributions to the
history of the Southwest. Each day of each month carries information, in both
English and Spanish, about the events that have taken place on that date.

APPENDIX A

DISTINGUISHED MEXICAN-AMERICAN

PERSONALITIES

DISTINGUISHED MEXICAN-AMERICAN PERSONALITIES

INTRODUCTORY NOTE

The achievements and contributions of Mexican Americans to our society are reflected in this brief biographical section. The selective entries include only a few of the many Mexican Americans who have had distinguished careers at the local, state, national, and international level in government, business, education, and social movements. The listing of writers, artists, entertainers, recording artists, and sports figures shows the varied areas to which Mexican Americans have contributed their knowledge and skills.

Names for entry in this section were selected from the literature, journals, and newspapers, and through extensive personal interviews with the Spanish-speaking students on campus at Texas Woman's University, Denton, Texas. The names were then researched using such biographical tools as *Biography Index, Current Biography, Who's Who in Government, Who's Who in American Politics, Who's Who in the South and Southwest, Who's Who in America,* and others.

GOVERNMENT FIGURES

Banuelos, Romana A. (1925–)
    Born: Arizona
    Education: Public schools
Mrs. Banuelos was chosen by President Nixon on September 20, 1971, to be the 34th Treasurer of the United States. She is also President of the Board of Ramona's Mexican Food Products Company, a company started and developed by Mrs. Banuelos. She is Chairman of the Board of the Pan American National Bank of East Los Angeles, which she helped to found in order to aid Mexican Americans.

Castro, Raul Hector (1916–)
    Born: Cananea, Sonora, Mexico
    Education: B.A., Arizona State College, 1939; LL.B., University of
               Arizona, 1949; Doctor of Laws, Northern Arizona Univer-
               sity, 1966
Lawyer and civic leader, Castro practiced law in Tucson, Arizona (1949-1951) and became Deputy County Attorney, Pima County, Arizona (1951-1954). He was elected County Attorney of Pima County, Arizona, and served from 1954 to 1958, when he was appointed Judge Superior Court, Tucson (1958-1964). He was also Judge of the Juvenile Court, Tucson (1961-1964), and was appointed Ambassador to San Salvador, El Salvador, where he served from 1964 to 1968 before going to La Paz, Bolivia (1968-1970), as U.S. Ambassador. Raul Castro is now practicing international law in Tucson. Awards: Outstanding Naturalized Citizen Award, Pima Bar Association, 1963; Americanism Award, D.A.R., 1964; Distinguished Public Service Award, University of Arizona, 1966; Matias Delgado Decoration, Government of El Salvador.

Chavez, Dennis (1888-1962)
    Born: Los Chavez, New Mexico
    Education: LL.B., Georgetown University, Washington, D.C., 1930
Dennis Chavez, one of eight children born into an old New Mexico family, was
appointed to the Senate in 1935 to complete the unexpired term of Senator
Bronson Cutter. The people of New Mexico elected Mr. Chavez to the U.S.
Senate for over 25 years. He served as Chairman of the Public Works Committee
and as a member of the Appropriations Committee. Senator Chavez was a
champion of civil rights and equality.

Garcia, Alex P. (1929–)
    Born: El Paso, Texas
    Education: Los Angeles City Schools; East Los Angeles Junior College;
              University of California at Los Angeles Extension; Southern
              California College of Business
Alex P. Garcia became the first Mexican American to be elected to the California
Legislature (1968) to serve the 40th Assembly District. He was field representative
for Congressman Edward R. Roybal of Los Angeles and a member of the California State Committee on Public Employment and Retirement. He has concerned himself with the interests of minority groups.

Garcia, Hector P. (1914–)
    Born: Llera, Tamaulipas, Mexico
    Education: B.A., University of Texas, 1936; M.D., University of Texas,
              1940
Serving in the U.S. Army Medical Corps during World War II, where he received
the Bronze Star and six battle stars, Garcia became interested in Mexican-
American veterans and was instrumental in founding the American G.I. Forum;
he is currently Chairman of the Board of the Forum. Dr. Garcia is President of
the International Radio Company, Corpus Christi, Texas; organizer and national
coordinator of the "Viva Kennedy Clubs"; alternate delegate to the United
Nations with the rank of Ambassador (1967); a member of the U.S. National
Commission for UNESCO (1968); a Commissioner of the U.S. Commission on
Civil Rights (1968); and National President of the Political Association of
Spanish Speaking People (1960-64). Dr. Garcia is the recipient of the Out-
standing Democracy Forward Award, Texas Conference of Negro Organizations,
1955, and the Gold Medal of Merit for organizational work with the American
G.I. Forum. He is a practicing physician in Corpus Christi, Texas.

Garza, Eligio de la (1927–)
    Born: Mercedes, Texas
    Education: Mission High School; Edinburg Junior College; St. Mary's
              University, San Antonio; LL.B., St. Mary's University School
              of Law, San Antonio, 1952
Mr. Garza is an active member of the League of United Latin American Citizens
(LULAC); was elected to the Texas House of Representatives for six consecutive
two-year terms; and has been the U.S. Congressman from Texas since 1964. He
is a member of the Mexico-United States Inter-Parliamentary Union and an
active civic leader.

Gonzalez, Henry B. (1916–)
>Born: San Antonio, Texas
>Education: Thomas Jefferson High School, San Antonio; San Antonio
>>Junior College; University of Texas; LL.B., St. Mary's Univer-
>>sity School of Law; LL.D. (Honorary), St. Mary's University,
>>1965

Henry B. Gonzales became a member of the San Antonio City Council (1953-
1956); was Mayor Pro-Tem of San Antonio (1955-1956); and was elected to
the Texas State Senate in 1956. He was the first Texan of Mexican ancestry
ever to be seated in the U.S. House of Representatives (1961–); was Co-
Chairman of the Viva Kennedy Organization in 1960 and Viva Johnson in 1964.
Henry Gonzalez has written numerous articles and has worked for better education, better housing, benefits for farm workers, and minimum wage.

Hernandez, Benigno Carlos (1917–)
>Born: Santa Fe, New Mexico
>Education: B.A., University of New Mexico, 1941; D.J., De Paul University,
>>1948

Hernandez practiced law in Albuquerque, New Mexico (1949-1951), until he
was appointed Special Assistant U.S. Attorney (1951-1952). He was appointed
U.S. Ambassador to Paraguay in 1967 and was Chairman of the New Mexico
Chapter of the National Conference of Christians and Jews (1964-1965). He
served on the National Citizens Advisory Committee Vocational Rehabilitation,
Department of Health, Education and Welfare (1963-1967).

Lujan, Manuel, Jr. (1928–)
>Born: San Ildefonso, New Mexico
>Education: B.A., College of Santa Fe, 1950

A partner in the Manuel Lujan Insurance Agency, Albuquerque (1950-1968),
Lujan became a member of the 91st and 92nd Congresses from the first New
Mexico district. He served as a member of Indian Affairs Subcommittee and the
National Parks and Recreation Subcommittee. Lujan is past president of the
New Mexico Independent Insurance Agents Association, a member of the Interior
and Insular Affairs Committee, and was president of the Santa Fe Community
Council (1964-1965).

Mondragon, Robert A. (1940–)
>Born: La Loma, New Mexico
>Education: Albuquerque High School, 1958

Mondragon became New Mexico State Representative, Bernalillo County (1967-
1970); he was elected Lieutenant Governor of New Mexico in 1971. Mr. Mondragon
presented the seconding speech at the 1972 Democratic Convention for Senator
McGovern. He is a member of the American G.I. Forum, the Fraternal Order of
Police Association, and the Executive Committee for Albuquerque Goals for
Progress.

Montoya, Joseph M. (1915–)
>Born: Pena Blanca, New Mexico
>Education: Bernalillo High School, Bernalillo, New Mexico; attended

Regis College, Denver Colorado; LL.B., Georgetown University, Washington, D.C.

At 21 Montoya became the youngest man to be elected to the New Mexico House of Representatives; he served in this capacity for 12 years. He was elected Lieutenant Governor of New Mexico for eight years (1947-1951, 1955-1957). Montoya was appointed to fill out the term of the late Dennis Chavez as U.S. Senator and was then elected to the Senate in 1965. He served as a member of the Appropriations Committee, Public Works Committee, and Air and Water Pollution Subcommittee; he was the Official U.S. Observer at the Latin American Parliamentary Conference, Lima, Peru, 1965, and a delegate to the Democratic National Convention, 1968.

Muniz, Ramsey (1943–)
    Born: Corpus Christi, Texas
    Education: B.A., Baylor University, 1966; LL.B., Baylor University, 1971.
Ramsey Muniz was the 1972 La Raza Unida Party candidate for governor of Texas. Muniz received his law degree but has not practiced law, since he was hired as Administrative Assistant to the Director of the Model Cities Program in Waco. He resigned this position late in 1971 to work on his gubernatorial campaign. Muniz joined La Raza in 1968, when he was still a student, and worked as the party's unpaid North Texas organizer. He is now a resident of San Antonio.

Roybal, Edward R. (1916–)
    Born: Albuquerque, New Mexico
    Education: Roosevelt High School, Albuquerque, 1934; University of
        California at Los Angeles; Southwestern University; LL.D.
        (Honorary), Pacific States University, 1966
When he was a young man, Roybal worked with the California Tuberculosis Association as a public health educator until reporting for service in the Army. After his service in the U.S. Army in World War II, he was elected a City Councilman in Los Angeles—the first American of Mexican descent to be elected in California's history. Roybal represented his district as Councilman for 13 years before his election to the U.S. Congress in 1962. He has been a member of the Foreign Affairs Committee (1965), a member of the Veteran Affairs Committee (1965-1967), and a member of the Committee on Appropriations (1971–). Edward R. Roybal stresses the need for progress in education, health, and community needs.

Sanchez, Leopoldo G. (1926–)
    Born: Los Angeles, California
    Education: Attended high school in Los Angeles; attended St. Mary's
        College and Southwestern University, receiving his LL.B.
        in 1954
As a young man, Sanchez worked as a laborer in the steel mills to finance his education. Serving in the U.S. Army, he became a Technical Sergeant. On his return to civilian life he was elected in 1960 to an office in the Municipal Court and in 1966 to the judgeship, Superior Court of Los Angeles. He is an active civic and community leader.

Sanchez, Phillip Victor (1929–)
    Born: Pinedale, California
    Education: B.A., Fresno State College, 1953; M.A., Fresno State College,
        1971
Mr. Sanchez served as administrative assistant, U.S. Property and Disbursing
Office, State of California (1950-1954); in the Personnel Office (1954-1956); as
an administrative analyst, Fresno County (1956-1957); as senior administrative
analyst (1957-1962); in the Administrative Office (1962-1971); and as Assistant
Director for Operations of the Office of Economic Opportunity, Washington,
D.C. (1971). Mr. Sanchez was nominated by President Nixon, September 1971,
to be Director of the Office of Economic Opportunity (1971–).

Telles, Raymond L. (1915–)
    Born: El Paso, Texas
    Education: Cathedral High School, El Paso; attended the University of
        Texas at El Paso; International Business College, El Paso
Mr. Telles served as an officer in the U.S. Air Force during World War II. Afterward, he served as an aide to both President Truman and President Eisenhower
during visits to Mexico City. With the coming of the Korean War, Telles served
as Executive Officer of the 67th Tactical and Reconnaissance Group. He holds
the Bronze Star and Commendation Ribbon. Returning to El Paso, he served as
mayor of that city from 1957 to 1961, and became Ambassador to Costa Rica
from 1961 to 1967. From 1967 to 1969 he served as the United States Chairman of the U.S.-Mexico Border Commission, and in 1971 he became Commissioner
for Equal Employment Opportunity Commission.

Teran, Carlos M. (1915–)
    Born: El Paso, Texas
    Education: Los Angeles public schools; Juris Doctoris degree, University of
        Southern California, 1949; B.A., University of Southern Cali-
        fornia, 1953; M.A., Claremont College Graduate School, 1966
For the past ten years, Teran has been a Superior Court Judge in Los Angeles.
He served for four years as a member of the Governor's Advisory Committee on
Children and Youth, was a delegate in 1960 to the White House Conference of
Children and Youth, and was President of the Pomona Boys Club. He holds the
rank of Colonel in the U.S. Air Force Reserve.

Ximenes, Vincente T. (1919–)
    Born: Floresville, Texas
    Education: Floresville High School; B.A., University of New Mexico, 1950;
        M.A., University of New Mexico, 1951; study under a scholar-
        ship at Fisk University Race Relations Institute, 1955
Ximenes was appointed research economist at the University of New Mexico and
worked there for 10 years. For outstanding service during World War II, he received the Distinguished Flying Cross and the Air Medal. He became National
Chairman of the American G.I. Forum (1956-1958) and was National Director
of the Viva Johnson group in 1964. In 1967 he became Commissioner of the
Equal Employment Opportunity Commission.

LEADERS OF SOCIAL MOVEMENTS

Bravo, Francisco (1910–)
>Born: Los Angeles, California
>Education: University of Southern California, 1938

Francisco Bravo, as a young man, was determined to rise above his job as a fruit picker in Santa Paula, California. He worked his way through college and in Los Angeles in 1941 he opened the Bravo Free Medical Clinic, where, with the help of his wife, he has aided many Mexican Americans. The Bravo Foundation has awarded numerous scholarships to young people for study in professional schools and colleges.

Calderon, Tony (1933–)
>Born: San Antonio, Texas
>Education: Durham's Business College, 1961; attended San Antonio
>College, 1962-1964; completed extension courses at the Air
>University Institute at Maxwell Air Force Base and at Ohio
>State University

Mr. Calderon became interested in helping Mexican Americans who were not citizens of the United States to obtain old age assistance. He formed a group to work toward changing the Texas law which made it mandatory for the aged to become naturalized citizens before being eligible for the assistance. This law was changed in 1967. Mr. Calderon is the founder and president of IMAGE, Involvement of Mexican-Americans in Gainful Endeavors, a non-profit corporation dedicated to the improvement of the status of Mexican Americans through better housing, education, and wages.

Carrasco, Raymond (1936–)
>Born: El Paso, Texas
>Education: Ysleta High School, Ysleta, Texas; attended the University
>of Texas at El Paso, 1954-1957; B.S., Sacramento State
>College, California, 1965

Carrasco has been a research assistant with Dow Chemical Company (1960-1965); Consultant for the California Department of Social Welfare (1966); and chief of Relocation and Community Redevelopment Services for the Sacramento Redevelopment Agency from 1967 to 1969. He was a co-founder of the Sacramento Concilio, Inc., a council of local Spanish-speaking organizations. Carrasco served as Chairman of the Steering Committee for a proposed Mexican Commercial and Cultural Center in Sacramento and as Deputy Director, Inter-Agency Committee on Mexican-American Affairs. He received the Community Award for Service, Sacramento Community Council, 1969.

Chavez, Cesar E. (1927–)
>Born: Yuma, Arizona
>Education: Through seventh grade

Chavez's parents were farm workers and followed the crops from state to state. Cesar Chavez understands farm workers and is today the champion of the farm worker in the Southwest. He became the General Director of the Community

174

Service Organization in 1958 and worked with this organization until 1962, when he founded the National Farm Workers Association. This self-financed union joined an AFL-CIO union of farm workers, with Chavez named head of the alliance. Chavez believes that worker unions and employers should cooperate peacefully to establish good working conditions. He is probably best known for the Delano grape-pickers' strike, the famous 300-mile protest march from Delano to Sacramento in 1966, and his fast in 1968 that lasted 25 days.

Corona, Bert (1918–)
> Born: El Paso, Texas
> Education: El Paso City Schools; attended the University of Southern
> California and the University of California at Los Angeles

A social reformer, Corona is a founder of the Mexican Youth Converence (1936), the Community Service Organization (1948), and the Mexican-American Political Association (MAPA) in Phoenix, Arizona, in 1958. He has held the office of California State Secretary, State Vice President, and State President in the Mexican-American Political Association.

Gonzales, Alfonso Z. (1931–)
> Born: Sacramento, California
> Education: Sacramento Public Schools; A.A., Sacramento City College,
> 1951; B.A., University of California at Berkeley, 1956; LL.B.,
> University of California at Berkeley, 1960

A community leader, a lawyer, and a Vice President of the Mexican-American Educational Association, Alfonso Gonzales has worked to improve the conditions of his fellow Mexican Americans. Gonzales has become affiliated with various health, education, and welfare agencies in California and was Commissioner and Chairman of the Human Relations Commission of the City and County of Sacramento. In 1969 he received the Dos Rios Parent-Teacher Club Appreciation Award.

Gonzales, Robert E. (1936–)
> Born: Fresno, California
> Education: Selma High School, Fresno, 1955; B.A., University of Cali-
> fornia at Berkeley, 1959; LL.B., Hastings College of Law,
> University of California, 1962

Robert E. Gonzales was admitted to the California Bar in 1963 and has since been active in the Mexican-American community, where he has used his legal experience effectively. He was Vice President and Director of the Mexican-American Legal Defense and Education Fund, and was San Francisco City and County Supervisor (1969).

Gonzalez, Rodolfo ("Corky") (1929?–)
> Born: Colorado
> Education: Colorado public schools

The organizer of the United Crusade for Justice in Denver, Gonzalez, a former prizefighter with a national ranking and once a businessman, heads the first organization of Mexican Americans in Denver to strive for the social and economic betterment of the Mexican-American people. A recent delegate to the La Raza Unida Party Convention in El Paso, he is the author of *I Am Joaquin*, an epic poem that begins with the pre-Columbian heritage and concludes with the plight of Chicanos today (see numbers 488 and 786).

Hernandez, Rodolfo P. (1931–)
    Born: Colton, California
    Education: Fowler Elementary School, California; attended Fresno City
           College
Young Rodolfo Hernandez joined the Army in 1949 and served his country in Korea. He was awarded the Congressional Medal of Honor on May 31, 1951—our nation's highest military honor for individual heroism. A credit to his country, Hernandez has become involved in community affairs.

Lozano, Ignacio E. (1927–)
    Born: San Antonio, Texas
    Education: Central Catholic High School, San Antonio, 1943; B.A.,
           University of Notre Dame, 1947
Ignacio E. Lozano is the publisher and editor of the newspaper *La Opinion* in Los Angeles, California—the only Spanish language daily serving the Southwest. He has served on the California State Advisory Committee to the U.S. Commission on Civil Rights; as Consultant to the U.S. Department of State's Bureau of Educational and Cultural Affairs (1964), and as Executive Director, Commission of the Californias, 1967.

Montez, Philip (1931–)
    Born: Los Angeles, California
    Education: B.A., University of Southern California, 1956; M.A., University of Southern California, 1958
Philip Montez, an educator and civil rights advocate, was a founder and first President of the Association of Mexican-American Educators of California; a teacher at Cathedral High School in Los Angeles; and Director, Western Field Office, U.S. Commission on Civil Rights.

Sierra, Tony N. (1924–)
    Born: Santa Barbara, Chihuahua, Mexico
    Education: B.S., University of Arizona, 1951
This community leader and businessman not only has developed his own pharmacy but is active in professional and civic organizations, serving as the Director of the Imperial County, California, School Boards Association; President of the Board of Trustees, Calexico Unified School District; and member of the California State Board of Education. The American Pharmaceutical Association honored Sierra in 1968 for his contributions to business and education in Los Angeles.

Tijerina, Reies Lopez (1926–)
    Born: Falls City, Texas
    Education: Fragmentary early education; Bible College, Ysleta, Texas
A Spanish American social activist and former clergyman, Tijerina founded the

Alianza Federal de Mercedes (Federal Alliance of Land Grants)—now the Alianza de los Pueblos Libres (Federal Alliance of Free City States)—to advance claims of impoverished Spanish Americans of New Mexico to land which was granted to their ancestors by Spanish viceroys in Mexico and the Mexican government, but was taken from them after the Mexican War.

Valdez, Luis (1940?—)
    Born: Delano, California
    Education: San Jose State College
Luis Valdez is the director of the Teatro Campesino Centro Cultural. He grew up in the field, a child of campesinos. As soon as he was old enough, he picked grapes in Delano, California, where he was born. He left the Valley when he was 14, searching for a better way of life. His search led him to San Jose State College. Valdez has been described as "a young man with grandiose Pancho Villa moustache, a Brechtian poet, a union organizer, a sometime college teacher, and alumnus of the San Francisco Mime Troupe." In November 1965, just two months after the Huelga in the San Joaquin Valley began, he established the *commedia dell'arte* of the farm workers: El Teatro Campesino. In makeshift union halls and at roadside picket lines, with no scripts, no props, no stage, Luis Valdez created a theater. El Teatro's actors were farm workers—his stage, the vineyards. Valdez has said, "We are not a theater for farm workers; farm workers are our theater."

Vallaescusa, Henrietta (1920—)
    Born: Tucson, Arizona
    Education: A.B.A.A., Los Angeles City College, 1941; R.N., Mercy
            College Nursing, San Diego, 1944; B.A., Immaculate Heart
            College, 1945
Public health nurse for the Los Angeles Health Department (1947-1955); Health Service Director, Los Angeles Times Boys Club (1950-1951); supervisory public health nurse, Los Angeles (1955-1959). Ms. Vallaescusa has served as Executive Secretary to Rep. George E. Brown, Jr. (1963-1964); Human Resources Development Officer, AID, Washington, D.C. (1964-1965); Community Development Advisor for the Latin American Bureau (1965-1967), and Community Development Advisor in Panama City (1967-1971).

EDUCATORS

Acosta, Robert J. (1939—)
    Born: Los Angeles, California
    Education: John Marshall High School, Los Angeles, 1957; B.A., Cali-
            fornia State College at Los Angeles, 1961; B.A., California
            State College at Los Angeles, 1967
Robert J. Acosta is the founder of the Blind College Students of Southern California; the Blind Teachers of California; and co-founder of the Northern California Blind Student Organization. A teacher of the blind, Acosta, blind since birth, was named as one of America's Ten Outstanding Young Men of 1968 by the United States Jaycees.

Galarza, Ernesto (1905–)
>Born: Tepic, Nayarit, Mexico
>Education: Sacramento High School, Sacramento, California; B.A.,
>>Occidental College; M.A., Stanford University; Ph.D., Columbia
>>University

Dr. Galarza, a teacher, writer, and sociologist, was also the Director of Research and Education, National Agricultural Workers Union, AFL-CIO; Chief, Division of Labor and Social Information, Pan American Union; and a Consultant to the Bolivian Government, the National Farmers Union, and the Ford Foundation. Dr. Galarza is now retired and resides in San Jose, California.

Gonzales, Eugene (1925–)
>Born: Glendale, California
>Education: B.A., Whittier College, 1950; M.S., University of Southern
>>California, 1955; LL.D., Whittier College, 1968

Eugene Gonzales, an educator, has been active in professional, community, and civic organizations. He is the holder of Life Diploma Credentials in general administration, general elementary and secondary, and pupil personnel services. He has served as Supervisor of Child Welfare and Attendance, and Coordinator of Child Welfare Services for the Santa Barbara County Superintendent of Schools; District Supervisor of Child Welfare and Attendance, and Vice Principal of Walter F. Dexter Intermediate School, Whittier City Schools, California; and Associate Superintendent of Public Instruction and Chief, Division of Instruction, California State Department of Education.

Gonzalez, Efren W. (1929–)
>Born: New York City, New York
>Education: Cardinal Hayes High School, 1947; attended Syracuse Univer-
>>sity, New York; A.B., Iona College, New Rochelle, New
>>York, 1951; M.Sc., Columbia University, School of Library
>>Service, 1952

Efren Gonzalez, who began his professional career as a librarian with the Military Sea Transportation Services in 1952, has been in the pharmaceutical library field since 1955. He is currently manager of Science Information Services in the Research and Development Laboratories of Bristol-Myers Products. As a member of Special Libraries Association, New York Chapter, he has served on the Finance Committee (1967-1971); the Special Committee for Translations (1969); the Special Committee for the Reserve Fund (1968-1969); and the Board of Directors (1967-1970). Gonzalez was President of the Special Libraries Association for 1971-1972.

Martinez, David (1931–)
>Born: Montrose, Colorado
>Education: Montrose County High School, 1949; B.A., University of
>>Colorado, 1954; M.A., University of Colorado, 1961

David Martinez became the first American of Mexican descent to hold the office of elementary principal in the Sacramento Unified School District. He was principal of Washington Elementary School, Sacramento (1968); President of the Sacramento Area Economic Opportunity Council (1969); and is presently principal of Ethel Phillips Elementary School, where he administers a bilingual education program.

Martinez, Gilbert T. (1931–)
    Born: Redlands, California
    Education: B.A., San Jose State College, California, 1955; M.A., San Jose
        State College, California, 1960
Gilbert Martinez, an educator, was coordinator and director of five staff schools for the Creole Petroleum Corporation, Tia Juana, Zulia, Venezuela (1964-1967); a consultant for the Bureau of Instructional Planning and Development, California State Department of Education. As an author, he has published *Mexican-Americans, a Hyphen in History*.

Montez, Miguel (1933–)
    Born: El Paso, Texas
    Education: Cathedral High School, Los Angeles, 1951; Loyola University,
        Los Angeles, 1951-1954; D.D.S., School of Dentistry, Univer-
        sity of Southern California, 1958.
Dr. Montez is a distinguished dentist, educator, and civic leader. He formulated a plan to provide for the educational needs of the pre-school underprivileged Mexican-American children in Pacoima and in San Fernando as a beginning of the federal Head Start Program. He was founder and President of the Latin American Civic Association, co-founder and Chairman of the Board of Directors of the Joint Venture Project, and has been a member of the California State Baord of Education since 1966.

Nava, Julian (1927–)
    Born: Los Angeles, California
    Education: Los Angeles Public Schools; A.A., East Los Angeles Junior
        College, 1949; B.A., Pomona College, 1951; M.A., Harvard
        University, 1952; Ph.D., Harvard University, 1955
Julian Nava has been a Fulbright Lecturer, Universidad de Valladolid, Spain; Founding Director, Great Lakes Colleges Association Center, Bogota, Colombia; President, Pacific Coast Council on Latin American Studies (1965-1966); and a member of the Los Angeles City Board of Education Office No. 3. Nava, the author of many articles, has also written *Mexican-Americans–Past, Present, and Future*. He is currently Professor of History at San Fernando Valley State College, California.

Palomares, Uvaldo H. (1936–)
    Born: Indio, California
    Education: B.A., Chapman College, Orange, California, 1960; M.A., San
        Diego State College, 1962; Ed.D., University of Southern
        California, 1966
Uvaldo Palomares, a clinical psychologist, is a specialist in designing tests that accurately measure the aptitudes and abilities of Spanish-speaking students. He founded the Human Development Training Institute to develop programs for

pre-school children. Palomares was the Consulting Psychologist, Palm Springs Unified School District, California (1965-1966); Assistant Professor of Education, San Diego State College (1966-1969); and President of the Institute for Personal Effectiveness in Children.

Rodriguez, Armando M. (1921–)
  Born: Gomez Palacio, Durango, Mexico
  Education: B.A., San Diego State College, 1949; M.A., San Diego State
      College, 1951; graduate work at the University of California
      at Los Angeles
An outstanding educational leader, Armando Rodriguez is Assistant Commissioner for the Regional Office Coordinator of the United States Office of Education. He has held positions as Consultant, California State Department of Education (1965-1966); Chief of the Bureau of Intergroup Relations, California State Department of Education (1966-1967); First Chief of Mexican American Affairs Unit of the United States Office of Education (1967); and Director, Office for Spanish Speaking American Affairs, U.S. Office of Education (1970).

Samora, Julian (1920–)
  Born: Pagosa Springs, Colorado
  Education: B.A., Adams State College of Colorado, 1942; M.S., Colorado
      State University, 1947; Ph.D., Washington University, St.
      Louis, 1953
Dr. Samora, Head of the Department of Sociology, University of Notre Dame from 1963 to 1966, has done field work on problems of acculturation and health attitudes of the Mexican American. He has written numerous articles and is the author of *La Raza: Forgotten Americans* (1966) and *Mexican-Americans in a Midwest Metropolis—A Study of East Chicago* (1967). Dr. Samora was a visiting professor at the National University of Colombia and a Consultant to the Ford Foundation and other agencies.

Sanchez, George I. (1906–)
  Born: Albuquerque, New Mexico
  Education: Public schools in Arizona and New Mexico; B.A., University
      of New Mexico, 1930; M.S., University of Texas, 1931; Ed.D.,
      University of California at Berkeley, 1934.
George Sanchez is one of the foremost experts on the educational and social problems of the Mexican-American in the United States and Latin America. Appointed by President Johnson to the Community Relations Service Committee; invited by President Johnson to witness the signing of the National Defense Education Act (1964); and an invited delegate to President Johnson's Conference on the Peace Corps (1965). He was author and editor of the Inter-American Series published by Macmillan.

ARTISTS

Camplis, Francisco
Grazia, Nick de
Hernandez, Manuel
Montona, Jose Ernesto
Montoya, Malaquios

Rodriguez, Dave
Trujillo, Hernandez
Villa, Esteban
Yanez, Rene

WRITERS

Morin, Raul R. (1913-1967)
    Born: Lockhart, Texas
    Education: San Antonio Trade School, San Antonio, Texas; Frank
            Wiggins Trade School, Los Angeles, California
Raul Morin served his country during World War II in the 79th Infantry Division
in the European Theater of Operations; he received the Purple Heart, two Bronze
Stars, and the U.S. Army Infantry Badge. His book, *Among the Valiant*, records
the deeds of Mexican-American servicemen. In his memory the Los Angeles
City Council dedicated to him the "Raul Morin Memorial Square" in East Los
Angeles (1968).

Acuna, Rudolph
Romano, Octavio
Salas, Floyd
Salazar, Ruben
Vasquez, Richard

The Story of the Mexican American
El Grito
Tattoo the Wicked Cross
Writer for the *Los Angeles Times*
Chicano

SPORTS FIGURES

Plunkett, Jim (1947–)
    Born: San Jose, California
    Education: San Jose public schools; Stanford University, Palo Alto,
            California
Plunkett was an all-around athletic star from the time he was a fifth grader in
San Jose. In high school he excelled at basketball, wrestling, track, and baseball,
and he discovered his ability as a passer in football. In 1964 and 1965 he was
named to the All-League team and the North Shrine All-Star team. Many colleges and universities offered Plunkett football scholarships when he graduated
from high school in 1966. He chose Stanford University. In 1970, he sparked
the Indians to an 8-3 season, the Pacific Eight Championship, and a trip to the
Rose Bowl. His three-season totals with Stanford were 530 out of 962 passes
completed, for 7,544 yards and 52 touchdowns, and his career record of 7,887
yards in total offense was by far the highest in the history of the NCAA. On
November 24, 1970, the Downtown Athletic Club in New York City awarded
Plunkett the Heisman Memorial Trophy. In January 1971, Plunkett was chosen
by the Boston Patriots (now the New England Patriots) in the pro draft.

Trevino, Lee (1939–)
>Born: Dallas, Texas
>Education: Through eighth grade

Lee Trevino was forced to leave school after the eighth grade to help support his family. Lying about his age, he joined the U.S. Marine Corps when he was 17 and became golf champion of the Corps. He obtained his Class A Card in 1966 and entered the United States Open at the Olympic Country Club in San Francisco. In 1968 Trevino won the United States Open Championship and became the third man ever to make the United States Open his first major tournament victory. The Open was worth a small fortune to him in endorsements and business deals; later in the year, winning his second major tournament, the Hawaiian Open, he received an additional $25,000 first prize. In February 1969, Trevino had his third big win in the Tucson Open. Children as well as adults belong to the immense following known as "Lee's Fleas." A generous, wisecracking man, Trevino usually writes a check for several thousand dollars to a local orphanage or charity following a tournament victory.

Aguirre, Hank	Professional baseball
Jackson, Reggie M.	Professional baseball
Kapp, Joe	Professional football
Napoles, Jose	Boxing champion
Olivarez, Ruben	Boxing champion
Ramos, Mando	Lightweight boxing champion of the world
Rodriguez, Aurelio	Professional baseball
Torres, Alacran	Boxing champion
Villanueva, Danny	Professional football

ENTERTAINERS

Limon, Jose Arcadio (1908–)
>Born: Culiacan, Sinaloa, Mexico
>Education: University of California at Los Angeles; New York School of
>>Design, 1928; Doris Humphrey-Charles Weidman Studio,
>>(1930-1940); Honorary Doctor of Fine Arts, Wesleyan
>>University, 1964

Jose Limon, concert dancer, choreographer, and instructor, has toured most of North America, South America, and Europe in concert. In addition, he has taught at numerous colleges and universities. He studied at the Doris Humphrey-Charles Weidman Studio in New York (1928) and by 1930 was dancing in the chorus of Norman Bel Geddes' modernized version of *Lysistrata* on Broadway. Limon's first choreographed composition to be performed publicly was a solo to two preludes of Reginald de Koven (1931); in 1942 Limon took his place unquestionably as one of the important artists in contemporary dance and reached the height of his powers as a dancer by 1950. In 1950 he was invited by the Mexican government to teach, choreograph, and perform with his company at the Instituto Nacional de Bellas Artes in Mexico City. In the fall of 1954, the Jose Limon Company became the first group to travel under the State Department-

ANTA Cultural Exchange Program, performing in four South American cities. In 1957, again under the auspices of the State Department, they made a five-month tour of Europe and the Near East. The government sent them to South and Central America for 12 weeks in 1960, and to the Far East in 1963. Limon received the *Dance Magazine* Award in 1957 and the Capezio Award in 1964. In 1966 he was awarded a $23,000 grant for choreography by the National Council on the Arts. In recent years Limon has been a member of the dance faculty at the Juilliard School of Music in New York City.

Lopez, Trinidad ("Trini") (1937–)
    Born: Dallas, Texas
    Education: Dallas public schools
Lopez was only 11 when, with his father's encouragement, he decided he would become a musical star. His father purchased a twelve-dollar guitar and Lopez taught himself to play and sing. As an adolescent he formed his own combo and worked his way up to engagements in the larger nightclubs. In 1960 Lopez took his combo to Los Angeles, but the only booking he could get was a single for himself at "Ye Little Club." His engagement there, originally for two weeks, lasted for one year. In April 1963, Lopez signed an exclusive contract with Reprise Records. In late 1963 and early 1964 Lopez toured Europe where his performances drew standing-room-only audiences. He has been a guest star on the television shows of Jack Benny, Ed Sullivan, Carol Burnett, Andy Williams, and Dean Martin, and on August 8, 1967, he was host on the CBS television network show *Spotlight*. Lopez appeared in a number of movies in 1965 and 1967. Honors bestowed on him include a Golden Record for his success with "If I Had a Hammer" in 1963 and the Dallas Man of the Year Award in 1967.

Quinn, Anthony (Rudolph Oaxaca) (1916–)
    Born: Chihuahua, Mexico
    Education: Attended public schools in Los Angeles, California
The character actor Anthony Quinn won two awards from the Academy of Motion Pictures Arts and Sciences for the best supporting role in *Viva Zapata!* (1952) and for his role in *Lust for Life* (1956). He played in the Italian-made motion picture *La Strada*, which won an Academy Award in 1956 as the best foreign language movie of the year. Quinn started his movie career at an early age playing the part of a juvenile Tarzan in a jungle film. From 1936 to 1947 Quinn remained in Hollywood taking all parts that came his way. In December 1947 he made his Broadway debut. For nearly two years he played in the road company of Tennessee Williams' *A Streetcar Named Desire*. Quinn played in summer stock on the East Coast, taking the part of "Texas" in Lynn Rigg's play *Borned in Texas*, in 1950. During recent years he has devoted his time and energy to moviemaking in Hollywood and Italy.

Carr, Vicki   Roland, Gilbert
Montalban, Ricardo   Santana, Carlos
Navarro, Ramon   Sunny and the Subliners
Rene y Rene

POPULAR RECORDING ARTISTS

Beltran, Lola
Feliciano, Jose
Fernandez, Vincente
Jimenez, Jose Alfredo
Lopez, Sonia
Los Dandys
Los Johnny Jets
Muriz, Marco Antonio

Negrete, Jorge
Rafael
Santanera, Sonora
Solis, Javier
Tapatia, La Rondalla
Trio Los Panchos
Vargas, Mariachi

APPENDIX B

MEXICAN-AMERICAN ORGANIZATIONS

MEXICAN AMERICAN ORGANIZATIONS

INTRODUCTORY NOTE

Traditionally, Mexican Americans have organized numerous social and mutual-aid societies to provide a social life which retains the Mexican culture and which is separate from the Anglo. In recent years, new organizations have been founded on state, regional, and national levels dedicated to the needs of the Mexican American people. Civic and political activity has increased as young Mexican Americans learn how to use political institutions and practices, through membership in such organizations as American G. I. Forum, Mexican American Political Association (MAPA), Political Association of Spanish-Speaking Organizations (PASSO), Community Service Organizations (CSO), Mexican American Youth Organization, and others.

The material in Appendix B was gleaned from extensive reading on the Mexican-American people in both books and journals. *The Directory of Spanish-Speaking Community Organizations* (U.S. Cabinet Committee on Opportunity for the Spanish Speaking, 1970) was especially helpful in identifying the organizations as to scope. The following were useful in selecting the political organizations: Kaye Briegel's *The History of Political Organizations Among Mexican Americans in Los Angeles Since the Second World War* and "Politics and Policies of the Mexican American Community," by Ralph Guzman (in *California Politics and Policies* by E. P. Dvorin and A. I. Misner).

MEXICAN AMERICAN ORGANIZATIONS

Advisory Committee on Education of
Spanish and Mexican Americans Est. 1967
    400 Maryland Ave., S.W. Scope: National
    Washington, D.C. 20202 Membership: Mexican American,
Cuban, Puerto Rican
This Committee, an arm of the U.S. Office of Education (with Gilbert Chavez as Chief), advises the Commissioner of Education on policies for educational programs for Mexican Americans and other Spanish-speaking persons. The First National Conference on Educational Opportunities for the Mexican American was sponsored by this Committee in April 1968, with a published report available. (Formerly known as Advisory Committee on Mexican American Education.)

Alianza Est. 1894
    55 East Broadway Scope: Primarily Southwest
    Tucson, Arizona 85701 Membership: Mexican American
Formerly known as Alianza Hispano-Americano. A fraternal benefit insurance society organized in 1894. The organization publishes a magazine, *Alianza*, which reports organizational affairs and news of interest to the Mexican-American community.

Alianza Federal de Pueblos Libres   Est. 1962
 1010 Third St., N.W.   Scope: Statewide
 Albuquerque, New Mexico   Membership: Spanish American
Originally named Alianza Federal de Mercedes, this group was organized and led
by Reies Lopez Tijerina, a leader of social reform in New Mexico. The group
demands the land lost by the original settlers of the Southwest following the
Treaty of Hidalgo.

American G. I. Forum Auxiliary Est. 1948
 621 Gabaldon Rd., N.W.   Scope: National
 Albuquerque, New Mexico 87104 Membership, Mexican American
The organization is made up of the wives and relatives of American G.I. Forum
members and other Mexican-American women over the age of 21 (married
women under 21 may also join). Their objective is to promote equality for
Mexican-American members and to aid and assist local chapters of the Forum.

American G. I. Forum of U.S.   Est. 1948
 620 Gabaldon Rd., N.W.   Scope: National
 Albuquerque, New Mexico 87104 Membership: Mexican American
An organization of the veterans of the Armed Forces of the United States, of
primarily Mexican origin, and their families. Their objective is to "foster and
perpetuate the principles of American democracy based on religious and political freedom for the individual and equal opportunity for all." The Forum is
active in programs of general interest to the Mexican American community,
and it publishes the *G. I. Forum Bulletin.*

American Spanish Committee Est. 1962
 P.O. Box 119   Scope: National
 Canal Street Station   Membership: American Spanish-
 New York, N.Y. 10013   surnamed citizens
An organization to protect the civil rights and Christian beliefs of all Spanish-
surnamed American citizens.

American-Spanish Film and Television Center Est. 1968
 16632 Lucia Lane   Scope: Local
 Huntington Beach, Calif. 92647 Membership: All Spanish-speaking
            people
This organization produces programs of cultural, social, and historical value to
the Spanish-speaking community and also aids Spanish groups in making documentary and publicity films.

Arizona Social Club   Est. 1964
 1100 Cummins   Scope: Local
 Broderick, California   Membership: Mexican American
A social club for activities of the Mexican-American community. The club meets
monthly and is supported by membership dues.

Association of Mexican American Educators (AMAE)

2950 National Avenue
San Diego, California

Est. 1965
Scope: Statewide
Membership: Mexican American

The objective of the AMAE is to encourage boards of education and school administrators to understand and work more effectively with the education of the Mexican American. The organization also serves as a clearinghouse for current research relating to the education of Mexican Americans. Funded by membership dues.

Auxiliary Mexican Border Veterans

1074 Buckner Road
Memphis, Tennessee 38122

Scope: National (but primarily Southwest)
Membership: Mexican-American women

The Auxiliary is composed of 250 women relatives of the federalized National Guard Volunteers who served on the Mexican border in 1916-1917. Mrs. Viola Helsapple is the National President. The Auxiliary holds an annual convention and meetings.

Barrios Alianza de Latinos Americanos (BALA) Est. 1968

12937 Venice Blvd.
Los Angeles, Calif. 90291

Scope: Local
Membership: Mexican American

An organization of volunteer members working in the barrios to aid in preventing youth from participating in gang warfare through educational programs.

Los Barrios Unidos

3219 Herbert St.
Dallas, Texas 75212

Scope: Local
Membership: Mexican American

Los Barrios Unidos was formed originally to get West Dallas streets paved; however, the group now conduct marches in downtown Dallas to demand day-care centers, community clinics, and other facilities for the Mexican-American community. Peter Martinez is founder of the organization.

Brown Berets

National address unavailable

Est. 1968
Scope: Primarily Southwest
Membership: Mexican-American youth

A militant youth organization (composed of Mexican-American students at colleges, universities, and even high schools) which has staged walk-outs, sit-ins, and boycotts to underline demands for Mexican-American study programs and for greater recognition in history books of Hispano cultural contributions.

California Chicano Law Student Association (CCLSA)

Community Participation Center
UCLA School of Law
405 Hilgard Avenue
Los Angeles, Calif. 90024

Est. 1969
Scope: Statewide
Membership: Mexican American

189

This student association makes legal services available to the Mexican-American community and works with various issues within the community. Branch offices and organizations are established in some ten other law schools within the universities of California.

The Campesinos Forum   Est. 1967
    P.O. Box 61   Scope: Local
    Hillsboro, Oregon 97123   Membership: Mexican American
The members of the Campesinos' Forum act as representatives of migrant workers in public agencies and work toward improvement of labor camps and workers' rights. The Forum also sponsors a Spanish-language radio program.

Central California Action Associates (CCAA)   Est. 1967
    1044 Fulton Mall   Scope: Statewide
    Fresno, California 92721   Membership: Mexican American
Conducts and sponsors educational programs to teach basic skills and subjects which will contribute to economic betterment of the Mexican American. CCAA, funded by the Economic Opportunity Act, has five branch offices in California.

Centro Chicano Cultural (CCC)   Est. 1968
    P.O. Box 291   Scope: Statewide
    Woodburn, Oregon 97071   Membership: Mexican American
The CCC acts as a Chicano service center promoting the education and cultural heritage of the Mexican Americans. Partially funded by the Catholic Church.

Club Mexico Bello (Beautiful Mexico)   Est. 1924
    710 Skylark Road   Scope: Local
    Pasadena, Texas 77502   Membership: Mexican American
Club Mexico Bello (Club Cultural Recreativo Mexico Bello) is the oldest and most elite Mexican American social club in the Houston area. The club motto is "The Pride to be Mexican: Homeland, Race, Language." It views itself as an association of brotherhood built upon qualities and customs existing only in Mexican culture.

Club Sembradores de Amistad de Houston   Est. 1964
    P.O. Box 1786   Scope: International
    Houston, Texas 77001   Membership: Mexican American
Club Sembradores de Amistad is composed mainly of wealthy Mexican-American professionals who help students obtain scholarships, either through direct aid or by providing information on other sources of financial assistance.

Club Verde Mar   Est. 1953
    1001 Main Street   Scope: Local
    Houston, Texas 77001   Membership: Mexican American
Composed of young Mexican American adults, the club emphasizes the preservation of Mexican culture. Sponsors a Baile Ranchero on September 16 each year.

Community and Human Resources　　　Est. 1967
Agency (CHRA)　　　Scope: National
　　751 South Figueroa Street
　　Los Angeles, California 90017
The Community and Human Resources Agency is a non-profit organization
funded by private industry and foundation grants. The Agency helps implement
manpower training programs and provides direct service for manpower information in the community. The Agency has a branch office in Long Island City, N.Y.

Community Service Organization, Inc. (CSO)　　Est. 1947
　　714 California Avenue　　　Scope: National
　　Venice, California 90291　　　Membership: Primarily Mexican
　　　　　　　　　　　　　　　　　　American
The CSO grew out of a committee formed in 1947 to elect Edward Roybal to
Los Angeles City Council. The CSO, despite its role in Roybal's campaign, is
not primarily interested in electing Mexican Americans to public office. Its
basic aim is to provide political representation for those who would be otherwise
unrepresented. The CSO has carried on an active campaign for Mexican Americans
"to guard and further our democratic rights; to become more aware of our re-
sponsibilities as citizens; to better discharge our civic duty," and, as the constitution of one chapter declares, to promote "the general welfare in Spanish-speaking
neighborhoods."

Council of Mexican American Affairs　　Est. 1966
Project Head Start　　　Scope: Local
　　3930 North Mission Road　　　Membership: Mexican American
　　Los Angeles, Calif. 90031
Operates Head Start Program as a delegate agency according to contractual
relationship with the federal government, with nine branch offices in California.

Crusade for Justice　　　Est. 1966
　　1567 Downing Street　　　Scope: Local
　　Denver, Colorado　　　Membership: Spanish American
This crusade, led by Rodolfo "Corky" Gonzalez, stresses autonomy. It runs a
bilingual school which teaches neglected bits of history, directs its own security
force, operates several small businesses, and plans for Chicano farms that will
supply a Chicano market. The organization also protests publicly when it feels
that Chicano people have been dealt with unjustly.

Educational Laboratory for Inter-　　Est. 1967
American Studies (ELIAS)　　　Scope: International
　　18111 Nordhoff, Box 96　　　Membership: Mexican American
　　Northridge, Calif. 91324
Provides administrative and instructional services as well as materials for school
districts serving Mexican-American students. Supported by fees for services and
donations.

Ford Foundation Doctoral Fellowships for Black Americans, Mexican Americans, Puerto Ricans, and American Indians
    320 E. 43rd Street
    New York, N.Y. 10017

Est. 1968
Scope: National
Membership: Black Americans, Mexican Americans, Puerto Ricans, American Indians

A fellowship program seeking to increase the number of minority students in graduate schools who intend to make college teaching a career. Forty-five awards are given to college seniors and recent graduates selected from approximately 600 applicants. The recipients will begin full-time graduate study leading to doctorates in the humanities, social sciences or natural sciences at graduate schools of their choice. The awards are renewable annually for up to five years to complete degree requirements. A bi-racial advisory committee, composed of nationally prominent scholars in the humanities, social sciences, and natural sciences, assists the Foundation in making the selections. (Formerly titled Ford Foundation Doctoral Fellowships for Black Students.)

Governor's Committee on Mexican American Affairs
    c/o Mr. Anibol Mejia
    1306 Capitol Way
    Olympia, Washington 98501

Est. 1968
Scope: Statewide
Membership: Mexican American

This committee studies, recommends, and prepares policies for the state government.

Hispanic American Institute
    100 East 27th Street
    Austin, Texas 78705

Est. 1966
Scope: Regional
Membership: Mexican American

The institute prepares research papers, conducts leadership and citizenship classes, and works to promote bilingual and bicultural programs.

Industry/Mexican American Action Committee (IMAAC)
    Address unknown

Est. 1969
Scope: National
Membership: Mexican American

The IMAAC was established to aid the Spanish-speaking in northern California in economic development. Funded by private contributions from industry.

International Institute of Los Angeles
    435 South Boyle Avenue
    Los Angeles, California 90033

Est. 1914
Scope: Local
Membership: Primarily Mexican American

The International Institute of Los Angeles provides services such as counselling for non-English speaking students, immigration counselling classes, and inter-group relations program for children 5 to 12 years of age and their parents. The Institute is supported by United Way, fees, and membership dues.

Justicia
    Hollywood, California

Est. 1969
Scope: Local
Membership: Mexican American

This association was organized to help remedy the injustices existing in the casting practices of the motion picture industry and the stereotype role of the Mexican American in movies. The Academy Awards ceremony in the spring of 1970 was the organizations' first target. Ray Martel and Ray Andrade were the organizational leaders.

Latin American Club
    511 Elba
    Burley, Idaho 83318

Est. 1965
Scope: Local
Membership: Mexican American

The Latin American Club assists the Spanish-speaking community in social, cultural, and economic efforts.

Latin American Educational
Foundation (LAEF)
    4100 West 38th Avenue
    Denver, Colorado 80212

Est. 1949
Scope: Statewide
Memberships: Spanish American

The LAEF organization assists Spanish-speaking students in securing financial aid for college through guidance to agencies providing grants and loans. A non-profit corporation.

Latin American Research and
Development Agency (LARADA)
    820 Oxford Lane
    Colorado Springs, Colorado 80906

Est. 1970
Scope: Local
Membership: Spanish American

The Agency is interested in the culture, the heritage, and the general well-being of the Spanish-speaking people of the area. It is supported by the Catholic Churches of Colorado Springs and the Archidiocese of Denver.

League of Mexican-American Students
(LOMAS)
    University of Houston
    Houston, Texas

Est. 1967
Scope: Local
Membership: Mexican American

LOMAS, an organization made up of university students, is comparable to the Latin American Clubs. The members of this organization visit high schools to inform Mexican-American students about procedures in applying for college and financial aid; teach citizenship classes for adults; tutor children; participate in voter registration drives; and sponsor a dance to raise money for scholarships for Mexican-American college students.

League of United Chicanos (LUCHA)
    Los Angeles, Calif.

Est. 1968
Scope: Statewide
Membership: Mexican American

The primary objective of LUCHA is to help addicts in and out of prison by providing counseling services and employment services. Headed by "Moe" Aguirre, LUCHA developed and became known as an organization that specialized not only in drug addiction problems but also in problems of ex-convicts. It eventually became the recipient of federal funds.

League of United Latin American Citizens
(LULAC)
   2918 South Birch Street
   Santa Ana, California 92707

Est. 1929
Scope: National
Membership: Primarily Mexican
American

This national league was founded in Harlingen, Texas, and is one of the oldest and most notable Mexican American organizations in the United States. LULAC has developed a number of educational programs and has provided extensive aid to less fortunate Mexican Americans. In the 1960s, under new leadership, the LULAC association joined other associations in challenging discrimination and endorsing many of the demands of the new movements. However, the organization remains firm in its policy of political non-partisanship, and does not support individual political candidates.

Medical Society of the United States
and Mexico
   333 West Thomas Road
   Phoenix, Arizona 85013

Est. 1954
Scope: International
Membership: Doctors of medi-
cine in the U.S. and Mexico

The Society is composed of doctors of medicine in the United States (800) and in Mexico (400) who promote international goodwill, sponsor research and educational programs, and foster interchange of doctors. It disseminates information through the *Arizona State Medical Journal*, the official organ of the group.

Mexican American Documentation and
Educational Research Institute
   1229 East Cypress Street
   Anaheim, California 92805

Est. 1969
Scope: National and international
Membership: Mexican American

The objectives of this institute are to increase goodwill between Mexico and the United States, to develop a better understanding between the cultures, and to aid in the education of Mexican-American students. Funded by contributions.

Mexican American Educational
Association (MAEA)
   P.O. Box 1047
   Sacramento, California 95805

Est. 1963
Scope: Local
Membership: Mexican American

MAEA promotes goals for the general welfare of the Mexican American community by acquainting and including Mexican Americans in educational programs and community actions. Scholarships are awarded to needy students. Supported by fund raising activities and donations.

Mexican American Legal Defense and
Educational Fund (MALDEF)
   145 Ninth Street
   San Francisco, California 94103

Est. 1968
Scope: National
Membership: Mexican American

Funded by the Ford Foundation, its purpose is to protect, by legal action, the constitutional rights of all Mexican Americans, and to help educate young Mexican-American lawyers so they can join in the work of MALDEF. Counsels individuals and groups concerning their legal rights, and conducts seminars for Mexican American lawyers. The group maintains a 2,000-volume library.

Mexican American Political
Association (MAPA)
   353 North Mednick Avenue
   Los Angeles, California 90022

Est. 1959
Scope: Statewide
Membership: Mexican American

A non-profit, non-partisan organization working for improved economic, cultural, and civic interests of the Mexican American through political action. Self-supporting.

Mexican American Student Association
(MASA), University of Arizona
   715 North Park
   Tucson, Arizona 85720

Est. 1967
Scope: Local (MASA, National)
Membership: Mexican American

The purpose of the organization is to advance and promote belief in the value of education. This group gives an annual Cinco de Mayo Ball for funds. It serves as a liaison between the University and the community.

Mexican American Student Confed. (MASC)
   San Jose State College
   San Jose, California

Est. 1967
Scope: Primarily Southwest
Membership: Mexican American

An organization of students in colleges and universities throughout the Southwest, this organization was formed to deal with Mexican-American educational problems. Originally developed in California.

Mexican American Unity Council (MAUC)
   615 Perez
   San Antonio, Texas 78207

Est. 1967
Scope: Local
Membership: Mexican American

A tax-exempt corporation chartered under the non-profit laws of Texas. The activities of the organization center around rehabilitating homes, developing neighborhood plans and the economics of development. An economic development specialist and a manpower specialist are available.

Mexican American Youth Organizations
(MAYO)
   2701 South Flores Street
   San Antonio, Texas 77018

Est. 1967
Scope: Local (part of national organization)
Membership: Mexican American

This Texas organization is involved in educational, economic, political, and community development in South Texas.

Mexican American Youth Organization
(MAYO)
   Rehabilitation Center (CRC)
   Corona, California

Est. 1968
Scope: Statewide
Membership: Mexican American

This MAYO group is a non-profit, non-funded organization in California composed entirely of Chicano ex-addicts. Formed at the California Rehabilitation Center in Corona, California, mainly as a drug prevention organization, it also deals with employment, housing, education, and the many other problems related to the barrio.

Mexican Chamber of Commerce of the   Est. 1921
United States   Scope: National
   60 Wall Street   Membership: Mexican American
   New York, N.Y. 10005
Consisting of 600 members, this organization publishes a semi-monthly Digest
and Membership Directory. Meets annually in April in New York City.

Mexican Pilgrims' Foundation (MPF)   Est. 1948
   441 Lexington Avenue   Scope: National
   New York, N.Y. 10017   Membership: See description
The organization is composed of American citizens who have lived or traveled
in Mexico or who have interests there. Purpose is to provide gifts for educational,
charitable, scientific, and religious institutions in Latin America.

Movimiento Estudiantil Chicano   Est. 1967
de Aztlan (MECHA)   Scope: Local
   5151 State College Drive   Membership: Mexican American
   Los Angeles, California 90032
The members of MECHA are interested in the area of education, endeavoring to
strengthen Mexican American Studies Department and the Educational Opportunity Program. Self-supported.

National Latin American Federation   Est. 1956
   6305 Corgiat Drive South   Scope: National
   Seattle, Washington 98108   Membership: Mexican American,
                                            Puerto Rican, Cuban
This Federation promotes equal employment opportunities, social and political
justice for the Spanish speaking, and improved educational programs. Funded
by assessment of each member organization.

National Mexican American Anti-Defamation
Committee   Est. 1968
   Dupont Circle Building   Scope: National
   1346 Connecticut Avenue, N.W., Suite 321 Membership: Mexican American
   Washington, D.C. 20036
This Committee is made up of individuals, non-profit organizations, religious
groups, foundations, business, and industry to promote Mexican-American
relations by seeking to eliminate defamatory characterizations of Mexicans by
the media. Their activities include consultations, seminars, broadcasting activities, and public opinion polls.

New Hispano Movement, Inc.   Est. 1966
   1478 South Moline   Scope: Regional
   Aurora, Colorado 80010   Membership: Spanish Americans
This group "founded the first ethnic political party in the United States." It
supports independent candidates for public office. Supported by private contributions.

Nostros—We
    Los Angeles, California

Est. 1970
Scope: Local
Membership: Spanish-speaking
actors and actresses

A group of Spanish-speaking actors and actresses in Los Angeles chose Ricardo Montalban, an internationally known actor, as president of their new organization called Nostros—We. The main objective of this organization is to bring new opportunities to its members and to fight discrimination. Another objective of the group is to help change the "terrible image of the Mexican which advertising in newspapers, magazines, and television has created."

Padres Asociados Para Derechos,
Religiosos, Educativos y Sociales
    3313 Fredricksburg
    San Antonio, Texas 78201

Est. 1969
Scope: Southwest
Membership: Mexican American
priests

Membership of 325 in 20 chapters. Members are priests working with Mexican Americans. Their aim is to improve conditions for Mexican Americans, and their programs include: mobile team ministry (a team of Catholic priests and Protestant ministers); federation of existing Chicano organizations to work together for Mexican American people; and the establishment of a center of Hispano-American religious studies. The association conducts annual retreat-seminars and a three-week symposium on anthropology and government programs. Publishes the *Padres' Executive Newsletter* (weekly) and *Padres' Directory*.

El Partido de la Raza Unida (La Raza Unida)
    c/o Jose Angel Gutierrez, Chairman
    Crystal City, Texas 78839

Est. 1969
Scope: Primarily Southwest
Membership: Mexican American

Conceived as a political party to educate and stimulate Chicanos to a greater involvement in their destiny. The party selects candidates for office and takes stands on issues and laws. El Partido began in Crystal City, Texas, through the efforts of Jose Angel Gutierrez. Since its inception on November 9, 1969, it has grown in popularity and importance. A national platform has been tentatively approved. Mexican American Youth Organization of Texas has been very instrumental in developing the La Raza Unida Party.

Political Association of Spanish-Speaking
Organizations (PASSO)
Address unknown

Est. 1960
Scope: Texas
Membership: Primarily Mexican
Americans; also Puerto Ricans,
Cubans, and South Americans

PASSO is to Texas as MAPA is to California. The members of this political organization attempt to place Mexican Americans in public office by participating directly in federal, state, and local elections. They stress voter registration and get-out-the-vote drives.

El Porvenir Development
    33071 W. El Progresso Avenue
    Cantua Creek, California 93608

Est. 1965
Scope: Local
Membership: Mexican American

An organization funded by the Office of Economic Opportunity to give assistance in housing to the Mexican-American farm laborers.

El Pueblo   Est. 1971
    5228 E. Whittier Blv.   Scope: Local
    East Los Angeles, California   Membership: Mexican American
A community organization with the following statement of purpose: "We desire to establish a day in memory of the battle which occurred in East Los Angeles on August 29, 1970, resulting in the death of three Chicano brothers at the hands of the law enforcement officers of this country." The members of El Pueblo voted to establish August 29 as the first Chicano holiday, "El Dia Del Chicano" (The Day of the Chicano).

La Raza Unida   Est. 1968
    P.O. Box 336   Scope: Local (part of the
    Mendota, California 92640   national organization)
    (one of many local chapters)   Membership: Mexican American
La Raza Unida aids the Mexican-American community in improvements such as water and sewer lines, road pavement, income tax preparation, promotion of school lunch programs, and voter registration drives.

Los Sembradores de Amistad   Est. 1964
    P.O. Box 1786   Scope: International
    Houston, Texas 77007   Membership: Mexican American
Composed mainly of wealthy Mexican American professionals, this organization believes that lack of education is the most important issue facing the Mexican American today. This group helps students obtain scholarships, either through direct giving or by providing information on other sources of financial aid. They work to promote cultural and civic improvements in the community.

Sociedad Mutualista de Mexicanos Americanos Est. 1968
de Granger   Scope: Local
    P.O. Box 453   Membership: Mexican American
    Granger, Washington
The members of this society offer aid and assistance to other Mexican Americans, act as a liaison with schools, and maintain two scholarship funds. Supported by members.

La Sociedad Mutualistica Obrera Mexicana
    207 Charles Street   Scope: Local
    Houston, Texas   Membership: Mexican American
This society, with six branches in Houston, is a fraternal, mutual-aid society which awards scholarships to Mexican American high school students and supplies emergency funds for accidents, sickness, and death.

Southwest Council of La Raza (SWCLR)   Est. 1968
    11 West Jefferson   Scope: National
    Phoenix, Arizona 85003   Membership: Primarily Mexican
                                            Americans

The Council aids and assists the Mexican-American community by providing support to affiliated Mexican-American organizations. Funded by the Ford Foundation.

Special Task Force on Opportunities for
Spanish-Surnamed Americans (OSSA)
    Social Security Administration
    1710 U.S. Courthouse Building
    Los Angeles, California 90012

Est. 1970
Scope: Regional (Region IX)
Membership: Mexican American

An advisory group to make recommendations to the Director of the U.S. Department of Health, Education and Welfare on ways and means to improve services to the Mexican American community. Federally funded.

El Teatro Campesino
    North Van Ness
    Fresno, California

Est. 1966
Scope: Local
Membership: Mexican American

El Teatro Campesino, formed by Luis Valdez of the United Farm Workers, was organized to explain the problems of farm workers and to keep the values of Mexican culture alive through skits, one-act plays, and other theatrical means.

Teatro Urbano
    San Jose State College
    San Jose, California

Est. 1967
Scope: Local
Membership: Mexican American

Teatro Urbano, another dramatic group, was formed by San Jose State students and deals with the problems of Chicanos living in cities. The group endeavors "to keep the values of Mexican culture alive in an Anglo controlled society."

Texans for the Educational Advancement
of Mexican Americans (TEAM)
    P.O. Box 9372
    San Antonio, Texas

Est. 1969
Scope: Statewide
Membership: Mexican American

TEAM is active in the promotion of educational programs for Mexican Americans, working on college admissions, assistance, and curriculum revision.

Texas Institute for Educational
Development
    124 West Edwards
    Crystal City, Texas 78879

Est. 1969
Scope: National
Membership: Primarily Mexican American

The Institute is a training center for community development through education.

Tricolor Group
    103 Marshall Place
    Longmont, California 80501

Est. 1969
Scope: National
Membership: Mexican American

Tricolor aids the migrant Mexican-American families in job placement, better housing, and improved working conditions. Supported by fund-raising activities.

United Farm Workers Organization
P.O. Box 62
Keene, California 93531

Scope: Statewide
Membership: Primarily Mexican
American

This organization, led by Cesar Chavez, is not just a union, since it has an insurance program, its own credit union, and its own newspaper (*El Malcrido*). A special grievance committee investigates problems connected with the workers' jobs and files insurance claims for members who cannot read or write English. This little union that started out alone has now joined a large established union— the AFL-CIO.

United Mexican American Students (UMAS)
National address unavailable

Est. 1967
Scope: National
Membership: Mexican American
students

UMAS is a confederation of clubs of college students in which each has individual autonomy to determine its degree of militancy. This group is concerned primarily with the problems in education such as inferior educational facilities, increasing the number of Mexican American students in colleges. It stresses the value of education.

U.S.-Mexico Border Public Health
Association
509 U.S. Court House
El Paso, Texas 79901

Est. 1943
Scope: Southwest
Membership: See description

An association composed of physicians, public health administrators, nurses, sanitary engineers, veterinarians, scientists, laboratory workers and other health officers from the four American and six Mexican states fronting on the border between the two countries. Their primary concern is to improve public health along both sides of the border.

Vesta Club, Incorporated
P.O. Box 7149
Phoenix, Arizona 85011

Est. 1953
Scope: Local
Membership: Mexican American

The Vesta Club is supported by fund-raising activities and private contributions. The Club has awarded over $30,000 in scholarships given annually to outstanding Mexican-American students of Arizona. Its purpose is to attain greater social, cultural, and moral standards for the Mexican American.

Voluntarios de Aztlan—Raza Unida
124 West Edwards Street
Crystal City, Texas 78839

Est. 1970
Scope: Local
Membership: Mexican American

"Created to provide an opportunity to utilize Chicano talent, energies and strengths to liberate our people; to realistically work toward the goal of self-determination; to provide our own answers to our problems as we perceive them. . . . One of the basic objectives of Voluntarios de Aztlan is to provide manpower to solidify and ensure Chicano control of those areas in South Texas where Chicanos are in majority; the other objective is to provide experience and training in political organization . . . so they may . . . work to effect social change."

APPENDIX C

CHICANO PRESS ASSOCIATION
AND PERIODICALS AND NEWSPAPERS
OF INTEREST TO
THE MEXICAN AMERICAN

CHICANO PRESS ASSOCIATION AND PERIODICALS AND NEWSPAPERS OF INTEREST TO THE MEXICAN AMERICAN

INTRODUCTORY NOTE

The titles for periodicals and newspapers for this bibliography were selected by examining literature on Mexican Americans. The entries used were those for which complete bibliographic information could be verified either by direct contact with the publisher or through standard reference tools

The bibliographic information concerning the newspapers and journals listed in this appendix was partially obtained by a questionnaire sent directly to the publisher. Out of the large number of questionnaires mailed, fewer than one-fourth replied giving the complete information requested. As a result, the following reference tools were searched in an effort to complete the necessary information: *N. W. Ayer and Son's Directory of Newspapers and Periodicals, The Standard Periodical Directory, Ulrich's International Periodicals Directory, Foreign Language and Nationality Press, From Radical Left to Extreme Right* (Vols. 1 and 2), and *Encyclopedic Directory of Ethnic Newspapers and Periodicals in the United States.*

Few entries for Spanish-speaking people were included in older standard reference tools. What entries there were were difficult to locate and were often incomplete. *The Foreign Language and Nationality Press* (1970) contains a fairly large number of publications for the Spanish speaking; however, the entries do need updating. The most valuable and easily used reference book on ethnic periodicals and newspapers is the new *Encyclopedic Directory of Ethnic Newspapers and Periodicals in the United States* (1972), by Lubomyr R. Wynai.

A great many titles were omitted from this bibliography because information could not be verified.

CHICANO PRESS ASSOCIATION

The newspapers listed here are all members of the Chicano Press Association, a mutually cooperating group of papers that publish in various parts of the nation. They are dedicated to the dissemination and exchange of information, stories, cartoons, and photos that are very relevant to Mexican Americans.

Adelante
  2019 Summit Street
  Kansas City, Missouri 64108

El Alacran—Mecha
  California State College
  Long Beach, California

Basta Ya!
  P.O. Box 12217
  San Francisco, California

Carta Editorial
  P.O. Box 54624, Terminal Annex
  Los Angeles, California 90054

La Causa
5116 East Whittier Blvd.
Los Angeles, California 90054

El Chicano
c/o 4021 First Avenue
San Bernardino, California

Compass
1209 Egypt Street
Houston, Texas 77009

El Coraje
c/o Mexican American Liberation
   Committee
Tucson, Arizona

El Deguello
P.O. Box 37094
San Antonio, Texas

The Forumeer
435 Hubson Street
San Jose, California 95110

El Gallo
1567 Downing Street
Denver, Colorado 80218

El Grito Del Norte
Rt. 2, Box 5
Espanola, New Mexico 87432

La Guardia
635 South Fifth Street
Milwaukee, Wisconsin 53204

Lado
1306 North Western Avenue
Chicago, Illinois 60622

El Machete—Mecha
Los Angeles City C
Los Angeles, California 90029

El Malcriado
P.O. Box 130
Delano, California 63215

Nuestra Lucha
110 N.W. Fifth Avenue
Del Rey Beach, Florida 33444

El Paisano
P.O. Box 155
Tolleson, Arizona 85353

El Papel
P.O. Box 7167
Albuquerque, New Mexico 87104

Papel Chicano
5141 Clay
Houston, Texas 77023

El Popo—Mecha
Cal State College
San Fernando
Northridge, California 91324

La Raza
P.O. Box 31004
Los Angeles, California

La Raza Nueva
2815 West Commerce
San Antonio, Texas 78205

El Rebozo
P.O. Box 37207
San Antonio, Texas 78237

La Revolucion
Box 1852
Uvalde, Texas 78801

La Verdad
P.O. Box 13156
San Diego, California 92113

La Vida Nueva
East Los Angeles College
Los Angeles, California

La Voz de los Llanos
1007 A Avenue G
Lubbock, Texas 79403

La Voz Mexicana
P.O. Box 101
Watoma, Wisconsin 54982

El Yaqui
P.O. Box 52610
Houston, Texas 77052

PERIODICALS AND NEWSPAPERS OF INTEREST
TO THE MEXICAN AMERICAN

Alianza (Alliance)   1909—
P.O. Box 1671
Tucson, Arizona 85702

Monthly   Membership dues   Spanish

The official publication of Alianza, a fraternal benefit insurance society, which reports organizational affairs and material of interest to the group.

American Spanish News (America)   1959—
2448 Mission Street
San Francisco, California 94110

Bi-weekly $10.00/year   Spanish-English

Provides general, national, international, and local news coverage. Film reviews, advertising, charts, and illustrations are included.

Americas   1949—
Sales and Promotion Division
General Secretariat of the Organization of American States
Washington, D.C. 20006

Monthly $5.00/year   Spanish-English

Americas, published in both English and Spanish editions, includes articles, essays, fiction, poetry, book reviews and news of inter-American activities. A wide range of topics is covered, from pre-Columbian times to the present. Well illustrated.

Aztlan: Chicano Journal of the Social Sciences and the Arts   1970—
Mexican American Culture Center, University of California
405 Hilgarde Avenue
Los Angeles, California 90024

Quarterly $4.00/year   Spanish-English

The content is academic and scholarly. The articles deal with the problems of the day. No illustrations. Good format.

Belvedere Citizen   1934—
3590 East First Street
Los Angeles, California 90063

Weekly $5.00/year   Spanish
General national and international news of interest to the Spanish speaking.

Bernalillo Times   1931—
  P.O. Box B
  Bernalillo, New Mexico 87004

  Weekly $2.50/year   Spanish-English

A general news weekly of interest to the community.

Blanco y Negro   1891—
  Prensa Espanola
  Serrano 61, Madrid 6, Espana

  Weekly $16.00/year   Spanish

A Spanish journal similar to *Time* magazine, carrying articles on world affairs,
sports, and the arts. Many color photographs.

Box y Lucha   1951—
  P.E.S.A.
  Tenayuca 55, Mexico

  Weekly $0.25/copy   Spanish

Similar to *Sports Afield* in format but devoted to boxing and wrestling. Popular
presentation.

Bronce   1969—
  1560 34th Avenue
  Oakland, California 94601

  Monthly $4.00/year   Spanish-English
A social science periodical of Mexican-American interest.

Buen Hogar (Good Home)   1966—
  5535 N.W. Seventh Avenue
  Miami, Florida 33127

  Monthly $6.00/year   Spanish

A family magazine with articles on fashion, home, food, children, health.
Also includes novels and feature stories.

El Centinela y Heraldo de la Salud
(Sentinel and Herald of Health)   1895—
  1350 Villa Street
  Mountain View, California 94040

  Monthly $4.00/year   Spanish

This monthly publishes national and international news with general articles
on health and religious liberty.

Chicano Community Newspaper   1969—
  1257 North Mt. Vernon Avenue
  Colton, California 92324

Weekly	$7.50/year	Spanish-English

Tabloid format. Contains book reviews, advertisements, and general news of interest to the Chicano group.

Chicano Student Movement   1968–
    P.O. Box 31322
    Los Angeles, California 90031

Bi-monthly	$3.00/year	Spanish-English

A barrio newspaper serving the Mexican-American student movement in Los Angeles and the Southwest. "It expresses in militant terms the anger and bitterness with which the Mexican American views white 'racist' middleclass society, a society which he feels ignores him." Discusses local politics, meetings, and makes recommendations on candidates.

Chicano Times   Vol. 3, 1970–
    719 Delgado
    San Francisco, California 94118

Quarterly	$0.35/copy	Spanish

Discusses local politics, meetings, candidates, and propositions related to the San Francisco area.

Civil Rights Digest   1967–
    1405 Eye Street, N.W.
    Washington, D.C. 20425

Quarterly	$0.35/copy	English

Published by the Commission on Civil Rights. The digest includes articles on civil rights of Mexican Americans, such as "Equal Administration of Justice," "Reflections of a Spanish-Speaking Interpreter" (Spring 1970 issue).

Claudia   1965–
    Pisa
    Mexico 1, D.F.

Monthly	$0.55/copy	Spanish

The Mexican equivalent of *McCall's Magazine*, containing articles on food, health and skin care, fashion modes, interviews, and some fiction.

Confidencias   1943–
    P.U.M.E.X.A., Apdo 55
    Hermosillo, Sonora, Mexico

Weekly	$12.00/year	Spanish

A "popular romance" type of journal of particular interest to women.

Con Safos   1968–
    P.O. Box 31085
    Los Angeles, California 90031

    Quarterly $2.50/year   Spanish-English

"Reflections of Life in the Barrio." Contains feature articles, fiction, poetry,
a glossary of barrio language, and a barriology examination in each issue.

El Continental (The Continental)   1925–
    909 East San Antonio Street
    El Paso, Texas 79901

    Daily $10.00/year   Spanish

The objectives of this daily are to provide "general information to the public
with news from all over the world." A modern daily newspaper in Spanish.

Corpus Christi Americano. Robstown Americano.   Vol. 5, No. 34
Alice Americana. Harlingen Americano.   (9-23-72)
    1012 Leopard Street
    Corpus Christi, Texas 78401

    Weekly $10.00/year   Spanish

These weekly newspapers, with editorials, advertising, and announcements,
carry items of primary interest to the Mexican American. The four papers are
published by Ochoa Newspaper Company (P. R. Ochoa, editor).

Costilla County Free Press   1948–
    P.O. Box 116
    San Luis, Colorado 81152

    Weekly $2.00/year   Spanish-English

This independent weekly, in Spanish and English, publishes general and local
news.

El Crepusculo   1949–
    P.O. Box 1005
    Taos, New Mexico 87571

    Weekly $7.00/year   Spanish-English

An independent paper which carries local news of primary interest to the
citizens of the area.

Defensor-Chieftain   1904–
    P.O. Box Q
    204 Manzanares N.E.
    Socorro, New Mexico 87801

    Semi-weekly $6.50/year   English

A local newspaper carrying items of interest to the locality with some national
and international news.

El Diario–La Prensa (Formerly **La Prensa)**   1913–
181 Hudson Street
New York, New York 10025

Daily $28.00/year   Spanish

This daily newspaper is published for the Spanish-speaking population of New York and surrounding areas. Coverage is local, national, and international.

Diario de Las Americas (Daily of the Americas)   1953–
4349 N.W. 36th Street
Miami, Florida 33166

Daily $24.00/year   Spanish

Local news of interest to the Spanish-speaking community, plus national and international news coverage.

East Los Angeles Tribune   1930–
4928 Whittier Boulevard
East Los Angeles, California 90022

Weekly   Free   Spanish

Appears in the Sunday issue of the *East Los Angeles Gazette.* This supplement contains articles of interest to the Spanish-speaking people of Los Angeles.

Entrelineas   1971–
Penn Valley Community College
560 Westport Road
Kansas City, Missouri 64111

Monthly $5.00/year   Spanish-English

Articles of interest to Mexican Americans, with book reviews, advertisement, charts, illustrations, and index.

La Espana Libre (Free Spain)   1936–
231 West 18th Street
New York, New York 10011

Bi-monthly $5.00/year   Spanish-English

Published by the Confederated Spanish Societies of the United States. A bi-monthly carrying group news of interest to Spanish-speaking people.

Futbol   1970–
Editorial Andax, Noucalpan de Juarez
Edo. de Mexico

Weekly $0.30/copy   Spanish

A sports journal, with numerous photographs and illustrations.

La Gaceta (The Gazette)   1922—
  2015 Fifteenth Street
  Tampa, Florida 33605

  Weekly $5.00/year   Spanish, English,
                                                          Italian
A general news weekly with one page in Italian, the remainder in Spanish and
English.

Grafica   1947—
  705 North Windsor Boulevard
  Hollywood, California 90038

  Bi-monthly $3.50/year   Spanish

A journal published for the Spanish-American people of the Hollywood and
Los Angeles area containing features on world affairs, movie news and gossip,
and local affairs from the community.

El Grito   1967—
  Quinto Sol Publications, Inc.
  P.O. Box 9275
  Berkeley, California 94719

  Quarterly $4.00/year   Spanish-English

"A journal of contemporary Mexican American thought." The articles reflect
historical, anthropological, and sociological viewpoints. Contains poetry, art
portfolios, fictional stories, and the leading issues of concern to Chicanos.

The Healdsburg Tribune   Vol. 104, 1970—
  P.O. Box 518
  Healdsburg, California 95448

  Weekly $5.00/year   Spanish-English

Publishes local interest news, with Chicano efforts publicized.

El Heraldo de Brownsville (Brownsville Herald)   1892—
  13th and Adams Streets
  Brownsville, Texas 78520

  Daily (except Saturday) $26.00/year   Spanish-English

A general newspaper sponsored by Freedom Newspaper, Inc.

Highlights   1971—
  Office of Youth and Student Affairs
  U.S. Department of Health, Education and Welfare
  Community and Field Services
  Washington, D.C. 20201

  Bi-monthly   Free   English

Edited by Alfredo J. Solano, this is one of the best sources, not only for news on Spanish-surnamed and Indian youths and student meetings, work programs, scholarships, but also for recent information on who is doing what for the Spanish-surnamed in federal and, to a lesser extent, state governments. Features photographs, brief biographies and descriptions of duties of key government officials dealing in programs of interest to the Spanish-surnamed and to Indian Americans.

El Hispano (The Spanish-American)   1966–
416 Luna N.W.
Albuquerque, New Mexico 87102

Weekly $3.50/year   Spanish

A weekly newspaper carrying local sports news, syndicated columns on women's and entertainment news as well as news of special interest to the Spanish-speaking population.

El Independiente (The Independent)   1885–
114 Grand Avenue, N.W.
Albuquerque, New Mexico 87101

Weekly $3.00/year   Spanish-English

"Legal newspaper containing political commentary and problems of the legal profession."

Informador   1963–
1510 West 18th Street
Chicago, Illinois 60608

Weekly $7.50/year   Spanish-English

Publishes items of Spanish-American interests, book reviews, film reviews, advertisements, charts, and illustrations.

El Informador (The Post)   1967–
2973 Sacramento Street
Berkeley, California 94701

Monthly $7.80/year   Spanish-English.

Provides general news and items of group interest.

Inside Eastside   1968–
P.O. Box 63273
Los Angeles, California 90063

Bi-weekly $2.50/year   Spanish

A Chicano paper serving the Mexican Americans in the East Los Angeles area.

Integrated Education: A Report on Race and Schools   1963–
   343 S. Dearborn Street
   Chicago, Illinois 60604

   Bi-monthly $8.00/year   English

Contains short, factual news items and quotes from many sources, which cover
the major developments in race relations throughout the United States. Feature
articles give in-depth exploration of the black community, primarily; however,
some attempt is made to examine the problems of other minority groups,
especially the Spanish American and the American Indian.

Journal of Mexican American History   1970–
   Box 13861
   Santa Barbara, California 93107

   Irregular annual $8.64/year   Spanish-English

"Mexican American history as used by the *Journal of Mexican American History*
is the history of the Mexican people in the United States from 1848 to the
present." Aimed at the solution of social and economic problems, the journal
includes documented research findings and scholarly articles, conferences, and
symposiums and book reviews.

La Justicia (Justice)   1933–
   1710 Broadway
   New York, New York 10019

   Monthly $2.00/year   Spanish

Primarily an organ of union information; sponsored by the International
Ladies' Garment Workers' Union.

La Luz   1972–
   1313 Tremont Place
   Denver, Colorado 80204

   Monthly $10.00/year   Spanish-English

La Luz, billed as America's first and only national magazine written by and for
Hispanos, made its debut on newsstands Thursday, April 6, 1972. Dr. Daniel
T. Valdes, publisher, stated that "the inaugural edition is being distributed to a
quarter million Spanish, Mexican and Puerto Rican Americans, as well as
Cuban and South American homes throughout the Southwest, and all principal
centers of Hispano populations in large American cities."

La Luz   1931–
   8259 Niles Center Road
   Skokie, Illinois 60076

   Monthly $4.00/year   Spanish

Covers current events and carries articles, short stories, poems, songs, and excerpts
from Spanish classics. Designed specifically for high school use, it is written in
simple Spanish.

La Luz Apostolica (The Apostolic Light)   1916–
  230 Meadowwood Lane
  San Antonio, Texas 78216

  Monthly $1.50/year   Spanish

This religious monthly is "the official organ of the Spanish Assemblies of God in all states west of the Mississippi River and also in Wisconsin and Michigan in the U.S.A."

Mecanica Popular   1947–
  5535 N.W. Seventh Avenue
  Miami, Florida 33127

  Monthly $3.50/year   Spanish

Popular Mechanics in Spanish.

Mexico This Month   1955–
  Altenos 42-601
  Mexico 6, D.F.

  Monthly $5.00/year   English

A guide to travel in Mexico, this is also a source for varied information about the country, published and edited by an author who knows the area well. The journal has a wealth of detail on Mexican arts, architecture, business and investment, events, and social problems. Usually an issue is centered on one topic or theme, which may range from the pinata to the problems of Mexican youth.

Mundo Hispano (Spanish World)   1970–
  2448 Mission Street
  San Francisco, California 74110

  Weekly $7.50/year   Spanish

This newspaper carries news of appeal to Spanish-speaking populations, with local, state, national, international news as well as syndicated columns.

New Mexico Historical Review   1926–
  Journalism 220
  University of New Mexico Press
  Albuquerque, New Mexico 87106

  Quarterly $6.00/year   English

As the official publication of the Historical Society of New Mexico, the Review carries Society membership information and several book reviews of titles directly concerned with the history of the Southwest. The articles are carefully documented accounts of significant areas of United States history.

El Nuevo Mexicano   1894–
  P.O. Box 1721
  Santa Fe, New Mexico 87501

| Weekly | $5.00/year | Spanish |

A weekly paper of local interest to the Spanish Americans in the area.

El Ojo, Chicano Newsletter 1971—
Montae Systems, Inc.
1700 K Street, N.W., Suite 1207
Washington, D.C. 20006

| Monthly | $1.50/year | Spanish-English |

The newsletter proposes to "direct itself to informing Chicanos through Aztlan of activities affecting Chicano programs." It presents information on curriculum development, program actions, fellowships and financial assistance, legislation, publications, employment and items of general interest that will aid Chicano education. Excellent source for current information on meetings and legislation.

La Opinion (The Opinion) 1926—
1436 South Main Street
Los Angeles, California 90015

| Daily | $24.00/year | Spanish |

A daily newspaper covering local, national and international news, emphasizing news of interest to the Spanish-speaking community of Southern California.

La Palabra Diaria (Daily Word) 1955—
Unity Village, Missouri 64063

| Monthly | $2.00/year | Spanish |

A non-denominational religious paper sponsored by the Unity School of Christianity.

Paladin & Don Quixote 1963—
21 East Santa Clara Street
San Jose, California 95113

| Bi-weekly | $4.00/year | Spanish |

Articles of general and local interest on a variety of subjects concerning the Spanish-speaking people.

El Porvenia (The Outlook) 1934—
200 East Third Street
Mission, Texas 78572

| Bi-weekly | $7.80/year | Spanish |

A bi-weekly paper in the Spanish language serving the Spanish Americans of the Rio Grande Valley of Texas.

La Prensa
Title changed to **El Diario—La Prensa** (q.v.).

Regeneracion   1970—
  P.O. Box 54624 T.A.
  Los Angeles, California 90054

  Bi-monthly $5.00/year   Spanish-English

Supersedes *Carta Editorial.* Contains the educational, political and sociological problems that face the Chicano today. Newsletter format. Announcements, book reviews and some poetry are also included.

Rio Grande Herald   1923—
  P.O. Box 452
  102 North Corpus
  Rio Grande City, Texas 78582

  Weekly $6.50/year   English

An independent newspaper with general and local coverage.

Rotarian: An International Magazine (Revista Rotaria)   1911—
  1600 Ridge Avenue
  Evanston, Illinois 60201
                                                               English or
  Monthly $2.50/year English; $3.75/year Spanish   Spanish

The official publication of Rotary International, this publication combines a breezy reporting of news of its clubs and their activities around the world with a series of articles in each issue directed to a special subject. "Mexico," "The City," and "Education," for instance, have been explored in recent issues by well-known experts and journalists. A popular browsing magazine.

Santa Fe News   1924
  232 Rosario Street
  Santa Fe, New Mexico 87501

  Weekly $5.00/year   Spanish-English

A Thursday weekly newspaper carrying local and national items of interest to the community.

Santa Rosa News   1924—
  P.O. Drawer P
  Santa Rosa, New Mexico 88435

  Weekly $4.00/year   English

A weekly newspaper dealing with the current local news and general news of interest to the Santa Rosa community. An English publication for Spanish-speaking Americans.

Selecciones del Reader's Digest   1948—
   Reader's Digest
   Mexico, D.F.   (116-12vo Piso)

   Monthly $4.00/year   Spanish

The Spanish language edition of *Reader's Digest*. The contents and format are similar to the English edition.

Siempre   1950—
   Nacional Distribuidors
   311 South Broadway
   Los Angeles, California

   Weekly $0.55/copy   Spanish

Emphasis is on Mexican material. The journal is similar to *Life* magazine in format, and carries articles and photographs on current events.

Siempre—New Orleans   1968—
   1224 Broadway
   New Orleans, Louisiana 70118

   Bi-weekly $6.00/year   Spanish

Latin American interest.

El Sol   1971—
   P.O. Box 583
   Crystal City, Texas 78839

   Quarterly $5.50/year   Spanish-English

Newest creative arts magazine. Publishes poetry and usually one short story. Photographic illustrations.

El Sol—Dallas   1966—
   801 Core Street
   Dallas, Texas 75207

   Weekly $6.00/year   Spanish

A weekly independent paper publishing items concerning problems of the Spanish-speaking people of Dallas.

Sucesos   1960—
   Editorial Sucesos para Todos
   Calzada de Tacubaya 103
   Mexico 18 D.F., Mexico

   Weekly $0.40/copy   Spanish

Carries articles of current national and international news. Similar to *Time* magazine. It is illustrated, and has book reviews and film reviews.

The Taos News (Las Notecias de Taos)   1959—
 P.O. Box 1005
 Taos, New Mexico 87571

Weekly $7.00/year   Spanish-English

A weekly newspaper containing local and national news.

Temas (Themes)   1950—
 1560 Broadway
 New York, New York 10036

Monthly $4.00/year   Spanish

A popular magazine containing general information, special features, enter-tainment news, women's features, health and beauty items, etc.

Texas Observer: A Journal of Free Voices   1906—
 600 West Seventh Street
 Austin, Texas 78701

Bi-weekly $7.00/year   English

This journal carries critical articles on current issues, book reviews, play reviews, advertising, charts, and illustrations. "A window to the South."

El Tiempo   1963—
 Mecha-Foothill College
 12345 South El Monte Avenue
 Los Altos Hills, California 94022

Daily $3.00/year   Spanish

A daily newspaper of general news coverage, national, international and sports.

El Tiempo de Laredo (Laredo Times)   1880—
 111 Esperanza Drive
 P.O. Box 29
 Laredo, Texas

Daily (except Saturday) $0.10 weekdays; $0.25 Sunday   Spanish-English

A standard daily newspaper with Spanish pages giving local news coverage.

The Times (El Tiempo)   1935—
 P.O. Box 856
 683 West Main Street
 Raymondville, Texas 78580

Weekly $3.00/year   English

An English publication for Spanish-speaking Americans. It contains local and general news coverage.

Times of the Americas   Vol. 4, 1970
  P.O. Box 1173
  Coral Gables, Florida 33134

  Weekly $8.00/year   English

An English-language publication specializing in news of Latin America.

Todo   1933–
  Calle de Hamburgo 36
  Colonia Juarez, Mexico 6
  Mexico, D.F.

  Weekly $6.00/year   Spanish

A popular news magazine emphasizing Mexican and world news. Many black and white photographs.

La Tribuna de North Jersey (North Jersey Tribune)   1950–
  70 Kossuth Street
  Newark, New Jersey

  Monthly $2.00/year   Spanish

General interest news for the Spanish-speaking population with special editorials on various subjects.

La Trompeta (The Trumpet)   1912–
  905 Bluntzer Street
  Corpus Christi, Texas 78405

  Monthly $1.00/year   Spanish

Religious news published by the Christian Triumph Company for the Spanish population.

Vanidades (Continental)   1961–
  Publicaciones Culturales de Mexico
  Salamanca 102, Mexico

  Bi-monthly $0.60/copy   Spanish

A woman's magazine similar to *Good Housekeeping*. Carries articles on health and beauty, fashion, and some fiction.

La Verdad (The Truth)   1940–
  910 Francisco Street
  Corpus Christi, Texas 78405

  Weekly $3.50/year   Spanish-English

This weekly contains local news but primarily editorials on labor, welfare, education, and economics.

La Voz (The Voice)   1959–
   6201 Biscayne Boulevard
   Miami, Florida 33138

Weekly $5.00/year   Spanish-English

This official publication of the Catholic Archdiocese of Miami reports on
developments within the Church to the people of South Florida; it also
carries articles concerning migrants, political refugees, and social problems.

APPENDIX D

REFERENCE

REFERENCE

GENERAL REFERENCE

Bancroft, Hubert H. **History of Mexico.** 6 vols. New York: McGraw-Hill Book
      Company, 1967. (San Francisco, 1883-1888). The works of Hubert
      Bancroft.
Despite passage of time, this monumental work continues to serve as an important reference work and gold mine of bibliographic information. It can serve as
a point of departure for virtually any topic in Mexican history between 1824
and 1887.

Grebler, Leo, Joan W. Moore, and Ralph C. Guzman. **The Mexican American
      People: The Nation's Second Largest Minority.** New York: The Free
      Press, 1970. 777p.
This volume is the result of a study designed by the Mexican American Study
Project at the University of California, Los Angeles, and executed in cooperation
with scholars at other institutions of higher learning. The aim of the work is to
depict factually and analytically the present realities of life for Mexican Americans
in today's society. The book draws on a great variety of research material, from
census data, household surveys, and informal interviews to books, journal
articles, and government publications. An extensive bibliography is included.

McWilliams, Carey. **North From Mexico: The Spanish Speaking People of the
      United States.** Westport, Conn.: Greenwood Press, Inc., 1968. 304p.
Originally published by Lippincott in 1949, this is still the definitive, though
dated, study of the Mexican in the United States. The work includes some primary
source material relating to Los Angeles.

Moquin, Wayne, ed. **A Documentary History of the Mexican Americans.** New
      York: Frederick A. Praeger, 1971. 399p.
A history of the Mexican American presenting a view of the people's story from
1536 to 1970. The work is arranged chronologically; the 65 documents collected
here are grouped into five chapters that provide an account of the Mexican
American experience in Anglo America. Included are reprints of official documents and reports, excerpts from early manuscripts and journals, and from letters
and essays by modern historians on Mexican Americans and by participants in
the Chicano movement. The recommended readings include fiction and general
selections.

BIBLIOGRAPHIES, DIRECTORIES, GUIDES, AND HANDBOOKS

Altus, David M. **Bilingual Education, A Selected Bibliography.** Las Cruces, New
      Mexico: New Mexico State University, 1970. ERIC-CRESS.
Covering items listed in *Research in Education* through June 1970, this bibliography
includes the abstract of each title and covers research in the area of bilingual
education done primarily in the 1960s.

Bibliografia de Aztlan: An Annotated Chicano Bibliography. Compiled by
 Ernie Barrios and others. San Diego, California: San Diego State College,
 Centro de Estudios Chicanos, 1971.
A topically arranged annotated bibliography compiled by a group of Chicano
professors and Chicano leaders. The stated purpose of the bibliography "is to
objectively review the literature that has been written on the second largest
minority, the Chicano."

Bryant, Shasta M., comp. **A Selective Bibliography of Bibliographies of Hispanic
 American Literature.** Washington, D.C.: Pan American Union, 1966.
 48p.
The author compiled this bibliography on Latin American Literature for the
Pan American Union in the Division of Philosophy and Letters. Although it is
dated, some excellent bibliographies on Mexican literature may be found through
it.

Campbell, Walter S. **The Book Lover's Southwest: A Guide to Good Reading.**
 Norman, Oklahoma: University of Oklahoma Press, 1955. 287p.
A survey of books representing the literature of the Southwest in history,
folklore, poetry, fiction and humor. A good companion to Frank Dobie's
Guide to Life and Literature of the Southwest. The annotations are not
scholarly; however, they are interesting and to the point.

Caselli, Ron, comp. **The Minority Experience: A Basic Bibliography of American
 Ethnic Studies.** Santa Rosa, California: Sonoma County, Superintendent
 of Schools, 1970. 61p.
Approximately 950 books and periodicals published between 1940 and 1969 are
cited in this bibliography prepared for teachers and students of American
minority ethnic groups. Afro-Americans, Mexican Americans, and native Americans are the three groups specifically covered in the bibliography. Areas of
concern are sociology, economics, and psychology. The majority of citations
included provide a historical approach to current problems.

Castillo, Guadalupe, and Herminio Rios. "Toward a True Chicano Bibliography:
 Mexican-American Newspapers: 1848-1942." **El Grito,** III (Summer
 1970), 17-24.
A bibliography of 193 Mexican-American newspapers in publication between
1848 and 1942. A note states that the bibliography is to be brought up to date
in the near future. The newspaper titles are listed by state, with date of establishment and date of termination given (if the publication has ceased publishing),
for each entry.

Charno, Steven M., comp. **Latin American Newspapers in United States
 Libraries: A Union List.** Conference on Latin America History Series,
 No. 2. Austin, Texas: University of Texas Press, 1969. 632p.
Compiled in the Serial Division, Library of Congress, this is a record of the
holdings of 70 United States libraries of some 5,500 titles for 20 Latin American
republics and Puerto Rico. Included is a selective bibliography.

Crosby, Muriel Estelle, ed. **Reading Ladders for Human Relations.** 4th ed.
National Council of Teachers of English. Washington: American
Council on Education, 1963. 242p.
Books annotated in this fourth edition of *Reading Ladders for Human Relations*
develop six themes representing central ideas into which differences among
people can be integrated or resolved. Within the arrangement of the ladders,
books are "alphabetically arranged by theme and in order of maturity and
difficulty, ranging from those for the very young child to those for only mature
readers. Some books at the end of each ladder demand emotional maturity
beyond the grasp of the average high school level." A list of publishers, author
index, and title index are included.

Cumberland, Charles C. "The United States-Mexican Border: A Selective Guide
to the Literature of the Region." Supplement to **Rural Sociology**,
XXV, No. 2 (June 1960), 1-236.
An extensive bibliographic essay and guide to the literature relevant to the
United States-Mexican border. The purpose of the guide "is to indicate both
the areas which have been covered in the literature and the subjects which have
been inadequately studied." The work is primarily intended to aid researchers
dealing with contemporary situations. The material included covers only the
period after Mexican Independence and up to 1958.

Dobie, J. Frank. **Guide to Life and Literature of the Southwest.** Rev. ed.
Dallas, Texas: Southern Methodist University Press, 1952. 222p.
A subjective choosing of the works which seemed to Dobie to be the best
sources on life in the Southwest. Titles are grouped by subject (Indians, badmen,
range life, etc.) and are annotated; fiction and folklore are also included.

Esquenazi-Mayo, Roberto, and Michael C. Meyer, eds. **Latin American Scholarship Since World War II: Trends in History, Political Science, Literature, Geography, and Economics.** Lincoln, Neb.: University of
Nebraska Press, 1971. 335p.
Latin Americanists offer an overview of book-length works and, when applicable,
periodical literature, mimeographed studies, and dissertations.

Foester, Merlin H. **Index to Mexican Literary Periodicals.** Metuchen, N.J.:
Scarecrow Press, Inc., 1966. 276p.
The 16 periodicals chosen for indexing represent a varied selection from among
recent journals of Mexican literature and culture. The 16 journals are *Antena,
Contemporaneos Estaciones, Fabula, La Falange, Forma, El Hijo, Prodigo,
Mexico Moderno, Poesia, Prometeus, Romance, Ruta, Sagitario, Taller, Tierra
Nueva,* and *Ulises.*

Gomez-Q, Juan. **Selected Materials on the Chicano.** Los Angeles: Mexican-
American Cultural Center, University of California at Los Angeles,
1970.
Unannotated bibliography with such subject headings as statistical materials,
journals, law and justice, films, artists, etc.

Griffin, Charles C., ed. **Latin America: A Guide to the Historical Literature**. Publication No. 4, Conference on Latin American History. Austin, Texas: University of Texas Press, 1971. 700p.
This volume is intended to provide a selective scholarly bibliography, accompanied by critical annotations, covering the whole field of Latin American history. The basic organization of the guide is chronological, with main divisions devoted to the colonial, independence, and post-independence periods. Within these major parts, separate sections deal with the various geographical areas.

Gropp, Arthur E. **A Bibliography of Latin American Bibliographies**. Metuchen, N.J.: Scarecrow Press, Inc., 1968. 528p.
Arrangement is by subject, with principal subject groups subdivided geographically by country. The bibliography contains works both in Spanish and in English. The work is an updating of Cecil Knight Jones's *Bibliography of Latin American Bibliographies* (2nd ed., 1942).

Gropp, Arthur E. **A Bibliography of Latin American Bibliographies—Supplement**. Metuchen, N.J.: Scarecrow Press, Inc., 1971. 277p.
This work is a continuation of Mr. Gropp's *A Bibliography of Latin American Bibliographies* (1968). The supplement contains more than 1,400 references to bibliographic information published in monographic forms, the majority published from 1965 to 1969. Arrangement is by subject, with principal subject groups subdivided geographically by country. A detailed index to names of persons, corporate bodies, government agencies, titles of series, and subjects is provided.

Handbook of Latin American Studies. Gainesville, Florida: University of Florida Press, 1936— .
Published annually, this exhaustive reference on all aspects of Latin American civilization covers the social sciences in the 1971 edition. The yearly editions alternate coverage of the social sciences and the humanities.

Haro, Robert Peter. **Latin Americana Research in the United States and Canada: A Guide and Directory**. Chicago: American Library Association, 1971. 122p.
The major acquisition programs and catalogs of Latin American collections in the United States and Canada are described, and research centers that have continuing programs dealing with one or more aspects of Latin America are listed and annotated.

Hebblethwaite, Frank P. **A Bibliographic Guide to the Spanish American Theater**. Pan American Union, Basic Bibliographies, No. 6. Washington, D.C.: GPO, 1969. 84p.
A highly useful collection of references to the theater in various countries and in Spanish America in general. Does not include references to specific plays or dramatists.

Hedman, Kenneth, and Patsy McNiel. **Mexican American Bibliography: A Guide to the Resources of the Library at the University of Texas at El Paso.** El Paso, Texas: University of Texas, The Library, 1970.
A topically arranged bibliography basically of the holdings of the university library. Included is a useful section on bibliographies.

Hilton, Ronald, ed. **Handbook of Hispanic Source Materials and Research Organizations in the United States.** 2nd ed. Stanford, California: Stanford University Press, 1956. 448p.
The term "Hispanic" is used in the title to embrace Spain, Portugal, and Latin America of the pre- and post periods; Florida, Texas, the Southwest, and California are included until their annexation by the United States. The material surveyed belongs to the humanities, the fine arts, the social sciences, and, in some exceptional collections, the natural sciences. The handbook is arranged by state and locality under which the various collections are described. For precise items reference to the index is necessary.

Hispanic Society of America. **Catalog of the Library.** 10 vols. Boston: G. K. Hall and Company, 1962.
Four supplements, beginning in 1970, have been added to the original ten volumes. The Society's library contains over 100,000 volumes, covering the cultures of Spain, Portugal, and colonial Hispanic America. Emphasis is on the art, history, and literature of these countries, including music, social customs, regional costumes, and description and travel, but excluding Indian subjects. The card catalog has at least an author card for every book in the collection printed since 1700. Manuscripts, most periodicals, and pre-1700 books are not included.

Humphreys, Robin A. **Latin American History, A Guide to the Literature in English.** London: University Press of Oxford, 1958. 197p.
An annotated bibliography covering general reference works, bibliographies and guides, periodicals and the literature of both ancient history and modern history to 1958. The fields of archaeology or ethnology are not covered, nor is the bibliography a guide to parliamentary and congressional papers.

Johnson, John J., ed. **The Mexican American, A Selected and Annotated Bibliography.** Stanford, California: The Center for Latin American Studies, Stanford University, 1969. 139p.
The 274 titles included in this bibliography are annotated in consistently excellent abstracts which primarily emphasize the social sciences.

Jones, Cecil Knight. **A Bibliography of Latin American Bibliographies.** 2nd ed. Washington, D.C.: GPO, 1942. 307p.
This volume gives references to approximately 3,500 publications, monographs, indexes, catalogs, articles from periodicals, general books containing bibliographies, and some reference and miscellaneous works.

Keating, Charlotte Matthews. **Building Bridges of Understanding Between Cultures.** Tucson, Arizona: Palo Verde Publishing Comapny, Inc., 1971. 233p.
Lengthy annotations with age level are provided in this very excellent bibliography. Works are arranged under subject headings and subdivided as to preschool and primary levels, upper-elementary levels, and junior high and high school levels. Mexican-American material may be found under the headings "Spanish-Speaking Americans," "Multi-Ethnic Representation," "Bilingual/Bicultural Children," and "Mexico." An author index and a title index are included in the work.

Los Angeles County Superintendent of Schools Office. **Portraits: The Literature of Minorities.** Los Angeles, California, 1970. 70p.
An annotated bibliography developed to "identify printed materials of literary quality by and about four ethnic groups in the United States for students in junior and senior high schools." The work contains fiction, poetry, drama, folk tales and legends, biographies, autobiographies, essays, letters, and speeches. Lengthy annotations are valuable to the bibliography.

Mayer, Brantz. **Complete History of Mexico, Aztec, Spanish Republic With Biographies of the Viceroys of New Spain.** 2 vols. Chicago: Rio Grande Press, 1971. Repr. of 1897 ed.
A reprint of the 1897 masterpiece of this extensive and complete history of Mexico. Excellent biographical material on the viceroys of New Spain.

Mexican American Directory, 1969-1970 Edition. Washington, D.C.: Executive Systems Corporation, 1969.
A who's who among Mexican Americans. The directory contains information only on those who filled out biographical data sheets.

Mexican American Study Project. **Revised Bibliography.** With a bibliographical essay by Ralph Guzman. Advance Report 3, Los Angeles, Division of Research, Graduate School of Business, University of California, 1967. 99p.
This bibliographical essay introduces the work and gives a discourse on the major works on the Mexican Americans from the 1920s to 1967. The bibliography, though not annotated, is an extensive listing of books, pamphlets, journal articles, dissertations, and unpublished materials.

The Mexican Americans: Books for Young People. Oakland, California: Oakland Public Schools, Division of Instructional Media Library, 1969. 27p.
An annotated bibliography for young people, divided into sections ("In the United States," and "Mexican Roots, Past and Present"), then further subdivided into fiction and non-fiction. The titles are graded as to appropriate level.

Navarro, Eliseo. **The Chicano Community: A Selected Bibliography for Use in Social Work Education.** New York: Council on Social Work Education, 1971. 57p.
The purpose of this bibliography is to provide resource material for social workers, teachers, students and anyone in need of material for a better understanding of the Chicano community. Each item in this annotated bibliography is coded to indicate the subject matter of the material. The code categories cover such topics as historical background, acculturation, education, health, religion, racism, politics, economics, family life, social welfare, and literature. Many of the annotations are critical, while others examine and analyze the material.

Pan American Union. Columbus Memorial Library. **Index to Latin American Literature, 1929-1960.** 8 vols. Boston: G. K. Hall and Company, 1962.
Photo-reproduced from card catalog cards, this work is based on broad selective indexing.

Potts, Alfred M., comp. **Knowing and Educating the Disadvantaged: An Annotated Bibliography.** Alamosa, Colorado: Adams State College, Center for Cultural Studies, 1965.
This extensive annotated bibliography, sponsored by the Office of Education, was compiled to aid the planning research and demonstration projects related to the education of agricultural migratory adults. The bibliography is available through ERIC (Educational Resources Information Center).

Revelle, Keith. **Chicano: A Selected Bibliography of Materials by and about Mexico and Mexican Americans.** Oakland, California: Latin American Library of the Oakland Public Library, 1969. Addendum 1970. 21p.
A bibliography "designed for general use by anyone interested in Mexican American problems and culture or anyone wishing to establish a Mexican American collection." Revelle's introductory remarks are of interest to one beginning a Mexican American collection. The work contains sections on books (partially annotated), newspapers, periodicals, and articles, reports and speeches.

Rivera, Feliciano. **A Mexican American Source Book.** Menlo Park, California: Educational Consulting Associates, 1970. 196p.
A valuable collection of Mexican American sources. Included is the Treaty of Guadalupe-Hildago, historical outline, history of the missions, and portraits of Mexican-American leaders.

Ross, Stanley R. "Bibliography of Sources for Contemporary Mexican History." **Hispanic American Historical Review,** XXXIX (May 1959), 234-38.
An excellent listing, although dated, of important bibliographies and sources for Mexican history.

Sanchez, George Isidore, and Howard Putnam. **Materials Relating to the Education of Spanish-Speaking People in the United States: An**

Annotated Bibliography. Latin American Studies, No. 97. Austin, Texas: University of Texas Press, 1959. Repr. Westport, Conn., Greenwood Press, 1971. 76p.

The author states that "this bibliography is concerned primarily with the education of those Spanish speaking people in the United States who are of Mexican descent." Some 882 annotated items are arranged alphabetically under six headings: books; articles; monographs, bulletins, and pamphlets; courses of study; bibliographies; unpublished theses and dissertations. The compilation was done by graduate students but judiciously selected by Sanchez and Putnam. The bibliography is heavy on educational items, although many other areas are covered, from the 1920s through 1956.

Schramko, Linda Fowler. **Chicano Bibliography, Selected Materials on Americans of Mexican Descent.** Sacramento, California: Sacramento State College Library, Bibliographic Series No. 1, 1970. 124p.

Representing relevant library holdings to the spring of 1969, this extensive bibliography is topically arranged and includes books, journal articles, ERIC items, government publications, a list of Chicano periodicals, and an index.

Spache, George D. **Good Reading for the Disadvantaged Reader: Multi-Ethnic Resources.** Scarsdale, N.Y.: Garrard Publishing Co., 1970. 201p.

An unannotated bibliography divided under broad subject headings and further divided by primary level, intermediate level, junior high, and high school level. A one-sentence description usually follows the bibliographic entry. Some of the unusual headings are: audiovisual resources, professional resources, adult literacy, materials for basic education of adult illiterates and school dropouts. There is one chapter on Mexican Americans and migrant workers, an author and title index, and a listing of names and addresses of publishers.

Stanford University. Center for Latin American Studies. **The Mexican American.** 2nd ed. rev. and enl. Ed. by Luis G. Nogales. Stanford, California: The Center, 1971. 162p.

This bibliography lists and annotates 444 works in anthropology, economics, education, history, law, linguistics, literature, philosophy, political science, psychology, public health and sociology. Contains an extensive bibliography with long critical annotations, a section listing Chicano periodicals, a subject index, and a field index.

Tash, Steven. **Selected Bibliography of Resources for Chicano Studies.** Northridge, California: San Fernando Valley State College Library, 1970.

A brief, 13-page bibliography of bibliographies. The work is topically arranged and is a useful reference tool to one starting on Chicano studies.

U.S. Cabinet Committee on Opportunity for the Spanish Speaking. **Directory of Spanish Speaking Community Organizations.** Washington, D.C.: GPO, July 1970. 231p.

A comprehensive list by state, giving address, scope, date established, and objective of the organization.

U.S. Cabinet Committee on Opportunity for the Spanish Speaking. **The Spanish Speaking in the United States: A Guide to Materials**. Washington, D.C.: GPO, 1971. 175p.
A bibliography of books, essays, and other materials dealing with Spanish-speaking affairs. It contains more than 1,300 individual citations on Mexican Americans, Puerto Ricans, and Cuban refugees and their role on the social, political, educational, and institutional development of this country. There are listings of books, periodical articles, government publications, theses, serials, audiovisual materials, and Spanish radio and television stations.

U.S. Department of Commerce. Bureau of Census. **Population Characteristics: Persons of Spanish Origin in the United States**. Washington, D.C.: GPO, 1971. 88p.
Important and useful data on the locale, age, economic status, education, and employment of Spanish-speaking people, based on a 1969 sample survey.

U.S. Department of Justice. **Directory of Organizations Serving Minority Communities**. Washington, D.C.: GPO, 1971. 88p.
Listed in the directory are the names and addresses of many federal agencies, private organizations, colleges and universities, newspapers and radio and television broadcasters serving women and Negro, Spanish-surname, American Indian, and Oriental communities. Arranged by state and subdivided by type of organization and group served.

U.S. Inter-Agency Committee on Mexican American Affairs. **The Mexican American, A New Focus on Opportunity: A Guide to Materials Relating to Persons of Mexican Heritage in the United States**. Washington, D.C.: GPO, March, 1969.
The types of materials in this bibliography have been classified into six broad categories: books, reports, hearings, proceedings and similar materials, periodical literature, dissertations and other unpublished materials, bibliographies, and audiovisual materials.

U.S. Library of Congress. Catalog. **Motion Pictures and Filmstrips: A Cumulative List of Works Represented by Library of Congress Printed Cards**. Washington, D.C.: Library of Congress, 1954– .
A printed quarterly with an annual cumulation. Includes entries for all motion pictures and filmstrips currently cataloged on Library of Congress printed catalog cards. The Library of Congress covers all films of educational or instructional value that are released in the United States or Canada. Data for the catalog are supplied mainly by film libraries, film producers, or distributors.

University of Texas. Latin American Collection. **Catalog**. 31 vols. Boston: G. K. Hall and Company, 1969.
In the library's 160,000 volumes dating from the fifteenth century to the present is information on virtually any subject relating to Latin America. Includes non-book materials and an extensive manuscript collection, some from the sixteenth century. This is a dictionary catalog of authors, titles, and subjects. Six supplements have been issued, adding to the 31-volume set.

AUTHOR INDEX

Includes names of authors, compilers, editors, illustrators, and translators. Numbers refer to entries, not pages, except when the letter "p" precedes the number. Entry numbers for all audio-visual material are followed by (A-V).

Aaron, J., 107
Acuna, R., 194-96
Adair, J., 113
Aiken, R., 526
Alba, V., 1
Alford, H. A., 197
Alisky, M., 234
Allen, S., 278
Almaraz, F. D., 563
Altus, D. M., p223
Alurista, 476
American Ethnological Society, 279
Anda, J. de, 198
Anderson, H. P., 370
Anderson-Imbert, E., 477
Andrews, M., 618
Anton, F., 389-90
Appel, B., 619
Arias-Larreta, A., 478
Arnold, E., 620
Aroul, G., 508
Arquin, F., 564
Ashford, G., 235
Atkin, R., 64
Avila, M., 94
Atwater, J. D., 565
Azuelo, M., 621-22

Baez, J., 566
Bagley, D., 623
Bailey, C., 445
Baker, B., 624-25
Baker, N. B., 567
Bakke, E. W., 280
Bakke, M. S., 280
Ballis, G., 281
Bancroft, H. H., p223
Bannon, J. F., 56
Barnstone, W., 25
Baron, A., 626
Barrio, R., 627

Barrios, E., p224
Barry, J., 628
Beals, C., 108-109, 622
Beals, R., 341
Beck, W. A., 236
Beckett, H., 629
Beckett, S., 507
Behn, H., 630
Beltran, A., 52, 148-49
Benitez, F., 57
Benson, E. P., 24
Benson, N. L., 65, 71
Bernal, I., 25, 391-94
Beteta, R., 568
Bishop, C., 631
Blacker, I., 39, 54
Blawis, P. B., 282
Bledsoe, T., 460
Bleeker, S., 110
Boatright, M. C., 527
Boggs, R. S., 528
Bolton, H. E., 237
Bongartz, R., 199
Bonham, F., 632-33
Boos, F. H., 395
Borrows, F., 462
Bourjaily, V. N., 634
Boyd, L. E., 480
Braddy, H., 529-30
Bradford, R., 635
Brand, D. D., 154
Brandenburg, F. R., 2
Brasch, R., 155
Brasher, C., 95
Bravo, M. A., 408
Bray, W., 111
Breck, V., 636
Brenner, A., 66, 396, 637, 692
Briegel, K., 283
Brinton, E., 747-48
Bristow, G., 638
Brock, V., 112
Brof, J., 485

233

AUTHOR INDEX

Dodge, D., 162
Dohman, B., 491
Dolch, E. W., 540
Dolch, M. P., 540
Dorner, G., 407
Dorson, R. M., 541-42, 552
Dozer, D. M., 11
Drumm, S. M., 163
Dufour, C. L., 73
Dunn, F. S., 97
Dunne, J. G., 290
Dunne, M. C., 653
Dunstan, F. J., 489
Dupery, E. E., 73
Duran, D., 27
Duran, F. D., 28
Du Soe, R. C., 654
Dvorin, E. P., 299
Dworkin, A. G., 373

Earle, P. G., 21
Edgerton, R. B., 377
Ediger, D., 120
Edmondson, G. C., 655
Edwards, E., 408
Egan, F., 164
Ekholm, G. F., 39
El Malcriado Staff, 277
Emmerich, A., 409
Enciso, J., 410
Erdman, L. G., 656
Ericksen, C. A., 346
Espinosa, J. E., 543
Espinosa, J. M., 544
Esquenazi-Mayo, R., p225
Evarts, H. G., 657
Ewing, R. C., 12

Fabrega, H., 374
Fagen, R. R., 121
Fagg, J. E., 13
Falconieri, J. V., 477
Faulk, O. B., 70, 239
Fedder, R., 347
Ferguson, W., 697
Fergusson, E., 122, 291

Ferlinghetti, L., 165
Fermaud, R. W., 158
Fernandez, J., 411
Fiedler, J., 658
Finney, J. C., 375
Fisher, H. T., 156
Fisher, M. H., 156
Flandrau, C. M., 166
Fogel, W., 240, 348
Forbes, J. D., 241, 349
Ford, N. D., 167
Form, W. H., 287
Forster, M. H., p225
Fromm, E., 123
Fuentes, C., 659-60

Galarza, E., 242, 292-93, 572
Galindo, S., 661
Gallegos, H., 242
Gallen, A. A., 662
Gamio, M., 294-95
Gannett, R., 721
Garcia, G. J., 205
Gardiner, C. H., 43, 53
Gardner, E. S., 168
Gardner, R. M., 206
Garro, E., 663
Garthwaite, M. H., 664
Gault, W. C., 665
Gavin, C., 666
Gay, C. T. E., 412
Gibson, C., 44, 124-25
Giffords, G., 545
Gilmore, B., 169
Gilmore, D., 169
Gillmor, F., 450, 573-74
Glazer, N., 305
Glubok, S., 45, 413
Gomara, F. L. de, 575
Gomez-O, J., p225
Gonzales, N. L., 243
Gonzalez, R., 488
Gonzalez Pena, C., 489
Goodman, M. E., 296
Gordon, A., 667
Gorostiza, J., 490
Goss, R. C., 546

AUTHOR INDEX

Granberg, W. J., 126
Grebler, L., 297, 350, p223
Greene, G., 668
Greenleaf, R. E., 46
Greenwood, M., 108, 567
Gregg, A. K., 244
Griffin, C. C., p226
Griffith, B. W., 298
Gringhuis, D., 594
Gropp, A. E., p226
Gual, E., 414
Guzman, D. de, 576
Guzman, M. L., 577, 669
Guzman, R., 299, p223, p228

Haddox, J. H., 578-79
Halliburton, W. J., 351
Hamilton, C. W., 74
Hancock, R., 14
Hanf, W., 15, 170
Hanna, A. J., 75
Hanna, K. A., 75
Hardy, J. E., 29
Harmon, M., 580
Haro, R. P., p226
Harrison, F., 464
Harrison, J., 464
Harss, L., 491
Hart, C. G., 670
Haslam, G. W., 492
Haslip, J., 581
Haug, M. J., 388
Hayner, N. S., 127
Hazelton, E. B., 671
Heaps, W. A., 300
Heath, G. L., 352
Hebblethwaite, F. P., p226
Hecht, P., 465
Hedman, K., p227
Hedrick, B. C., 171
Helfritz, H., 172
Heller, C. S., 301-302
Helm, J., 207
Henderson, L., 672
Henley, J. A., 558
Henry, R. S., 76
Herhard, P., 173

Hernandez, D., 208
Hernandez, L. F., 353
Heuman, W., 673
Heyden, D., 28
Hilborn, H. W., 501
Hill, G., 303
Hilton, R., p227
Hinkle, S. C., 245
Hispanic Society of America, p227
Hobart, A. T., 674
Hobart, L., 174
Hollon, W. S., 246
Holzapfel, T., 451
Horcasitas, F., 28
Horgan, P., 47, 247-48
Hudson, W. M., 547
Hulet, C. L., 493-94
Humphrey, N. D., 341
Humphreys, R. A., p227
Humphries, S., 639
Hurwitz, L., 436
Hutchinson, C. A., 249

Iduarte, A., 582
Iglesia, R., 583
Innes, H., 48
International Congress of Historians of
    the United States and Mexico, 98
Irwin, C., 128

Jackson, H. H., 675
Jagendorf, M. A., 548
James, D., 99
Jauss, A. M., 112
Jenkinson, M., 209
Johnson, D. L., 376
Johnson, H. S., 354
Johnson, J. J., p227
Johnson, M., 705
Johnson, W. W., 49, 77, 175
Johnston, E., 466
Jones, C. K., p227
Jones, E. H., 417
Jones, J., 418
Jones, M. S., 417

AUTHOR INDEX

AUTHOR INDEX

AUTHOR INDEX

TITLE INDEX

In addition to the titles of all entries, this index also includes the names of newspapers and periodicals listed in Appendix C (pages 203-219).

TITLE INDEX

Aztecs: The History of the Indies of
New Spain, 27

Aztecs, the Maya, the Incas—A Comparison
(A-V), 871

Aztecs Under Spanish Rule, 44

Aztlan: An Anthology of Mexican American
Literature, 479

Aztlan: Chicano Journal of the Social
Sciences and the Arts, p205

Ballet Folklorico de Ballas Danza Azteca
(A-V), 995

Barbarous Mexico, 91

Barrio Boy, 572

Basta!, 281

Basta Ya!, p203

Behind Spanish American Footlights, 452

Belvedere Citizen, p205

Benito Juarez: Builder of a Nation, 601

Bernalillo Times, p206

Best of Mexico by Car, 162

Beyond This Point Are Monsters, 703

Bibliografia de Aztlan, p224

Bibliographic Guide to the Spanish-
American Theater, p226

Bibliography for Olmec Sculpture, 418

Bibliography of Latin American Bibliographies, p226, p227

Bibliography of Latin American Bibliographies—Supplement, p226

Bibliography of Latin American Folklore,
528

Bibliography of Sources for Contemporary
Mexican History, p229

Bibliography of Spanish Plays on Microcards, 458

Bilingual Education, a Selected Bibliography, p223

Black Palace, 618

Black Pearl, 705

Blanco y Negro, p206

Blood of the Brave, 624

Blood on the Border, 69

Book Lover's Southwest: A Guide to
Good Reading, p224

Book of the Gods and Rites and the
Ancient Calendar, 28

Bounteous Earth (A-V), 962

Box y Lucha, p206

Bracero Program in California, with
Particular Reference to Health Status,
Attitudes and Practices, 370

Brave Bulls: A Novel, 689

Bridge in the Jungle, 728

Bright Summer, 713

Brill Among the Ruins: A Novel, 634

Broken Spears: The Aztec Account of the
Conquest of Mexico, 52

Bronce, p206

Brooklyn Goes to Mexico (A-V), 872

Brooms of Mexico (A-V), 758

Brothers under the Skin, 308

Buen Hogar (Good Home), p206

Buenos Dias, Teacher, 695

Builders in the Sun: Five Mexican
Architects, 434

Building Bridges of Understanding
between Cultures, p228

Burden of Poverty, 257

Burning Plain and Other Stories, 712

But I Am Sara, 699

Buying the Wind, 542

By the King's Command, 715

Cactus and the Crown, 666

Cactus Throne, 595

Cajititlan (A-V), 759

California's Dawn (A-V), 761

Californians of Mexican Descent (A-V),
760; (A-V), 996

Call Me Juanita, 658

Campus Challenge: Student Activism in
Perspective, 280

Captain Cortes Conquers Mexico, 49

Captain from Castile, 716

Carlos Fuentes, 576

Carreta: A Novel, 729

Carta Editorial, p203

Catalog of the Library (Hispanic Society
of America), p227

Catalog (University of Texas. Latin
American Collection), p231

Century after Cortes, 57

243

TITLE INDEX

TITLE INDEX

TITLE INDEX

Maya, 116, 793
Maya Archaeologist, 146
Maya Heritage (A-V), 794
Maya, Land of the Turkey and the Deer, 148
Maya of Ancient and Modern Yucatan (A-V), 795; (A-V), 971
Maya of Yucatan (A-V), 796
Maya World, 24
Mecanica Popular, p213
Medicine in Mexico, 143
Medusa, 448
Memoirs of a Bullfighter, 571
Memoirs of Pancho Villa, 577
Men of the Revolution, 604
Merchants of Labor, 292
Mexican Adventure, 72
Mexican American, 333, p230
Mexican American: A New Focus on Opportunity, 227
Mexican-American, a New Focus on Opportunity, 1967-1968, 232
Mexican American, a New Focus on Opportunity: A Guide to Materials Relating to Persons of Mexican Heritage in the United States, p231
Mexican American, a New Focus on Opportunity: The President's Remarks at the Installation of Commissioner Vincente T. Ximenes, 233
Mexican American, a Selected and Annotated Bibliography, p227
Mexican-American: An Examination of Stereotypes (A-V), 1003
Mexican-American and the United States, 202
Mexican-American Authors, 506
Mexican American Bibliography: A Guide to the Resources of the Library at the University of Texas at El Paso, p227
Mexican American Challenge to a Sacred Cow, 208
Mexican American Chronicle, 194
Mexican-American Culture: Its Heritage (A-V), 797
Mexican American Directory, 1969-1970 Edition, p228
Mexican-American Education, 367
Mexican American Family (A-V), 798

Mexican-American: Heritage and Destiny (A-V), 799
Mexican-American: Heritage and History (A-V), 800
Mexican American High School Graduate of Laredo, 344
Mexican American Literature, 505
Mexican American People, p223
Mexican-American Population of Houston, 296
Mexican American Series (A-V), 1004
Mexican American Source Book, p229
Mexican American Youth, 301
Mexican Americans, 259; (A-V), 902; (A-V), 972
Mexican Americans: A Brief Look at Their History, 215
Mexican-Americans: A Handbook for Educators, 349
Mexican-Americans: A New Focus on Opportunity, 231
Mexican-Americans: An Awakening Minority, 224
Mexican-Americans: An Historic Profile (A-V), 801
Mexican Americans and the Administration of Justice in the Southwest, 273
Mexican Americans: Books for Young People, p228
Mexican-Americans: Ethnic Isolation of Mexican-Americans in the Public Schools of the Southwest, 365
Mexican-Americans in a Midwest Metropolis, 222
Mexican Americans in School, 343
Mexican-Americans in Southwest Labor Markets, 240
Mexican Americans in the Southwest, 242
Mexican-Americans in the United States, 200
Mexican-Americans: Invisible Minority (A-V), 802
Mexican-Americans Make Themselves Heard, 234
Mexican-Americans of South Texas, 255
Mexican-Americans: Past, Present, and Future, 216
Mexican-Americans: Quest for Equality (A-V), 803

250

TITLE INDEX

Mexican Americans: Sons of the Southwest, 251

Mexican and Central American Mythology, 551

Mexican Archaeology, 30

Mexican Art (A-V), 1020

Mexican Art and the Academy of San Carlos, 1785-1915, 399

Mexican Art, Architecture, and Education (A-V), 903

Mexican Assignment, 694

Mexican Border Ballads and Other Lore, 527

Mexican Ceramic Artists—A Series: Talavera (A-V), 805; Donna Rosa, Potter of Coyotepec (A-V), 804

Mexican Ceramics (A-V), 806; (A-V), 973

Mexican Cession and the Gadsden Purchase (A-V), 904

Mexican Cities of the Gods, 172

Mexican Cookbook, 122

Mexican Corrido as a Source for Interpretive Study of Modern Mexico, 1870-1950, 470

Mexican Culture and the Mexican American, 198

Mexican Epic—Before the Conquest (A-V), 905; From Conquest to Nation (A-V), 906

Mexican Fishing Village (A-V), 974

Mexican Folk Dances (A-V), 1009

Mexican Folk Narrative from the Los Angeles Area, 550

Mexican Folkplays, 453

Mexican Folk-songs (A-V), 1016; (A-V), 1005

Mexican Foods—The American Way (A-V), 807

Mexican Handcraft and Folk Art (A-V), 808

Mexican Homes of Today, 430

Mexican House: Old and New, 431

Mexican Immigrant, His Life Story, Autobiographic Documents, 294

Mexican Immigration to the United States, 295

Mexican Immigration to the United States: The Record and Its Implications, 297

Mexican Impressions (A-V), 809

Mexican in Fact, Fiction and Folklore, 512

Mexican Indian Costumes, 403

Mexican Inquisition of the Sixteenth Century, 46

Mexican Interiors, 432

Mexican Jewelry, 405

Mexican Kaleidoscope (A-V), 907

Mexican Labor in the United States, 330

Mexican Maize (A-V), 810

Mexican Medusa, 451

Mexican Militarism, 78

Mexican Moods (A-V), 811

Mexican Mosaic, 525

Mexican Mural Renaissance 1920-1925, 400

Mexican Mural: The Story of Mexico, Past and Present, 174

Mexican Muralists, 425

Mexican Night: Travel Journal, 165

Mexican Novel Comes of Age, 496

Mexican or American (A-V), 812

Mexican Painting in Our Time, 421

Mexican People of Today (A-V), 908

Mexican Popular Arts, 439

Mexican Portfolio, 436

Mexican Potters—Clay Art in Old Mexico (A-V), 975

Mexican Rebel: Pascual Orozco and the Mexican Revolution, 1910-1915, 590

Mexican Rebellion (A-V), 813

Mexican Revolution: Federal Expenditure and Social Change since 1910, 150

Mexican Revolution, 1914-1915, 82

Mexican Revolution of 1910 (A-V), 909

Mexican Revolution: The Constitutionalist Years, 59

Mexican Serenade, 449

Mexican Society during the Revolution, 517

Mexican Story, 16

Mexican Town, Population 14,000: At School (A-V), 910

Mexican Ulysses, 610

Mexican Village, 704

Mexican Village Coppermakers (A-V), 976

Mexican Village Life (A-V), 814; (A-V), 977

Mexican Wall Paintings of the Maya and Aztec Periods, 392

Mexican War, 88; 89; (A-V), 1019

251

TITLE INDEX

TITLE INDEX

TITLE INDEX

TITLE INDEX

SUBJECT INDEX

Also indexed here are Appendixes A and B (pages 169-200).

259